Back in 1966, NBC began airing the first intelligent science fiction series the tube had ever seen. STAR TREK. Its impact was immediate.

Around the same time, a fellow named David Gerrold was discovering he wanted to be a writer. He was still in college when he saw his first STAR TREK episode, but he knew that was the market he wanted to crack.

He had never written anything professionally before so it is certainly among the more improbable events in creation that David Gerrold and STAR TREK should have gotten together. But then science fiction is full of the improbable made fact. And David Gerrold, with the single-minded dedication of a new talent making itself known, found a way to make the improbable happen. Not only did he sell the story, but he wrote the script as well for what turned out to be one of the most popular episodes of a series whose popularity itself has become a legend.

So this is a blow-by-blow account of how a TV story gets sold, how the script gets written, how it is translated into a final script despite the money (or lack of it), the censors (oh those touchy networks!): it is the story of the men who cut, and change, and re-write; it is the story of the men behind the scenes, and of the actors—all of whom have ideas on how to change, rearrange, rework. And it is of course the story of the man who has to pull all these elements together into a show that can be aired. It is, (no pun intended) an exhaustive and illuminating work.

Books by
David Gerrold

THE FLYING SORCERERS (with Larry Niven)

PROTOSTARS (ed.)

SPACE SKIMMER

WITH A FINGER IN MY I
  (short story collection)

WHEN HARLIE WAS ONE

THE TROUBLE WITH TRIBBLES

THE WORLD OF STAR TREK

THE TROUBLE WITH TRIBBLES

David Gerrold

Illustrations by
Tim Kirk

BALLANTINE BOOKS • NEW YORK

SBN 345-23402-2-150

First Printing: May, 1973
Second Printing: January, 1974
Third Printing: September, 1974
Fourth Printing: November, 1974

Printed in the United States of America

BALLANTINE BOOKS
A Division of Random House, Inc.
201 East 50th Street, New York, N.Y. 10022

This book should be dedicated to Irwin Blacker and Gene Coon and Gene Roddenberry and William Shatner and Leonard Nimoy and De-Forest Kelley and Jim Doohan and Walter Koenig and Nichelle Nichols and Majel Barrett and George Takei and all the other good people who made it possible.

But I'm sure they'll understand that this book is a special one—so it has to be for Betty Ballantine, who's pretty special herself.

The Trouble
With Tribbles

A Word to the Fore—

This book is the story of a television script, where it came from, how it was written, how it was eventually filmed and finally got onto the air as an episode of STAR TREK.

It's a peek into the techniques of writing for television, and it's a piece of lore about a popular TV show. But more than that, it's the story of how I began my career as a writer. And what I learned in the process.

And it's a book about STAR TREK.

The episode was "The Trouble With Tribbles", and from the very beginning it was an atypical example of television production.

But then again—STAR TREK was an atypical TV series.

For example, STAR TREK was the hardest series on the air to write for. Too many professional TV writers didn't understand science fiction—they couldn't handle the format. They didn't realize that science fiction is more than just a western with ray guns.

And the science fiction writers were almost defeated by the show too. They knew their science fiction, but they had to learn the exigencies of television production. Some of them couldn't handle a medium that kept interrupting itself for commercials, insisted on *exactly*—no more, no less—fifty-six-minutes worth of story, and needed three minor climaxes and a major one, no departures from form please.

These were the voyages of the good ship *Enterprise* and her crew: Captain Kirk, the interstellar womanizer; Mr. Spock, the pointy-eared logician; Dr. McCoy, specialist in sarcasm; Lieutenant Uhura, a really gorgeous communications officer; and Ensign Chekov, a Russian hot-shot at the helm. Each week this band of intrepids (and four hundred and thirty other odd crew members) set out to spread truth,

1

justice, and the American way to the lesser corners of the galaxy. Usually, they succeeded—once in a while, they deserved to.

STAR TREK was never a big hit in numbers—at least not in the numbers that meant anything to NBC: Nielsen, Arbitron, etc.—but it has undeniably carved itself a place in American folklore of the twentieth century.

STAR TREK has become a new mythology, and STAR TREK fandom has become a Phenomenon, almost a cult. The world-wide devotion of the show's followers sometimes borders on the fanatical.

There must be a reason for it.

I like to think that it's because STAR TREK was—despite its faults, and there were many—an imagination-stretcher. It tickled people's minds, it made them think—and most of all, it looked toward the future with a hopeful and optimistic eye. STAR TREK's very existence said, "There *will* be a future! And we must learn how to make it the best of all possible futures!"

And because of that, STAR TREK was for the young and for the young-at-heart—the people who would live in the future and the people who looked forward to it with anticipation and hope. STAR TREK provided a dream, and the viewers responded with intensity and enthusiasm.

One of the ways they responded was with story ideas and script outlines. In just one year, STAR TREK received more than six thousand scripts, outlines and stories from would-be STAR TREK writers.

Six thousand!

At best, a television show will buy thirty stories in a season.

On numbers alone, the odds against any new writer breaking into STAR TREK were 200 to 1. The odds against any *particular* new writer selling them a story were 6000 to 1. *Or more.* Remember, he's competing with more than just the other would-bes, he's also competing with all the professionals who are trying to sell *their* stories too. And the professionals have the edge—after all, it's their game.

And yet, the hopefuls keep trying.

It must be more than just the money—there are easier ways to get rich. It must be more than the credit too—who notices a TV writer? I suspect it's the desire to *share* in TV's special magic—a desire to be one of the magic-makers themselves. Every season, year after year, hundreds of amateur writers mail thousands of amateur manuscripts in to the Hollywood studios. The process is continual. But there was something about STAR TREK that attracted more of them than any other TV show in history.

Maybe it was STAR TREK's own particular kind of wizardry that intrigued them, or maybe it was the unlimited scope of imagination that the show's format allowed, or maybe it was the special rapport of the characters and actors who played them—but it had to be more than just the desire to break into the promised land of TV writing.

I believe that it was just plain wanting to get *closer* to your favorite TV series.

Once a week wasn't enough—you had to have more of STAR TREK, more! So you sat down and wrote your own stories—you acted out your private fantasies and put them on paper. And then even that wasn't enough, you had to share them—so you put them into an envelope and mailed them off to Gene Roddenberry at Paramount Studios in Hollywood and hoped that He too would recognize how *special* this dream of yours was—and He would reach down from the bridge of the *Enterprise* and say, "Yes, this is an official STAR TREK adventure. Yes, we'll share it with the rest of the world." He would anoint you and lift you up to join the ranks of STAR TREK's exalted—the special dreamers! And you would *glow* forever—because now *you too* were one of the people who actually *made* STAR TREK!

—The intensity of those who wanted to make that big leap was incredible. It still is. (They're still writing their STAR TREK stories even though there's no longer a STAR TREK to sell them to. But that doesn't stop them, not at all. To a real Trekkie, STAR TREK goes on forever.)

The difference between myself and all those other hopefuls is simple—I was the one who made it. (Hey, who's that gawky kid rubbing shoulders with the Vulcan?)

And the reason I made it is that I was training to write for STAR TREK long before there ever was a STAR TREK to write for. I had always been a reader of science fiction, I had always wanted to write it. I had wanted to make movies and work in television as well. And that's what I studied to do. STAR TREK provided the opportunity. And this is the story of it.

Some of these incidents are fun, some are funny—and several of them are very *special*. (And there's one in particular which makes me feel very very good every time I think of it—but I'm saving the telling of that one for the end.)

So, this book exists for a lot of reasons, but mostly for fun—I want to answer all of the questions that STAR TREK fans keep asking me. I want to tell the story of my very first sale as a professional writer. And I hope to bring back some of the sense of wonder that we all felt the first time we saw the *Enterprise* hurtling through space.

CHAPTER ONE:

From Winnie the Pooh to Aristotle
or
Getting Ready for Opportunity's Knock

In 1966, I was a rabbit.

I mention that fact in passing, only to explain why I missed most of STAR TREK's first season.

I was in my last year as a Theatre Arts student at San Fernando Valley State College (now Cal State at Northridge) and we were doing a children's show called *Winnie the Pooh*. I was the rabbit. Uncle Rabbit, that is; I wore a flowered waistcoat, wire-rimmed glasses, and a watch-chain with a little carrot-shaped fob. Under that, I also wore a six-foot rabbit costume and about twenty pounds of padding, tights and makeup.

STAR TREK's first episode was telecast on Sept. 8, 1966. It was "Man Trap," written by George Clayton Johnson. (My private name for that episode is "The Incredible Salt Vampire." I'm not being flippant, it just makes for quick mental identification.) I watched that episode eagerly—and also schizophrenically. Half of me was delighted that at last there was going to be another good science fiction show on television (there hadn't been one since the demise of "Twilight Zone")—and half of me was nit-picking, looking for things wrong with the show. (I found what I thought were a couple of real blunders too, but I was wrong.)

"The Incredible Salt Vampire" was my first exposure to STAR TREK—it was also to be my last for several months, a fact which produced no small amount of annoyance and a high degree of chafing at Thursday night rehearsals.

We rehearsed *Winnie the Pooh* for six weeks straight, from seven to ten every weekday evening. Then we had two weeks of "tech" rehearsals and dress rehearsals and lighting rehearsals, and then we had a month of performances on weeknights and weekends, and then we took the show on tour for two or three months of weekends to various schools and playgrounds throughout the Los Angeles area, so naturally we had to have regular brush-up rehearsals—

What I'm getting at is that I missed the next twenty episodes. At least.

I knew that STAR TREK existed, but that was about it. My chances to see the show had been limited, and I had no idea whether it had developed into a good show or a bad one. What I did know about STAR TREK were bits and pieces that had come to me through friends—and that was even more maddening because their opinions were so subjective.

I mean, it was like being Moses, and being taken to the top of the mountain—and then not being allowed to look at the promised land, instead having to listen to someone else describe it in highly emotional terms. To put it mildly, it was frustrating as hell.

Look, let's go back to the beginning. The very beginning.

I have been a science fiction fan for as long as I can remember. I grew up in the Van Nuys, California, Public Library, checking out the limit—ten books a week. My childhood companions were Robert A. Heinlein and Isaac Asimov and Theodore Sturgeon and Henry Kuttner and C. M. Kornbluth and Frederik Pohl and—well, you get the idea.

The first paperback books I ever bought were *Earthlight* by Arthur C. Clarke, and an Ace double novel: *One Against Eternity (The Weapon Makers)* by A. E. Van Vogt; and *The Other Side of Here* by Murray Leinster. And also a Dell collection called *Six Great Short Novels of Science Fiction.* I was just starting junior high school at the time—and it was like the opening of a whole new world. Suddenly there was Robert Sheckley and Phillip Jose Farmer and Alfred Bester and William Tenn and Ray Bradbury and Robert Silverberg and Gordon R. Dickson and Poul Anderson and Richard Matheson and—

—and then I discovered the magazines. *Fantasy and Science Fiction, Galaxy, If, Worlds of Tomorrow, Astounding* (which later became *Analog*), and also a couple which are only memories today: *Venture,* and *Beyond.* I was in high school by now, and my friends included Kurt Vonnegut and Brian Aldiss and Harry Harrison and John W. Campbell and Robert Bloch and H. L. Gold and Tony Boucher and L. Sprague DeCamp and Zenna Henderson and James Gunn and Daniel F. Galouye and Fritz Leiber and oh, yeah—a fellow named Harlan Ellison. I knew them only as names on the bindings of battered library books, or names on the covers of bright paperbacks, or names in the tables of contents in the magazines—but I knew those names. And they were magic. Those were people who were *dreaming*—and they were allowing *me* to share their dreams. How could I not help but think of them as my friends? They were letting me into their heads.

If I had to pick out one factor which has had the most influence in determining the shape of my life today, (with the possible exception of sex) I would choose science fiction. Books, novels, short stories, movies, comic books, what have you—if it dealt with anything even slightly out of the ordinary, I *had* to see it, do it or own it. (I have never quite forgiven Walt Disney for not completing Tomorrowland before he opened up Disneyland to the public in 1955—talk about disappointments . . .)

I can remember dragging my father to the worst possible

B-pictures on Tuesday evenings because that was the last night they would be played and I just *had* to see *Not of This Earth* and *The Incredible Shrinking Man* and *When Worlds Collide* and *It Conquered the World* and *Them* and *Tarantula* and *House of Wax* and (*sigh*) *Forbidden Planet.*

I remember the day we got our very first television set— and it opened up not just *Howdy Doody* and *I Love Lucy,* but *Tom Corbett, Space Cadet* and *Space Patrol* and *Tales of Tomorrow* and the occasional *Playhouse 90* or *Studio One* science fiction drama.

And I collected. I filled one whole wall of my room with books, then started on a second. Then I started packing them in boxes and filled the garage.

I took over my mother's 8mm movie camera and started making my own animated monsters—jerkily moving puppets and cartoons. I started drawing storyboards and reading voraciously on film techniques—not just to know how they were done, but so I could do them myself. I began to ache for the money and resources to do the kind of science fiction movies that I wanted to see, but no one else was making. (I still have a short piece of film left over from that period—and to me, it represents a triumph of will over technique. It's an 8mm wide-screen color shot of me stand-ing next to my workdesk and reacting to a little animated monster about three inches high—which in turn was looking up and reacting to me. Despite the crudeness of the anima-tion, I'm proud of this shot because there's neither matte line nor jerkiness, and absolutely no way at all to tell how the shot was done.)

I used to read a book a day. Like vitamins. I would take them to school and read them in class. School bored me—I was too busy exploring the universe to care about conjugat-ing verbs. And I was discovering that I knew more odd little bits of information about the world than my teachers did. (Like a math teacher at Van Nuys High who made fun of me in front of the whole class because I asked him to explain the terms *googol* and *googolplex.* They're mathematical terms for a couple of umpty-ump numbers—I still don't know for sure—but he'd never heard of them, so he just said, "Well, that's what you get from reading all that science fiction—") (From that day on, I stopped listening to the man. I ended up with a D in the course and had to repeat it in summer school.)

I used to haunt the newsstands and bookstores. I would make a point of stopping by Van Nuys' biggest stand every Tuesday and Thursday mornings to see if there were any new titles; and later on, I used to go down into Hollywood to the big stand at Hollywood and Cahuenga (it's still there)— and if there was anything on the racks I hadn't read yet, I would go burrowing for the copy that was in the very best condition. I collected and read and dreamt my way through junior high school and high school (first Van Nuys, then U.S. Grant) and six years of college. I was one of those kids who are called "walking encyclopedia" and "Einstein" and "egghead" and a lot of other things, less nice. I tried to ignore them. I didn't believe in fighting—can you imagine a pacifist in junior high school? In 1958? I got beat up a lot. But I felt superior because of all the wondrous things I had in my head, given to me by my special friends in the books and magazines—things that all those mundane-type people would never know. Never. They just couldn't get the message—and I wasn't going to try to share my private dreams with them because I didn't want to have to defend those dreams. And even so, I still had to. "Are you still reading that crap?" Science fiction just wasn't respectable. It still isn't very. Most people still equate science fiction with space opera, something for the kids, and smirk a bit about their intellectual "superiority."

But it was a normal condition of adolescence, and everyone solves the problem of growing up in his own way. Somewhere along the line, a little boy was deciding who he wanted to be and what he wanted to do—and one of those things would be to someday, somehow, join the ranks of the "special dreamers."

In short, science fiction was not just a casual decision for me. I did not stumble accidentally into it.

It was the logical culmination of a self-induced conditioning process—and I thank whatever deity I may be presently holding dear, for my existence in an environment which allows such a wide variety of opportunity and choice. (Say what you will about the faults of the United States of America—this country's high degree of technology and industry, as well as its literacy, makes it possible for a wide variety of subcultures to exist and flourish. And if you don't believe me, go back and reread *Future Shock* by Alvin Toffler.)

What I'm getting at, is that if you want to make a career in science fiction, or in writing, or in anything at all—you have to take it *seriously*. And when you do take it seriously, it becomes a way of life. Taking something seriously means immersing yourself in it and treating it with respect, and making it part of yourself.

Fred Pohl, who was then editor of *Galaxy*, put it all into one sentence the very first time I met him. He said, and it's really very simple, "If you want to write science fiction, you have to *read* science fiction."

So, I spent a lifetime training to be a STAR TREK writer—even before I *knew* there was going to be a STAR TREK. Apparently that was a lucky bit of prescience on my part. But even if it hadn't been STAR TREK, it would have been something, a contemporary equivalent perhaps. That was the direction I was moving in. And STAR TREK was the opportunity —but I couldn't have picked a better one if the gods themselves had called me in to design it.

And *most* luckily of all, I was ready for the opportunity when it did occur. The G*O*L*D*E*N   O*P*P*O*R*- T*U*N*I*T*Y isn't worth a damn thing unless you're prepared to meet it. Important Piece of Gerrold Wisdom (Number One): Once you make a decision to do something or to be something, *start preparing for it immediately*.

Somewhere in my life, probably while I was in junior high school, I knew I wanted to write. (I vaguely remember enjoying a couple of English classes that had put an emphasis on creative writing, and in one of which I produced my first "epic"—a fourteen page story—typed, of course; I was already thinking a little like a professional—about the oppression of telepathic human beings; mutants, of course. The story detailed the panic-stricken flight of a thirteen-year-old mutant from his junior high school, which bore an uncomfortable resemblance to the one I was then attending, and which the army had turned into a concentration camp where they were sorting the humans from the mutants—well, what do you expect from a hypersensitive Jew-boy who's just come up smack-bang against his first real anti-semitism? Your output is derived from your input. The story was an emotional statement, and heavily imitative of the last six books I had read. It had a "proper" ending too: the boy escaped to another planet or dimension where all the other mutants who had escaped had gathered together—but not to fight back, just to teach Earth people to love. i.e.—"We're not going to kill you; we're going to let you live with your consciences." The instructor was very disturbed by it—at first, he thought I had plagiarized it; he said it was too mature for a junior high school student to have written, and besides, I had used quotation marks too well. —Okay, so that was his way of being *impressed*. —Finally, I managed to convince him that I had written it myself, but he watched me warily for the rest of the semester.) (No, I did not try to submit the story anywhere—I knew I wasn't *that* good yet.)

High school got me into a journalism class, and if nothing else, I learned one thing from it:

It's not a learning experience, unless you can make mistakes.

And, boy, did we make mistakes! As many as were possible. We must have been staying awake nights thinking up new ones. We ran double-entendre headlines, we ran photographs sideways, we cut the editorials so we wouldn't have to leave out the jokes, we insulted members of the faculty at will, and a couple of times we came close to printing obscene photographs. Not quite, but almost.

But, as for learning about writing—?

Zero. Big fat round nothing. The instructor was even more inexperienced than us. We felt sorry for him. He was unable to teach us a thing.

The only thing we learned was that it's too easy to get into print. And that taught us a healthy disrespect for the printed page. We ended up being skeptical of everything we read, as well as most of what we heard. We turned into a classroom full of pre-pubescent iconoclasts—in fact, thinking back on it now, I don't think *any* instructor would have been able to cope with us; we had a collection of insanities, psychoses and fetishes that would have made the Camarillo State Home for the Bewildered proud to number us among its inmates. (Example: that class has since produced at least one Jesuit priest and two admitted felons, not to mention the speed-freak who *did* end up in a rubber room.)

What we *didn't* learn—and should have—was a sense of

responsibility toward the printed page. If you're going to put words on paper, they ought to be not just the prettiest ones you can think of, but the ideas behind them ought to be well thought out too. You should consider who you're writing for and what you want to tell them—and most of all, how you want them to react to it.

But, like I said:

Zero.

Big fat round nothing. That's what we learned.

So—onward to college. Look both ways and cross the street to Los Angeles Valley Junior College, a two-year establishment, notable for two facts only: first, there is no such place as Los Angeles Valley—it was the San Fernando Valley, but it was a Los Angeles College—*ahem,* Junior College. And second, it's a cheap place to pile up a lot of prerequisite courses before going on to the more expensive universities.

I don't know how other people feel about college, but to me, it's overrated. College gives you living experience in an environment where you have to be responsible for yourself—but very little more than that. If you learn anything, you've done it yourself.

Two years of Art and Journalism at the aforementioned Institute of Higher Learning taught me two things. I didn't want to be an artist. I didn't want to be a journalist.

What I wanted to do was *create.*

Let me digress for a moment from all this autobiographical bullshit.

There are only three kinds of job in the world. (Four, if you count godhood, but that may fall into the category of Services anyway.) They are: Producer, Serviceman, and Salesman. In that order of respectability.

Most people are either Servicemen or Salesmen. Servicemen are people like mailmen, telephone operators, truck drivers, tax accountants, secretaries, stock brokers, computer programmers, farm laborers, and so on; people who are performing jobs of *continuing* need; i.e. they are performing a service. Salesmen are advertising executives, cosmetic clerks, insurance men, and anyone else who takes money from your wallet in return for tangible value. (If the value is *in*tangible, he's a con man.) People who *sell.*

But *Producers* are special people. Not TV producers—I

mean Producers in the true sense of the word to *produce*. I mean artists, writers, filmmakers, rock singers, architects and inventors. People who are bringing something into existence that did not exist before. These are special people because these are the only people in the world who are *creating* wealth. Everybody else is either performing the service of bringing that wealth to the consumer, or making a living selling it to him.

And wealth is cumulative. Every bit produced is added to what has come before. As more and more wealth is produced, the human race becomes richer and richer—in ideas, and in the applied fruits of those ideas; culturally, technologically, industrially, and especially in that immeasurable something called "the quality of life."

And that's what I wanted to do—produce. Create. Bring something *new* into existence.

I wanted to write. I wanted to make movies. I wanted to act and direct.

And in that, I was only in competition with the entire city of Hollywood. And most of the surrounding suburbs.

In Southern California (there must be something in the air) *everybody* wants to write, make movies, act and direct. In fact, the greatest deals in town are being consummated on the unemployment line. (I know, I've set up a few myself.)

But we were talking about schools—if I had to pick just one school, just one *class*, just one *instructor* who taught me the most, it would be a very easy choice. There isn't anyone else who even comes close.

Irwin R. Blacker.

Beginning and Advanced Screenwriting.

The University of Southern California.

I mean, that's *it*. Right there, in one big package, all wrapped up in pretty paper and with bright red bows attached. And your name on it. It's all there in that man's head, and he's waiting to give it to you. If you can get into his class, he'll lay it out for you like a banquet before a barbarian, more information than you are ever likely to know how to handle.

You are going to find bits and pieces of writing wisdom and lore scattered throughout the pages of this book, nuggets of gold that you can take to your heart and cherish. But lest you think that they have sprung from my head fully grown, like Athena from the forehead of Zeus, let me put you straight, right here and now—I am only repeating the lessons that I learned at my Master's knee. These are precious bits of carefully garnered knowledge that have been handed down through generations of writers ever since Aristotle first wrote his *Poetics*.* I repeat them because they're worth knowing. They work for me, and a lot of other people too. And I want you to know where they come from. Irwin R. Blacker. And that other fellow—The Big A, Aristotle.

Oh—Blacker doesn't really teach writing. He teaches analysis. Nobody can teach you *how* to write—either you've got a piece of it or you haven't. But you *can* teach analysis —and that's what Irwin R. Blacker does better than anybody else.

He could even teach a dolt like me to understand the importance to drama of such seemingly disparate elements as Plot, Dialogue, Theme, Characterization, Spectacle and Music. Actually, those are Aristotle's six criteria necessary to drama, but their truth is such that even today's new-wave stories, widescreen spectaculars, screaming rock operas and hyperthyroid television commercials are still bound to the conditions imposed by those six basic elements.

Once you've learned to understand those criteria and recognized their importance to the success of a dramatic work, you've gained an all-important skill. Assuming you know how to use it properly, you can then examine just about any script presented you and spot its fatal flaws, if it has any. And if you have even the slightest degree of objectivity, you should be able to examine your own scripts and spot your own flaws.

And if you can do that, then it's only one short step to knowing what's needed to correct them.

But that's the hard part—

There is a plateau of professionalism that every writer who is going to make it must rise above—there's a level beyond which the amateurish*ness* disappears from his thought and sentence structure and he begins to display a sense of

---

*The first known analysis of the component elements of drama. An invaluable source book for writers, critics and students. Try to find it in the original Greek.

competence and skill in his approach to his material that will eventually win him the all-important compliment, the check. Once that plateau is passed, nearly every time that writer sits down at his machine, he will produce readable constructions of words.

The "unknown" is the person who will achieve and surpass that level of professionalism. The amateur is the one who will never come near.

The tools of analysis and understanding will not make it possible for an amateur to pass that plateau, not at all— but if a person does have it in him to get there, then those tools will get him there quicker. The more familiar with them he becomes, the more confidence and skill he will have in his craft.

Hence, the reason why I praise Mr. Irwin R. Blacker so highly. He made it possible for me to be ready when opportunity presented itself so coyly at my door.

Opportunity never uses a bludgeon when it comes calling, it never knocks with a battering ram. At best, it scratches lightly at the window pane, like a moth momentarily confused, then it flutters elusively away—and it's up to you to be there at that window listening for it, armed with net and field glasses, ready to drop everything and go chasing helter-skelter after it.

You can chase a lot of those little bugs that look like opportunities before you finally catch one that really is—but when you do catch it, you'd better know how to mount it and pin it. Otherwise you might as well save yourself the trouble.

So—I thank Mr. Irwin R. Blacker here and now for the tools that he gave me.

I am muchly appreciative.

CHAPTER TWO:

"Tomorrow Was Yesterday"

When STAR TREK telecast its first episode, I spotted two flaws right away. One was a scientific error, the other a characterization mistake.

The scientific error—a landing party "beamed" down to the planet, via a teleportation device called a "transporter." They materialized in thin air. I saw that and my immediate reaction was, "I don't believe it. You need a receiving booth for long distance teleportation."

The characterization mistake—there was this fellow named

Spock. He was supposed to be an alien, which I thought was a good idea, but when they said he was without emotions, I flinched. "Oh, hell—without emotions, he's going to be a thoroughly unlikable character. He might as well be a grumpy robot."

Okay. *Mea culpa.* I wasn't thinking according to the thoughts of Chairman Roddenberry. I was wrong.

On both counts. First, the transporter—from a scientific point of view, what right did I have to say that a teleportation device *needed* a receiving booth? How the hell did I know? Besides, and more importantly, the transporter made it possible to get the heroes of the show down onto the planet as quickly as possible and into the action of the story.

Remember, we only have one hour of television time. We can't waste it on repetitious landings and takeoffs. The important thing is the story. Besides, it's easier to believe in a transporter beam than in a spaceship that has to be built to cope with every possible kind of planetary condition in the universe so it can land on them at will—and also have the unlimited power it would need to take off again, especially against unknown higher gravities. No, the transporter beam makes a lot more sense.

Oh, the *Enterprise* could have used its shuttle craft as landing boats—but that still requires the versatility and power of the above. And it's still too time consuming. From a writing point of view, from a television point of view—and yes, even from a science-fiction point of view, Gene Roddenberry knew what he was doing.

Now, the second mistake. Mr. Spock. Boy, was I wrong about Mr. Spock!

How was I to know that he would turn out to be one of the series' most popular characters? (I would have said *the* most popular, but I have this sneaking admiration for Captain Kirk.)

What I hadn't realized was that the other characters on the *Enterprise* did have emotions—they *would* react to Mr. Spock's implacability, and the resultant interaction between them would make for some fascinating viewing. Besides, a character without emotions was a challenge for every scriptwriter who approached the show; they couldn't resist Mr. Spock.

But at that time, September of 1966, as a fan I had serious reservations about STAR TREK.* I liked what I had seen, but I wanted them to realize their full potential. I didn't want them to fall into the same trap of fantasy and pseudo-science fiction that had claimed—oh, say . . . *Lost in Space.*

Lost in Space was a thoroughly offensive program. It probably did more to damage the reputation of science fiction as a serious literary movement than all the B-movies about giant insects ever made—because *Lost in Space* was one full-color hour of trash reaching into millions of homes, regularly, once a week, for five achingly long years. The number of people that show must have touched—never mind, I'm getting nauseous just thinking about it.

With rare exception, the whole attitude of television network executives toward science fiction seemed to be that it was a convenient way to tell monster stories and wish-fantasies, something to be treated with all the respect of roller games, or wrestling. Gene Roddenberry had offered CBS a chance to buy STAR TREK—but their reaction had been, "But we already have a science fiction series—we have *Lost in Space.*" So much for CBS.

You see why I had doubts? There were too many minds in Hollywood that could not see the difference between a *Lost in Space* and a STAR TREK. (Please note that I use two different type faces.)

In an era which had produced such achievements as *Gilligan's Island, Green Acres,* and *The Flying Nun,* the only safe statement to make about American television was that it could not be underestimated.

---

*Look, I'm not the only one who had reservations about Spock. NBC was a little scared too. At one point, they had considered getting rid of his pointed ears and arched eyebrows because they thought that audiences might be repelled. They even made up and sent out publicity brochures with Leonard Nimoy in normal makeup, un-Vulcanized you might say. But by that time, Spock had begun to prove himself to be one of the show's strongest drawing points, so the idea was dropped. Later on, nobody at NBC would admit that they had ever been anything but 100 percent in favor of Mr. Spock being an alien, they had known Roddenberry was right all the time. The buck was passed so fast they wore it out.

Starting in 1965 sometime, I had begun pecking out outlines for submission to the various TV shows, dreadful things like "My Life Is My Own" for *Dr. Kildare,* and "The Saga of Swifty Morgan" for *Bonanza.* Whether these outlines showed any glimmer at all of my still-embryonic abilities with words and ideas is a moot point. They were of deservedly ill-repute, showing a degree of amateurishness that makes me cringe to look at them today and think that I ever submitted them for serious consideration. The nicest thing that can be said about them is that they provided valuable learning experience—especially in how to cope with rejection.

Fortunately, either my ego, or my determination, I'm not sure which, wouldn't let me quit. I kept pecking away —and in 1966, I met my first love. An IBM Selectric Typewriter. Such Beauty! Such Grace! Such a Joy to Behold! And it typed nice too.

The only reason I mention that fact is that the IBM Selectric was such a superior machine to the ten-year-old Smith-Corona portable it had replaced that my output zoomed up from six pages per eight hours of sweating to *thirty* pages —and no sweat at all!

Imagine that! A machine that could produce five times as much shit. Just what the world needed. More important though, the Selectric's efficiency made it possible for me to get my ideas down onto the paper with a minimum of physical effort. The typewriter had ceased to be an obstacle between me and the paper.

I tried to explain this once to a (would-be) playwright who still wrote his manuscripts longhand (I shudder to think of it), but he couldn't cope with the idea that an efficient typewriter is a *valuable* working tool.

Oh, well—try to explain your first love to someone else, they just won't understand.

Where were we? Oh, yes—the mechanics of submitting an outline to a television show. How do you do it?

First of all, you need an agent. Then let him worry about it. That's his job.

In fact, without an agent, you can't even get in the door. They won't read your manuscript at all.

Now, this may look like the agent-represented writers have an unfair edge over the unrepresented ones, but that's *exactly* the way it is. The unrepresented writer hasn't got a chance.

Look at it from a TV producer's point of view. He needs thirty good scripts. He needs them *now*. He hasn't got time to run a writing class, he hasn't got time to deal with unprofessionals and hopefuls on the off chance that one of them just *might* come up with something usable, he hasn't got time even to read their submissions to see if there's something in them worth stealing.*

He knows an agented writer is more likely to be *professional*. A man he can deal with. A man who will understand what is required of him and will turn out beautiful, non-offensive stories that can be filmed within the limits of the budget.

Now, I will tell you how I got my agent.

I called the Writers' Guild of America. They sent me a list of agents who were signatory to the Artists and Managers' Basic Agreement. Then I sat down at the telephone, and starting with the A's, called each one and asked if they were interested in representing new talent.

I had an agent before I'd made my fifth call.

Listen, if you try the same thing, start with the Z's. Please. And let me know what happens.

Most agents will say no. And the ones that will say yes aren't any too reputable. After all, how good can an agent be if he's willing to take on an unknown or amateur? Some may ask to read your material first.

But it's a chance you *both* have to take.

Some agents are masochists. They help new talent get started. So it was in this case. I now had someone to submit my manuscripts for me. They would at least be read.

This agent, a man whose name started with A, gave me one really dumb—but very profitable—piece of advice. It

---

*I say this as a joke. TV producers don't steal. It isn't worth the trouble; it's just as easy to hire the writer as it is to steal from him—but the possibility of such an accusation is one of the main reasons why they won't read an un-agented manuscript. There are too many amateurs willing to believe that a story with even the slightest similarity was plagiarized from theirs; they cannot conceive that ideas are *not* unique, and they will sue at the hint of a resemblance. So producers return their manuscripts unopened. A shame because a lot of good people lose out too, but lawsuits are a bloody nuisance.

went something like this: "Watch the new shows in September, and if you can come up with an idea, submit it very fast. Sometimes if a show is in trouble, they'll junk a bad episode in favor of a better script."

Don't you believe it. The odds are better in Russian Roulette. The only person who's going to win a gamble like that is somebody the producer knows and can depend on— say, like last year's Oscar winner for the best original screenplay.

But it sounded good at the time, and that was one of the reasons I was watching STAR TREK that first Thursday night when "The Incredible Salt Vampire" was on.

And I liked what I saw. It suggested so much. But it wasn't enough. And I had fears that they wouldn't be able to do it *right*. "Oh, no—" I said. "I hope they're not planning to turn this into a different-monster-every-week kind of series. The potential of this show is so much more." And then, I said: "Well, if you want something done right . . ."

So I went to my typewriter and started typing.

By Monday afternoon, I had produced a sixty page outline for a two-part episode, entitled, "Tomorrow Was Yesterday."*

"Tomorrow Was Yesterday" dealt with the discovery by the *Enterprise* of a giant "universe" or "generation" ship— that is, a slower than light spaceship that would take generations to reach its destination because they lacked the power to traverse the vast distances between the stars any faster. The *Voyager* was a colony ship that had been launched from Earth hundreds of years previously, but only now were Federation ships catching up to it, the *Enterprise* being the first.

Unfortunately, after hundreds of years, the people inside had forgotten that they were aboard a spaceship—instead they believed their enclosed world to be the totality of existence. Part of the reason for this stemmed from a mutiny in their long forgotten past, a mutiny that had left the *Voyager's* population divided into two armed camps. The elite were

---

*Absolutely no relation at all to the STAR TREK episode of later that season, "Tomorrow Is Yesterday." Although, I must admit, the similarity of the two titles did give me pause to think—but what the hell. What's a title or two among friends?

descendants of the well-educated, and they had a high standard of living in their part of the ship. The downtrodden oppressed were descendants of the mutineers.

Now, the *Voyager* was a giant sphere, or cylinder. Artificial gravity was provided by spinning the ship to create centrifugal force; therefore, from a shipside point of view, down was outward, up was toward the center. The upper levels in the center of the ship were where the control room was located— also where the elite "lightmen" lived. They had maintained themselves in very posh living quarters.

The lower levels, that is, those just inside the hull of the ship, had been intended as maintenance levels. They were unlit, and generally unlivable. There were miles of maintenance tunnels and the lower level men, believed to be "demons" by the lightmen, lived a nomadic existence, hiding in the darkness from the periodic raids from above. And raiding back too.

The lightmen, of course, considered themselves the chosen people of their universe because it was their sacred duty to protect the control room. The demons, however, were the only ones who had access to the ship's eight nuclear power plants which were located at the poles of the spinning sphere.

Naturally, neither group knew the truth of the whole situation and they were locked into a conflict which would prevent them from ever finding out. And because neither lightmen nor demons could conceive of *another* spaceship, each assumed that the men of the *Enterprise* were spies from the other levels, thus complicating Kirk's problem and making lots of possibilities for action and suspense, especially on the darkened lower levels.

Kirk's problem was simple: reestablish amity between the two camps, convince them that they were really on a spaceship, gain access to the control room, reactivate the nuclear propulsion units (which had been shut down in the mutiny) and change the course of the ship before it was too late to keep it from being drawn into a nearby star. And just to complicate it a little bit, the population of the generation ship was several thousand—just enough beyond the capacity of the *Enterprise* to make evacuation impractical.

The first hour of this proposed two-parter involved Kirk and Spock and assorted crewmembers getting chased and beaten up by both sides, and in the process, discovering the nature of the situation. In the second hour, Kirk solved the problem—and in a way that I thought especially symbolic, as well as visual.

Making friends with the dwellers of the "lower" or outer levels, via McCoy's medical help to the children (the lower levels had higher gravity and higher pressure than the levels above, as well as being generally uncomfortable), Kirk proposed that they reactivate the nuclear power plants to provide heat and light on the maintenance levels. The lower-men had been opposed to doing this because that would have given the dwellers of the upper levels the visual advantage they needed to come down and wipe them out. If the light was turned back on, the lower-men would lose their protection. But that would have been okay with them—all Kirk had to do was give them some phasers . . .

Kirk didn't like that idea at all.

Finally, Spock got an idea from observing a character named Specks, a librarian who wore glasses only as a historical badge of office. Scotty was ordered to fabricate filtered lenses for everyone to wear, and when the power plants were reactivated, they turned all the interior lighting so bright that no one could stand it. Everybody without glasses was effectively blinded as long as the lights were so bright. (I thought we might suggest this by over-exposing the film slightly and showing the control room raiding party as dark silhouettes in stark contrast.) In any case, Kirk and a group of men swiftly went up and took over control of the *Voyager* (it's all starting to come back to me now) and were able to change its course just in time—and also to begin the first steps toward ending the generations-long war between the two sides. A nice additional touch was that in order to accomplish this, the respective leaders of each side, older men with a stake in preserving the status quo, had to be removed (not killed, just removed) from power in order to let younger and saner heads prevail.

I was kind of proud of that story.* I had been trying to tell as meaningful and relevant a story as I could, a science fiction story that would also be appropriate for the limita-

---

*The retelling of it here does not do it justice, believe me. You can't shrink sixty pages down to six without losing something in the translation.

tions of television, and one that would utilize the characters and format of STAR TREK in what I hoped would be its maximum potential.

I had written it as a two-parter for two reasons. First, it would have meant more money for me if they had bought it —and second, it would have meant a greater spread of money in the budget for sets, costumes and actors. The budget for one episode wouldn't have been enough; I hoped the budget for two would be, thus making it possible to tell a story of wider scope.

I was wrong. Again.

STAR TREK rejected it. With one of the finest rejection letters it has ever been my pleasure to receive.

It is the only rejection letter I have ever pasted in my scrapbook:

October 3, 1966

Dear Mr. A——:

Herb Solow forwarded to me the outline entitled "TOMORROW WAS YESTERDAY" by David Gerrold.

Mr. Gerrold's outline was by no means inadequate. It is, as a matter of fact, very adequate. Unquestionably your young man can write. He has a good imagination and a good sense of structure. Unfortunately, his ideas of what is possible in television are somewhat grandiose. This is a fault which is found in the majority of vastly more experienced writers, so don't say I am picking on Mr. Gerrold. I am not. I am impressed by him. However, to film the two-part story outlined here would probably cost $6–700,000, in other words, the special effects, the sets, set decorations and so on are far too elaborate for television. What he has written is a good motion picture treatment for ideally a $2–3,000,000 picture.

However, because I am so impressed with his imagination and his ability, I would be delighted to meet with him and tell him more of our specific needs, this despite the fact that at the moment we are not buying scripts from anyone.

I am enclosing the outline. Thank you for letting me see it.

Sincerely yours,

Gene Coon
Producer
STAR TREK

cc: H. Solow
   G. Roddenberry

And *that's* how it all started.*

---

*Reacting to Gene Coon's comment that what I had written was ideally a $2–3,000,000 movie, my agent suggested that I turn the story into a movie outline. Just change the name of the space-ship and all of STAR TREK's characters to something else. I did, but it never sold. Then I tried to turn it into a novel—but that project bogged down too. The first eighty pages of manuscript of *Yesterday's Children* seemed to be heading in a totally different direction. After thinking about it for most of 1968 and '69, I decided to write the novel it was turning into instead of trying to preserve the one I had started with. The book sold to Dell at the end of '69, and I turned in the finished manuscript a year later. Dell published it in July of 1972. (*Yesterday's Children*, Dell Books #9780. You can probably get a copy by sending a dollar to Dell Publishing Co., 750 Third Ave., New York, 10017.) The last I heard, some studio was interested in buying the movie rights to it . . .

CHAPTER THREE:

"The Protracted Man" and "Bandi"

Before I went to meet Gene Coon, my agent carefully primed me on what to expect.

"David," he said. "Don't expect anything at all. He's got all his script assignments made for this season, he can't give you anything but encouragement. All he wants to do is talk to you and tell you more about the show. What he'll probably do is tell you to wait and see if the show is renewed for a second season, and if it is, then submit stories for it, because then he'll be in a position to consider them seriously."

I listened carefully, took it all in and practiced nodding my head at the right places.

Then I drove down to Hollywood for my prearranged appointment with Gene Coon. Needless to say, I felt like Dorothy being ushered into the presence of the Wizard of Oz. That Gene Coon was on a twenty foot throne surrounded by pillars of lightning and thunder didn't help much either. (That was a subjective view, of course, but it was one of those situations where I kept looking behind me to see if I was leaving a trail of little brown puddles.) I don't remember what his first words were. I was too awed by the effect of seeing them materialize in puffs of flame.

He told me he had been impressed by my outline, "Tomorrow Was Yesterday," and wanted to know where I had gone to school and what I had studied. I told him I had spent two years at the University of Southern California studying Cinema, and was working for a B.A. in Theatre Arts at San Fernando Valley State.

Apparently, that satisfied him as to the seriousness of my desire to write for television and movies, for he said, "David, I can't promise you anything at all. I've got all my script assignments made for this season, I can't give you anything but encouragement. But I did want to talk to you and find out a little bit about you and tell you more about the show. Now, if we're renewed for a second season—we won't know until February—then I want you to submit some more stories to us, because then we'll be in a position to consider them seriously."

Then we talked about possible story ideas, to see if I was thinking along the right track. One of the ideas I suggested was about small furry creatures that bred like crazy until they took over the *Enterprise.* Gene just smiled and shook his head. "Sounds cute, but it would probably cost too much. We'd have to build the creatures. No, think of something else."

And that was that.

I thanked him profusely for the opportunity to talk to him and promised to pray nightly for the show's renewal. He didn't insist that I back out of his office, bowing repeatedly; special dispensation had been granted.

Afterwards, on my way home, I realized I had done a dumb thing. I had forgotten to ask permission to visit the set.

Oh, well. If things worked out all right, I'd get plenty of opportunities later on.

Besides, as it happened, I'd had a quick glimpse of one of the actors. After the meeting, Ande, Gene's secretary, went digging for a copy of *The Star Trek Guide* for me. (Another bonus!) While she was doing that, I was gazing distractedly out the window . . . only to be startled by Leonard Nimoy, in full Vulcan makeup, calmly riding his bicycle down the Desilu back-street. My first real look at Mr. Spock—and he was doing something totally *human*. But I guess it was logical . . .

By now, the school situation was such that I was catching occasional episodes of the show—and liking it. Heavens! I was turning into a Trekkie.

And so was the girl I was hanging around with at the time. Actually, hanging around isn't the right way to describe what we were doing—*nattering* and *grommishing* comes a lot closer.*

Well, what do you expect from a couple of ex-rabbits? (Holly had also been in *Winnie the Pooh*. She had been an associate rabbit, while I had been the head bunny. She's only slightly crazier than me.)

We were both intrigued with the possibilities of my selling a story to STAR TREK, and in the next three months, we spent a lot of time talking over various story premises and how well they fit into the concept of the show as outlined in *The Star Trek Guide*. That was my bible.

By January, I had five story premises that I thought were suitable for STAR TREK.

One of them, I've forgotten. Which may be a blessing. It must have been so wretchedly handled that my subconscious mind has since suppressed all memory of it, and in one of my rarer moments of lucidity, I must have destroyed the last remaining copy. The only thing I do remember was that it

---

*I suppose this should be explained. Being theatre arts students, we were conscious of what all the extras—or "atmosphere people"—in any shot were doing. We had come to the conclusion that they were "nattering" and "grommishing." That is, in order to fake a conversation in the background, you mumble softly: "natter, natter, natter . . ." And your partner replies: "grommish, grommish, grommish . . ."

involved the capture of the *Enterprise* by a superior force and Captain Kirk had to play a game of chess for their freedom —using the officers and crew of the *Enterprise* as the chess pieces. (The crucial decision involved his knowing sacrifice of one of his officers in order to save the rest of the crew. I think the parallel I was trying to draw had something to do with the decisions a commander must make in battle. Sometimes they aren't always *nice*.)

The second premise was about a giant spaceship destroying, berserker machine. It was uncomfortably similar to an idea that Norman Spinrad was working on ("The Doomsday Machine") although I didn't know it at the time. My berserker was defeated by a careful use of illogic. Of course.

Two of the other premises were called "The Protracted Man," and "Bandi." I include them here, but with the caution that they are premises only, and not fully developed outlines. A premise is exactly that—a premise from which to develop a story.

Furthermore, these premises were written by a dreadfully inexperienced twenty-two-year-old—only my incredible enthusiasm and self-confidence kept me from spotting the many flaws and inconsistencies in them.

The Protracted Man

(A story premise by David Gerrold, February 1967.)

The *Enterprise* is temporarily assigned to aid a group of scientists who are in the final stages of a very important experiment. If the experiment succeeds, it will make it possible to cut down the traveling time from one part of the galaxy to another.

Even though faster-than-light travel is already possible (as evidenced by the *Enterprise* itself), the galaxy is so vast that many journeys are still impractically long. To get from one side of the galaxy to another, even at the *Enterprise*'s top speed, would take several years.

Consequently, this experiment is of considerable importance to the United Systems. If it succeeds they will be able to expand their explorations and colonies to the farthest reaches of the galaxy.

Basically, the idea is to set up a self-sustaining space warp through which a spaceship can take a "shortcut" from one part of the galaxy to another—a sort of tunnel in the sky. It is a long distance matter transport, achieved by a wrinkle in the very fabric of space.

Naturally, to set up this warp will require a great deal of energy and the math involved is so complex and sophisticated that it took a good many years just to program the computers for it. But all of these problems have already been solved and as the story opens, the scientists are in the final stage of preparations.

Because it will take a great amount of energy to actually fold the substance of space, the power will be drawn from a nearby star. The star itself has no planets and is of no conceivable use to anyone; it's a deserted backwater of the galaxy. Great energy screens have been constructed to tap its output of light and energy. They are like great sails hanging against the night.

But none of this needs to be shown. The *Enterprise* is light years away from the center of the action.

The *Enterprise* is assigned to be a retriever. Once the warp is established, a volunteer will pilot a shuttle craft through it. In a matter of seconds he will travel across four light years. The *Enterprise* is waiting to pick him up at his exit point. (This is a duty much akin to that of an aircraft carrier that picks up an astronaut after his capsule splashes down at sea.)

The *Enterprise* is hanging patiently in space. They are in the final stages of the countdown. Across the subspace radio they can hear the many different voices of the warp technicians.

Four light years away a switch is thrown, and aboard the *Enterprise,* they watch as the exit point of the warp takes shape several hundred miles off their bow. (This distance is a necessary safety factor.)

Slowly, the warp takes shape. It is a great flickering bright field against the darkness of space. (I envision a kind of hazy grid, wavering and slightly out of focus, superimposed against the backdrop of space. The three color negatives should be printed out of synch to give it a weird color effect. This is essential to the plot, but more about it later.)

However, something goes wrong. Perhaps it is a solar flare-up, or perhaps the great amounts of energy cause the dilithium crystals of the warp generators to fracture. In any case, the warp starts to flicker and seems to be shimmering out of control.

The chatter on the subspace radio indicates that the source of the trouble is at the other end, but it is too late to stop the experiment—the shuttle craft is already on its way through.

Indeed it is. Kirk and the others on the bridge can see a dim shape wavering within the warp, caught there, unable to escape. It is like a fly in a cosmic web.

Mr. Spock, who has been waiting in the transporter room, in case of just such an emergency, quickly activates the transporter. He is going to try to rescue the pilot of the shuttle craft by beaming him aboard the *Enterprise.* But as the transporter beam is activated, the warp starts to fade and seems about to flicker out of existence.

At first, Spock is unable to sense any life within the warp, then his sensors seem to go crazy, reporting conflicting data about the *number* of men in the warp. Although there is only supposed to be one, the transporter reacts as if there are several. Quickly, however, Spock does lock onto something—just as the shuttle craft explodes within the warp in a bright multi-colored flash.

The transport platform flickers. Something starts to take shape, but it is not one man, as expected—it is three! Yet, the three men seem strangely incomplete. As they take shape, it is possible to see that one of the three figures is a yellow phantom, one is red and one is blue. (One for each of the three color negatives.)

The three figures look at each other, then step together and unite to become one man, a normal man in normal color.

Something has gone terribly wrong. Apparently, the transporter has pulled the man out of the warp before he had come completely through it. It has affected him in some unknown way. As he steps down from the transporter platform, he seems to shimmer and as he moves, he shatters into his component colors.

(This is an easy effect to achieve—and probably the most inexpensive and effective of all special effects. The three color negatives are printed one or two frames out of synchronization. As long as the background does not move, it will appear normal, but any people within the shot will appear to shatter into their component colors every time they move. Later in the story, as the effect becomes more and more pronounced, the negatives are printed further and further out of synch. To show the protracted man in the same shot with an unaffected person, use a split screen or superimpose him.)

The affected man is quickly confined to the sick bay, where a puzzled Dr. McCoy scratches his head and tries to determine what has happened to him.

On the bridge, Kirk watches as the warp is shut down. It fades from the screen. He turns the controls over to a crewman and goes down to the sick bay to see the affected shuttlecraft pilot.

In sick bay, McCoy's instruments seem to have gone crazy. They are registering normal readings, not for one man, but for *several* identical men. As if one man has been superimposed upon himself three times.

Spock nods knowingly and says: "It is a logical development in view of the nature of the experiment." Kirk and
McCoy look at him, waiting for his inevitable explanation.
Spock, being the Science Officer, quickly theorizes: "The ex-
perimental warp is a fourth dimensional energy field. The
fourth dimension is *time*. Because the man was extracted
from the warp before he was completely through it, he has
been s-t-r-e-t-c-h-e-d along his time dimension."

Spock continues. The man has become a protracted man.
He exists across a time span of one complete second, as
opposed to a normal person who only exists during one nano-
second. Thus, he exists on several planes of existence. He
exists a half second ahead of a normal person, and a half
second behind. The crew of the *Enterprise* is able to perceive
three of these planes of existence.

Because of the doppler effect, the existence that is a half
second behind appears as a red phantom, the existence
which is a half second ahead appears as a blue phantom. The
yellow phantom is on the same plane of existence as the crew
of the *Enterprise*. Therefore, when the man moves, the blue
phantom moves first, followed by the yellow, then the red.
(Perhaps there are other existences beyond these, but reflect-
ing back light rays beyond the range of ordinary human
vision.)

McCoy asks Spock, at the end of this lengthy explanation,
what will happen to the man. Spock starts to explain about
entropy and certain other big words, but McCoy interrupts
and asks him to put it into words of one syllable. Spock stares
at him and comments that there are times when the good
Doctor can be most unscientific.

However, Spock continues, the man will probably stay
in this state if he is left undisturbed. If his time-protraction
is disturbed by any major upheaval of the local continuum,
it could have disastrous effects. Either he will be snapped
back to normal—or his time protraction will be increased.

Kirk asks Spock to explain. Spock theorizes that the man
is in a very delicate state. Any disturbance will probably
stretch him further and further along his time axis.

"What kind of disturbance?"

"I have no idea, Captain. It would probably be something
along the lines of a disturbance of the basic fabric of space.

Our warp drive might even have that kind of effect on him."

They go into the sick bay and talk to the man for a little bit. He sits up on the edge of the bed. Because he is still only a couple of frames out of synch, he can still perceive normal time, but when he speaks, he speaks with three voices. (This can be done by having the actor dub over his lines twice, or by using three tracks, each one in synch with one of the color negatives.)

However, the man is pretty well shaken up by his experience. The man, whom I shall call Jones (for convenience sake), reports that he perceives everybody in much the same way as they are perceiving him, although stationary objects seem to be normal.

Kirk is faced with the problem of what to do about Jones, but there is a complication to the problem. Jones' brother is a crewman aboard the *Enterprise*. Naturally he is worried and concerned about his time-protracted sibling. He is waiting for Kirk outside the sick bay.

He wants to know how soon they can cure his brother. How soon can they return him to normal?

Kirk replies. "We don't even know if we can."

Crewman Jones looks at him for a long moment, then asks to see his brother.

Kirk lets him into the sick bay, but with that one exception, nobody else is to enter the sick bay. It is off limits to all unauthorized personnel. They do not know if the effect is contagious (it could be) or if it is permanent or temporary. Worst of all, they are not even sure that they can return Jones to normalcy.

When Kirk returns to the bridge, he discovers from Mr. Scott that there is a power drain on the ship's matter-antimatter generators. The drain is localized in the sick bay. Apparently, the time protraction is an energy vacuum and draws power from the closest available source—in this case, the matter-antimatter generators.

Perhaps that is the answer to the problem. If Jones can be isolated from all energy sources, perhaps the time protraction will end and he will snap back to a normal condition.

In the wardroom, they talk to Mr. Scott about this possibility. He is doubtful that it can be done.

Spock suggests, "Wouldn't some kind of shielding work?"

Mr. Scott sees what Mr. Spock is suggesting. "I have some steel foil. It's collapsed steel—an inch thickness is equivalent to six inches."

"Do you have enough to shield the reactors?"

Scott shakes his head. "No, Captain. This stuff is so dense that we couldn't afford to carry that much. It would outweigh the rest of the ship."

"Well, so much for that idea—"

"But I do have enough to shield Jones," Scott suggests.

And that is the plan. A small cabin is quickly lined with the foil. It looks and handles very much like ordinary aluminum foil, but as a shielding, it stops radiations.

Jones is transferred to the shielded cabin and almost immediately the lights start to fade and the artificial gravity seems to lessen. All over the ship, reports come in that the power levels are falling.

"What's happening?" demands Kirk.

Spock answers, "Apparently, Captain, Jones' time protraction is stronger than we thought. He's drawing the power he needs right through the foil."

"But why so much?"

"Apparently, it takes a great deal of power to get through that foil. He's drawing it from the *Enterprise*. He's not conscious that he's doing it—he's just doing it. It's the time protraction."

Kirk orders Jones to be brought out of the unshielded cabin and returned to the sick bay. As they do so, they notice that his time protraction seems to have increased. By now, his time span covers a full second and a half. (Before, he was only two or three frames out of synch. Now, he is twelve to twenty-four frames out of synch. The blue phantom is twelve frames ahead of the yellow, the red is twelve frames behind.)

And the protracted man is very upset and dazed. He is confused because he is perceiving things that others can't. He is surrounded by multi-colored phantoms of Kirk and Spock and McCoy all moving and talking and gobbling at once. It is very disturbing. He can no longer communicate with them.

Crewman Jones, the brother of the affected man has noticed the increased protraction, and he is also upset.

Back in the wardroom, Kirk discusses the problem with his officers. Apparently, they cannot shield Jones, but they must cut him off from all available power.

Spock suggests, "The logical thing to do would be to shut down the *Enterprise*'s generators."

The others just stare at him.

Mr. Scott says, "That's impossible."

Spock just looks back at him and says, "Why?"

Mr. Scott explains, "Think of it, man! A ship without power is totally helpless. No gravity, no light, no heat, no air circulation, no defenses—nothing."

Spock suggests that they turn off the power for a short time only; a starship can maintain for at least half an hour before the life support situation becomes critical. That would be time enough to snap Jones out of his time protraction.

Scott shakes his head again. They are too close to a nearby star. The star puts out a good deal of hard radiation. The only thing protecting them from it is an electro-magnetic force field. If they shut down the power, they shut down the screen that deflects 99% of the radiation away from the *Enterprise*.

Spock suggests that they move the ship to a spot where the radiation is sufficiently low to permit this. A few light years away from any stars should more than do it.

Although doubts are expressed, they agree on the plan. The sooner they activate it, the better. The power drain of the protracted man has increased.

Kirk gives the order to move ahead at Warp Factor One. Almost immediately, McCoy is on the intercom, screaming: "Jim, you'd better get down here!"

In the sick bay, the strangest thing has happened. There are dozens of red and yellow and blue phantoms in the room, running and bumping into each other. Some escape into the corridor and go running up and down the halls, startling the crew of the *Enterprise*. Perhaps some of the phantoms are even negative images.

"What is it, Spock?" ask Kirk.

"I think I understand, Captain. We have to stop, immediately!"

Kirk orders a full stop. Gradually, the phantoms re-unite, until the protracted man is back to only three. But his time protraction has increased until he spans a full three seconds. (Perhaps he is now sixty frames out of synch, thirty ahead and thirty behind.)

Although the visible images are only a second out of phase, the non-visible images of Jones extend a good deal further. Spock is able to calculate this discrepancy and he reports that Jones' time protraction has been rapidly in-increased by their going into warp.

What had happened was that the *Enterprise*'s warp drive folds space in upon itself. It is a local disturbance of the basic continuum. Because Jones was in the center of it, his time line was folded back in upon itself over and over, and consequently, they saw many different phantom Joneses. When they came to a stop and the warp unfolded, it further stretched his time protraction.

Indeed it has. Before, Jones was perceptible as a human being, with colored fringes. Now, he is three overlapping phantoms, and his speech overlaps so badly that he is unintelligible.

Jones' brother blames Kirk for it. "If you hadn't ordered us into warp drive, he'd still be all right."

Kirk says, "Jones, I realize you're upset. You'd better go to your quarters before you say something that you'll later regret."

Jones stares at Kirk, almost hatefully, then he turns on his heel and walks away. Kirk nods to McCoy. "Keep an eye on him."

Back on the bridge, they discover that because Jones is stretched across a longer span of time, he is also using more power. They have also discovered that he drains more power from the matter-antimattter generators when he moves than when he stays in one place. The farther apart the three phantoms are in physical space, the more power they need to hold them together in the time continuum.

By now, the power drain is so severe that all functions of the ship are on emergency power.

"We've got to subdue him and keep him in one place," Kirk orders, but McCoy reports that Jones cannot be subdued by ordinary means.

"He can't be touched. He's just like so much fog."

"We'll have to use phasers then. Lowest level, stun him only."

A security squad is assigned to catch Jones and stun him. Meanwhile, Spock has come up with a solution to the problem. "Bring Jones to the transporter room."

But they cannot bring the man to the transporter room if they cannot find him. Jones sees the squad coming after him with phasers and he panics. To him, they look like multi-colored phantoms—an army of them.

All crewmen are alerted to stop Jones. "Use phasers. Shoot to stun."

Jones' brother arrives on the bridge, angry. He confronts Kirk. "You're trying to kill my brother!"

"It's him or us. We have no power left as long as he's moving around," Kirk answers. "You decide. Do we live or die?"

Jones doesn't speak for a long moment. Finally, he says, "Let me do it, then."

He takes his phaser and goes after his brother. Kirk orders all other crewmen to return to their quarters.

The *Enterprise* now becomes the scene of an eerie confrontation. The crewman confronts his brother, who is three bright colored phantoms.

"Robert," he says to the phantoms. "You've got to trust us." (His voice is being fed into the computer and garbled so that the protracted man can understand it.) With that, he pulls out his phaser and fires. One by one, the three phantoms collapse into each other. The protracted man lies unconscious on the floor.

Quickly, he is brought to the transporter room, where Mr. Spock is waiting. "Do we have enough power?" he asks.

"Not nearly enough," answers Mr. Scott.

Kirk orders all ship's functions shut down—everything except the transporter room. All available power must go into the transporter beam.

Spock is going to try an experiment. The clue to it is that when Jones materialized, he materialized not as one person, but as three different phantoms that had to reunite.

Spock feels that the transporter mechanism is able to differentiate between the different levels of Jones' time protraction and that they can use the transporter equipment to hold each plane of Jones' existence in a kind of limbo, then they can superimpose the three phantoms over each other and reunite them in the same time plane.

Spock explains, "We'll hold them apart until they've all dematerialized, then we'll adjust the phasing and try to materialize them all together in the same time orientation."

The command is given by Kirk to energize. Jones starts to dematerialize. He flickers through all kinds of different colors as each phantom is dematerialized out. When the last one disappears, Spock says, "Now!"

—And Jones reappears normally. He is no longer a protracted man. The desperate experiment has worked.

The tag for this one takes place in the bridge, as always. Kirk allows himself the luxury of a bad pun. He congratulates Spock on a *timely* solution.

Spock almost winces, and perhaps he complains that he will never understand an Earthman's concept of humor. "After all, there was a solution to the problem. It was only a matter of time."

Kirk gives him a look. "Mr. Spock, was that a joke you just told?"

"Who me? Captain!"

FADEOUT

Obviously, a premise is a very sketchy telling of the story. Continuity and characterization are overlooked. (We know who most of our characters are anyway, and there's no sense in developing continuity until the story is more fully fleshed.) In general, a story premise presents the problem to be solved, some of the complications, and its eventual solution—*plus* the writer's thoughts on how he intends to handle the material.

There's no point in doing any more than that until you know if the producer is interested. A story premise is to show him that your idea is feasible for his television show.

The origin for the idea of "The Protracted Man" is easy to trace. One of Hollywood's better special effects experts (and damn me for not remembering his name) had spoken to one of the classes I had taken while at U.S.C. He had also shown a reel with some of his more impressive tests and effects. Among them were matte shots from *It's A Mad, Mad, Mad, Mad World* and the overture/title from *Hawaii* which was never used with the picture. Also shown were some of the color tests he had made for *West Side Story*.

Remember all those shots in *West Side Story* of the juvenile delinquents dancing down the streets? Well, he had taken a couple of those and printed them with the color negatives out of synchronization. The backgrounds stayed the same—grim brick walls—but the people moving in the shots shattered into their component colors like an acid-freak's delusion. It was a startling and impressive effect—and he had tried it in a number of different ways, varying both the timing and the ordering of the negatives so that the spread of the images could be either more or less pronounced, and the order in which the color-images separated could be altered.

The effect was used only once in *West Side Story* (a truly commendable example of self-restraint on the part of someone), but in a way that never failed to make audiences gasp in surprise and delight. Remember, just before Maria, Anita, Tony, and Chino leave for the high school dance, Maria puts on her white dress and looks at herself in the mirror? She starts twirling for joy—and as she twirls, she fragments into brilliant colors, which further fragment and dissolve into the dance itself. If you've seen the picture, you remember the shot.

Anyway, it was that effect which triggered "The Protracted Man." I wanted an idea which could make full use of such a startling visual technique. STAR TREK was the natural place to use it, and the story grew out of the question, "What does this effect suggest?"

As a story, it is not perfect. Yet. If ever. That kind of battering and badgering of an idea is the result of the interaction between a producer and a writer, with a lot of memos from other people thrown in.

As an idea, "The Protracted Man" could be a good exploration of a spectacular special effect—but to make it a good STAR TREK episode too would require a level of personal conflict. Much more emphasis would have to be put on the conflict between Kirk and the protracted man's brother than is suggested here.

A greater danger to the *Enterprise* itself might also be suggested to heighten the overall tension of the show. Perhaps the long-distance warp that the shuttlecraft came through does not completely shut down—and the *Enterprise* is drifting toward it; they must destroy Jones' time protraction in order to destroy the power-drain on the matter-antimatter generators, and thus have enough power to avoid drifting into the dangerous warp.

Of particular advantage, I thought, was the fact that "The Protracted Man" took place entirely aboard the *Enterprise* and used only already existing sets. The shuttlecraft had already been established in previous episodes, and a special effect on the warp would almost be routine. (Routine for STAR TREK, that is.) Thus, the cost of the episode would have been well within limits. The only real problems would have been those of the director and the film cutters.

Actually, there are any number of ways that this idea could have been explored. A premise is only a jumping off point—a place from which to start the long process of developing a story into an episode.

The following premise, "Bandi," is a little simpler in concept, but the same basic conditions apply: Is it a good story? Is it for STAR TREK? And can we afford to do it?

Bandi

(A story premise by David Gerrold, February 1967.)

Kirk suddenly discovers that the *Enterprise* has a stowaway. It starts out with a couple of minor incidents: crew members claiming to have seen a three-foot teddy bear pacing up and down the corridors, or food disappearing from the galley, or strange noises.

Kirk disregards these stories as pranks until he and Spock meet the intruder face to face—or rather, face to muzzle. It is indeed a three-foot teddy bear. His fur is a lovely shade of golden brown and his eyes are big and soft and moist.

43

Kirk and Spock blink in surprise. The little creature stares at them for a long moment, then turns and runs, disappearing around a corner.

They follow it and find it hiding in the cabin of one of the crewmen. The cabin of crewman Jones.* (As convenient a name as any.) Jones has already come to Kirk's attention several times because of his laxness at his post in the transporter room.

Kirk asks for an explanation. Jones explains that at their last stop—an uninhabited pastoral planet—he discovered the little furry creature. He calls it Bandi.

Because they were there for some time, surveying the planet, he had time to grow attached to his pet and he could not bear to leave it behind. Working in the transporter room, he was able to bring Bandi up and hide him in his cabin. A couple of other crewmen also know about the little creature and have been sneaking food out of the galley for it.

Kirk's immediate reaction is one of anger. The creature will have to be destroyed. They are days from any convenient planet.

"Can't we keep him as a mascot?" asks the crewman.

"No. There are regulations against it." Kirk starts to order that the little beast be destroyed, but he finds it looking at him with its big soft brown eyes and . . .

For some reason, Kirk hesitates. There's no reason why they can't keep the animal as a specimen. He shrugs, "We'll lock him up in the biology section. There should be some cages there that will hold him."

Later, Spock asks Kirk why the sudden urge to save the creature's life. It is a disgusting show of emotionality. Kirk says that he hadn't planned to, but he had a sudden feeling of "strangeness." Something about the little creature kept him from ordering it put to sleep.

Spock shakes his head. He does not understand it.

Although Kirk has ordered that the creature be kept caged, for some reason, Bandi keeps getting out. The little furry keeps turning up in all parts of the ship. He is quiet and purrs when he is happy, which is nearly always. He is eager for attention and affection. (Think of Billy Barty in a mink coat.)

---

*Hey, this fellow Jones gets around, doesn't he?

Kirk keeps finding the creature in the galley, or in the engine room, and even on the bridge. Each time, he insists that the creature be locked up again. He even goes along to make sure—but somehow, people keep letting him out of his cage.

And other strange things are happening: minor miscalculations by crew members, careless accidents, and a lassitude that is infecting almost the whole ship. Kirk thinks it is the effect of Bandi.

But others disagree with him. Everyone thinks the little creature is harmless. He purrs, he's clean, he's neat, he eats very little. Even McCoy is surprised at the creature's lack of ill habits.

Yet Kirk is convinced that the creature's presence is a disturbing influence on the crew and he harbors a mild distaste for it. He will not allow Bandi to sit on his lap.

After one particularly dangerous accident—and Bandi, of course, was in the room—Kirk orders it locked up in a solitary cell in the ship's brig.

Bandi looks at Kirk for a long time. But this time, Kirk wills himself to not like the little furry beast. Bandi senses this dislike . . . Kirk is the only man on the ship who will not tolerate the little creature and keeps insisting that it be locked up.

That night Kirk has a nightmare. His sleep is troubled and uneasy; he is bothered by strange and unpleasant dreams. He wakes in a cold sweat—

—and finds Bandi, perched on the edge of his bed, staring at him. That's all, just staring . . . a baleful, malevolent stare.

Later, Kirk tells Spock about this and says: "I could swear that little beast knew I was responsible for it being locked up. And I had the strangest feeling that he was reading my mind."

But Bandi is not intelligent. McCoy's tests have shown that. His mind is about the same as a cat's.

Kirk knows that the creature is a menace. After the incident of the nightmare, he decides that Bandi must be destroyed, or Bandi will destroy the *Enterprise*.

Bandi is an empath.* He vibrates on the basic emotional

---

*No relation to "The Empath," by Joyce Muskat, written for STAR TREK's third season. She was using the word to have an entirely different meaning.

levels, and causes the people around him to do so also. He is a parasite, a quasi-telepathic leech; he is an emotional mirror. As long as he is fed and sheltered and loved, he will purr and give off warm empathic vibrations of love in return. In fact, his vibrations of love are so strong that they are hypnotic and have caused crewmen at their posts to grow lackadaisical and careless and—and an accident happens and a crewman is killed and Kirk decides that Bandi must go. But, when Bandi is menaced, he gives off waves of fear and anger. These waves of fear and anger are directed at Kirk. Kirk is the hate-object.

These semi-telepathic vibrations affect every member of the crew. Suddenly Kirk finds himself confronting not just a three foot teddy bear, but an armed and angry crew of the *Enterprise,* all reacting on their basic emotional levels. They don't know why, but they know that suddenly they hate their Captain very much.

Fortunately, Spock is unaffected by Bandi. Bandi's vibrations splash off him like so much water. Spock is able to kill Bandi, before the crew kills Kirk. (Saved in the nick of time!)

Immediately, the crew snap out of their emotional trances and sheepishly realize that they have done a no-no.

Order is quickly restored aboard the starship. Kirk reminds the crew: "I need not remind you that in the future we will leave all specimens where they belong. The *Enterprise* is not a zoo."

Spock turns to the Captain, "This is just an example, Captain, of what uncontrolled emotionality can do."

"Is it?" asks Kirk.

Spock nods. "Fortunately, Captain, I am not burdened by such a disrupting influence."

"Watch it, Mr. Spock. You're gloating. Pride is an emotion too!"

Spock looks at him, shocked.

FADEOUT

The "Bandi" premise was particularly skimpy, and would have needed a lot of fleshing out, perhaps a whole second plot, to make the story work. It needs a reason why Kirk *cannot* just kill Bandi outright—perhaps he is a valuable specimen that Kirk must transport from one planet to another.

I wouldn't want to superimpose an artificial danger onto this story; rather, I want one that is derived from the concept itself; thus, the old stopgap of the *Enterprise* being attacked by Klingons, or Scotty having trouble with the doubletalk generators, would not be satisfying. The characters should have to cope with only one *unified* conflict, the tension must be compressed into as concise a problem as possible.

So suppose we also postulate that Kirk has had to make a series of highly unpopular decisions—actions that particular members of the crew are bridling at. These decisions are allied with Bandi's presence in some way—thus Bandi would already have the crew's resentment of Kirk to feed on.

The whole idea is very touchy though—for one thing, the crew of the *Enterprise* is a loyal crew; to even suggest a capacity for mutiny seriously damages the overall concept of the show. So—try it this way: suppose Kirk has to temporarily take command of *another* starship on which Bandi is already established as a mascot. The reason for the assignment would be to investigate the reported laxity aboard that ship. Naturally, that crew might resent his presence and interpret his every command as an implied rebuke.

The name of the creature, Bandi, was chosen because it was halfway between Bambi and Banshee. I wanted to suggest a cute menace. Frankly, I don't like the name, I never did—and if the story had gone into development, I would have spent a lot of time trying to think up a better one.

What is interesting about the premise, though, is that it is a variation of the basic premise of "The Trouble With Tribbles," i.e.—a cute furry little creature that is actually a menace. I wanted to show that not all aliens would be horribly ugly,* and further, that if they are dangerous, the most dangerous aliens will be the cute ones—because human beings will not be able to recognize their inherent danger.

"Bandi" was one way to tell the story—who could resist a teddy bear? And who would believe him to be a menace to the ship?

---

*Somehow, in 1967, this seemed a very important point to make.

Again, the story was written to be as inexpensive as possible. No exteriors—unless you *want* to show the planet Bandi came from, and all the interiors are sets that are already in existence. The show would be fairly easy to shoot. The only costume that would have to be built would be the Bandi suit. I imagined that a midget would be best to play the part.

Like the other premises, I believed this to be a suitable idea for STAR TREK. In fact, I was kind of proud of all of them. They met the conditions imposed by the television medium—a set of limits that many writers do not understand—and I was trying to suggest conflicts that nobody else was thinking of.

I wanted very much to sell a story to STAR TREK, not just to break into television—but to write *good science fiction* for television. I wanted to do the best possible job.

I was *determined* to do the best possible job, because I was beginning to understand what I was up against. Not just six thousand other hopefuls, but also the three thousand members of the Writers' Guild of America, West—at least those of them who wanted to write for STAR TREK.

Gene Coon had a decision to make. I was trying to out-think him.

Let me digress for a minute and explain something. Gene Coon was STAR TREK's producer. Gene Roddenberry was the executive producer.

This means Gene Roddenberry *created* the show, decided who the characters would be, what actors would play them, what the *Enterprise* would look like, and what the general format would be.

Gene Roddenberry envisioned STAR TREK as "Hornblower in Space," the adventures of a kind of interstellar Mary Worth, traveling from planet to planet, solving problems and exploring the universe—and most important, because the vast distances of space have largely cut the *Enterprise* off from communication with its home base, the Captain of the ship is an independent entity, making his own decisions for each situation.

(This concept was partly unworkable. A spaceship captain does not put himself in the forefront of the exploration and scouting teams—any more than an aircraft carrier captain takes a plane up himself. Many fans objected to this one aspect of STAR TREK—they would have preferred that the

captain stay on the bridge and we follow a team of professional scouts down onto the planet. But William Shatner was
being paid a star's wages, so you don't waste him . . .)

Roddenberry developed the show through most of its early
episodes, shaping and guiding and making decisions—then he
turned it over to Gene Coon. Roddenberry was still the boss,
so to speak, but Coon was the guy who rolled up his sleeves
and got his hands dirty; think of him as the foreman.

It helps if you understand what a producer actually does:

He makes decisions.

If they're the right decisions, he's a good producer. If not,
he's not.

Both Gene Roddenberry and Gene Coon were good producers.

Most of the best producers started out as writers. This is
because almost all of a show's production problems can be
solved in the typewriter, long before the story ever gets to the
soundstage.

Your writer describes a mile-long valley with eighty-foot
high talking statues lining the walls and uttering proclama-
tions of doom? And your budget is only $191,000 for the
episode?

Change it. Turn it into a small flashing arch with a filtered
voice and newsreel stock shots superimposed in. Not quite
as effective, no—but more suitable for the twenty-one inch
screen and the twenty-one inch budget.

Television is an intimate, me-and-you, communication device. There's no room for Cecil B. DeMille and the parting
of the Red Sea. You have to forego the spectacles and
concentrate on the small stories, the soft ones.

When I went to school, the importance of the story was
that the incident it tells is *the most important* event that will
ever happen to this character. And that's true of movies,
novels and plays—whatever happens to the hero, whatever
he learns, will be the most important thing that he will ever
learn in his whole life. Whether he's Captain Ahab who
doesn't learn, or Captain Queeg who does, this is the reason
for his existence.

On television, however, you know that these characters
are going to be back next week—so you *know* that what
you're seeing this week isn't all that important, 'cause next
week's gonna be a whole new adventure.

You can't do high tragedy on a continuing series, or even *high* comedy. Because you can't sustain it week after week.

You can't run your characters in emotional high gear all the time. You'll burn them out, they'll cease to be believable.

And so, because the nature of the medium prevents you from being *great* week after week, many writers don't try to be great. They just try to be good. Instead of comedy and tragedy, they do melodrama and farce. They do the soft stories—the ones that are amusing, but not *totally* involving. They do the stories that are *not* about the most important incident in the characters' lives.

In a continuing series, you do stories that support the continuity of the series. And if you want to be good, every time you see yourself falling into a "formula" story—do the opposite.

One of STAR TREK's strengths was its flexibility. Because the format was so broad-based, it was almost *impossible* to tell the same kind of story week after week. STAR TREK was not going to fall into a formula easily.

On the other hand though, that same flexibility made the show the hardest show on television to write for. Both Gene Coon and Gene Roddenberry felt it was—and more than one writer of proven credits and ability found himself defeated by the need to be *totally original* for just one hour.

And if the problems were hard for the writers—well, think of the problems that the producers had. The buck stopped on their desks.

But that's what producing is. Decision-making. What stories to tell, how to tell them, and why they are worth telling.

Gene Coon was the producer I was trying to outthink. A writer of considerable skill himself, he is one of the few people who understand both science fiction and television and how the two can be fused most effectively. This was the man who was going to be looking at my work to see if it passed the all-important tests of professionalism and produceability.

Consider: a producer is handed two story premises. They're pretty much the same. Both are equally workable and would make good scripts. But neither is outstanding, just competent. He can only buy one of them; what does he do? He looks at the names of the writers.

If one is a pro and the other's a neo who's trying to break in, which one does he choose?

Which one would you choose?

If you said the neo, you're a hopeless idealist. Go back to square one, you're fired.

If you're a producer, you're a busy man, you haven't got time to run a writing class. You know that a fellow named Robert Bloch already understands television writing, he doesn't have to have it explained to him. He's a known quantity; all you have to worry about is getting him to fit *his* story into the concept of *your* show.

On the other hand, you've never heard of David Gerrold —who is this kid anyway? Why should we take a chance on him? He's not doing any thing better than anybody else we're already talking to.

And that's the key to breaking into television.

You're competing with the pros now. You have to be *better* than they are.

You have to do something outstanding to make the producers notice you. You have to do it on merit alone, because you have no previous credits and nothing else working for you.

If you're *almost* as good as a pro, or *only* as good as a pro, well . . . maybe. If they're desperate. If all their other writers have suddenly died of cirrhosis of the liver, and the story editor has run off to Rio de Janeiro with the petty cash, and it's a writers' strike and they can't find any scabs, and the producer's brother-in-law doesn't want to be a writer, and if the Pope suddenly converts to Judaism, then . . . *maybe,* they'll buy your story.

Otherwise, they'll buy it from someone who they know can deliver.

In television, a neo has to be better.

I had to put an idea on Gene Coon's desk that was so *good,* so *outstanding,* so *different*—without losing sight of STAR TREK's essential format—that he just *had* to use it. Or his teeth would ache for the rest of the season.

If the idea was good enough, he'd have to go to the source of it for the script. Me.

Of the five premises that I turned in (STAR TREK was renewed in February or March, and I immediately gave these premises to my agent), I believed "The Protracted Man" and "Bandi" to be the best. I expected one or the other of them to sell.

Although, to tell the truth . . . I had fond hopes for the fifth story too. I thought it might be fun. But, no, Gene Coon had already said he wasn't interested—

But the idea wouldn't go away. And I thought, well, maybe I can show him that it *can* be done—it really doesn't have to be *that* expensive, and maybe he can be convinced, it's worth a *try* . . .

I wasn't exactly sure how to tell it. The premise wasn't very well drawn. It may have been the worst written of the five—

—but it was the one that sold.

CHAPTER FOUR:

"The Fuzzies"

(A story premise by David Gerrold, January 1967.)

For centuries man has shared his homes and his cities with many other animals and creatures. Some of these animals have been man's partners—co-workers in the fields. Others have been pets—producing nothing, but returning love. Still others have been most unwelcome guests—parasites living off man and his families.

No matter how advanced the human race may become, it is not likely that men will ever lose their fondness for animals . . . nor is it likely that animals will ever lose their fondness for man . . .

However, it is doubtful that vermin will be able to follow man into space. A spaceship, or space station, would not ordinarily be plagued by vermin . . . unless, of course, the vermin are brought aboard willingly.

Such is the case in this story. The story is set at an interstellar trading post and aboard the *Enterprise.*

The trading post is a space station hanging in deep space at a point midway between seven star systems. As such, it is a valuable post for all the systems concerned.

The trading post is a cluster of life support modules joined together seemingly without rhyme or reason. It began as a single space platform, but as its supporting planets grew more prosperous, the station itself grew, adding new sections as needed. Perhaps it looks like a physicist's model of atomic structure.*

Because it is a structure in space, rather than on a planet, and because of its convenient location, the trading post is often an interplanetary marketplace. Large transfers of merchandise often occur at the trading post. Because of the convenient warehouse facilities, it is not uncommon for a delivery to wait in storage for several weeks before being picked up.

That was the first two pages of my original premise. When my agent read it, however, he said, "Oh, no—you have to set it on a planet. Space stations cost money. They'd have to build a miniature and a whole set of interiors. If the story looks too expensive, they won't buy it. Write it so they can use a stock frontier town."

I bridled at that. Two reasons—first of all, this was a story about little fuzzy creatures getting out of control. If they got loose on a space station, they could be easily controlled. And that pleased the conservationist in me. On a planet, the ecological damage would be catastrophic. Even though it was only a story, there was still something in my nature that would not allow me to destroy an innocent planet. I just couldn't do it.

---

*I was trying to think cheap.

Secondly—STAR TREK hadn't used a space station yet, and if this were truly a space-going culture, space stations would be a necessity. Hell, they'd be commonplace. And I wanted to see a story about one.

But my agent said no. Too expensive. He'd also disagreed with the "Bandi" outline. He couldn't find *empath* in his dictionary. Because the word didn't exist, there was no such thing. The producers of STAR TREK have problems enough already, don't confuse them with strange words.

Obviously, this agent did not understand science fiction. (Which was not the reason we later parted company, but it was one of the reasons why he was not the best possible agent for me.)

However, he did understand the mechanics of television. And if he said it was too expensive, then maybe he knew what he was talking about.

So, I rewrote "The Fuzzies." I changed only the setting and some of the grammar. Otherwise, the two versions of it were identical. This is the one that was turned in.

The Fuzzies

(A story premise by David Gerrold, February 1967.)

For centuries man has shared his homes and his cities with many other animals and creatures. Some of these animals have been man's partners—co-workers in the fields. Others have been pets—producing nothing, but returning love. Other creatures have not even returned that much.

What is the dividing line between pet and parasite? At what point does a creature cease to be a friend and begin to be a nuisance? This is the subject of this story.[1]

The story takes place at the "trading post," a small colony on a relatively undeveloped planet. Its culture is roughly that of a small frontier settlement of the 1870's.

Because of its location, the trading post is a convenient stopping place for ships bound from the civilized worlds of Earth to the less civilized worlds farther out on the frontier. Often, large transfers of merchandise take place here. Shipments of cargo destined for the worlds on the frontier are left for weeks at a time and picked up later.

One of these cargoes, waiting in a warehouse, is of special interest to Kirk. It is a shipment of grain—a quick-growing, mutated wheat with a high yield per acre. It is destined for a young, recently discovered agricultural planet.

The grain itself is harmless, but it has been the subject of a bitter feud for many months.

---

[1]After Gene Coon decided he was interested in "The Fuzzies," he went through the premise and made notes in the margin, pointing out the things I would have to change to make the story appropriate for STAR TREK, as well as NBC. These are included as footnotes.

The situation is this: the planet Barth is a fantastically fertile world. In just a few short years, the Barth Neo-Corn Corporation has become a multi-billion-dollar company.

The corporation has nearly 40% of the planet's usable land under cultivation and is able to export enough grain per year to feed ten worlds. The corporation, though, is a jealous monopoly.

A new company has been formed on Barth, planning to go into competition with the corporation. Their intention is to grow wheat. The shipment of grain is their seed crop.[2]

The Barth Corporation has made official protests that the wheat would destroy the ecological balance, but now that the company is going ahead with its plans, the corporation has been strangely silent.

Damon Jones,[3] the purchaser of the grain, is openly worried that the corporation may try to sabotage the crop. Kirk and the crew of the *Enterprise* have been called in to protect the grain and make sure that it reaches its destination safely.

Jones and an assistant have just accepted delivery of the grain. It is in a warehouse on the trading post planet.[4] They have to wait about three weeks for their own freighter to arrive in order to take the grain back to Barth.

Kirk, of course, does not object to this chore. The planet is a pleasant pastoral planet, and its gives the crew a chance for shore leave. Also, it gives Mr. Scott a chance to repair all the minor damage to the ship that has occurred in previous episodes.

The trading post city itself is a small westernish town.

---

[2]This was the first no-no. Gene's penciled notation was: *"Big business angle out. One planet against another."* Translated, this meant, "On American television, big business is *never* the villain. Make the conflict between two different planets instead."

[3]This character was originally conceived as being fairly sympathetic. Later, he became Nilz Baris, a pretentious, self-important bureaucrat.

[4]I repeat, it makes more sense to me to leave it in storage on a space station. If it's only waiting for transshipment, why expose it to possible planetary contamination? Furthermore, it seems like a waste of energy to beam it down and then beam it back up again—somewhere in that transaction, you'll be fighting the effects of the planet's gravity field and that will take power, a lot of it.

The buildings are quonset huts or wooden frame buildings, or even an occasional log hut.[5] (Anything that exists on the back lot that can be used to suggest a fairly young town.)

The trading post has a population of several thousand, and there are many interesting shops scattered about. As it is a jumping off place between the frontier and the civilized worlds, naturally many interesting artifacts and items are available in the shops. Many members of the *Enterprise* crew can be seen buying hand-carved chess sets, crystal earrings, fancy belts, and other souvenirs.

Kirk and Spock, however, have not had time to do much shopping. They have been busy watching for possible attempts to get at the grain.[6] One way is to keep tabs on all arrivals and departures.

Rather than a spaceport, the planet has a transport station of its own. All Kirk and Spock have to do is hang around it and see who beams down from a ship.[7]

When a small scout ship arrives at the trading post, Kirk and Spock hurry to the transport station to see who its pilot is. The pilot is a planet locater named Cyrano Smith.[8] He locates usable planets and sells the rights to them to large corporations.

Not all planets are worth exploiting—some are methane giants, like Jupiter, but occasionally a locater will discover a planet like Earth. A planet like that is worth a fortune— a locater can retire.

The situation is roughly akin to California gold mining in the old west. Like a prospector, a locater is a colorful, larger-than-life figure.

---

[5] I hated every line of this. I still do.

[6] *"Guards posted."* Gene was pointing out that Kirk and Spock would not be doing this task themselves. In my very first version, I had written: "At the request of Jones, Kirk agrees to post a guard over the warehouse. (The warehouse is like all of the trading post's living modules. It is a bubble of plastic, coated with foam. From the outside it is a blank sphere, but on the inside it can be subdivided to make apartments, or left empty to be a warehouse. This particular warehouse is three quarters filled with grain.)" But I had forgotten to include this when I rewrote it. Naturally Gene picked up on this immediately.

[7] *"Security would do this."* He was right, of course.

[8] The name Jones had already been used for someone else.

This particular locater is of the type who will do anything for a quick buck. Because of his roguish manner, Kirk and Spock have immediate suspicions about his motives at the trading post.

Kirk takes it upon himself to issue a general warning.[9] Cyrano protests—he insists that his motives are honorable. He has been in space a long time. He wants to rest a bit, take on supplies, and then he will leave again.

After Smith moves on, Spock comments: "A most unusual man. It would be logical to keep him under surveillance."

Kirk agrees. They follow Smith. As Smith is short on funds, he plans to sell some of his local artifacts for Interstellar Credit Units.[10] There are several ships that specialize in buying and selling unusual items from the frontier.

Kirk and Spock just happen to casually wander into one shop just in time to witness the transaction between Smith and the proprietor. Most of Smith's items are fairly commonplace, and do not bring a very good price, but Smith has brought with him something that is very unusual.

That something is a fuzzy. Apparently, Smith has found the creature on some planet during his explorations. It is a pet, he replies in answer to the shopkeeper's question.

Actually, Smith, being something of a con man, is just setting up the shopkeeper. Smith lets him hold the fuzzy. The shopkeeper takes it curiously. The creature throbs and purrs in his hand like a hedonistic kitten.

Kirk and Spock move in for a closer look. The fuzzy is a small colorful ball of fluff. This one is a particularly small one, only about the size of a tennis ball, but Smith notes that he has seen them as big as volley balls. The fuzzy is soft and warm and a bright green-gold color. It has no legs and no eyes—just a small soft mouth.

When stroked, it throbs and purrs. It loves being held, and it loves the warmth of the human hand. It moves by pulsing and flexing its body, or by rolling, depending on how

---

[9]This was rather high-handed of Kirk, I thought. And a bit presumptuous too. Had it been allowed to stand, it would have been bad plotting.

[10]This was an assumption on my part. STAR TREK hadn't touched on the question of money at all.

fast or how far it wants to go. It is a simple life form with only two senses, a heat detection sense and a food detection sense.

(The fuzzies, as I imagine them, are like those balls of fluff available in novelty shops, though not so garishly colored.[11] They can be hollow gloves so that the actor who is holding the fuzzy can manipulate it like a hand puppet.)

The shopkeeper queries Smith about the creature. Kirk and Spock listen interestedly. As the shopkeeper questions him, it becomes apparent that the man is thinking in terms of a possible profit. Smith, being a con man, is noncommittal. High pressure tactics are bad sales techniques.

"Is it dangerous?" asks the shopkeeper.

"Harmless as a newborn babe. I'd sooner sleep wearing a coat of fuzzies than a blanket."

"Does it eat much?"

"It will eat as much as you want to feed it—this particular one has gone for a week without being fed."

"What happens when you don't feed it?"

"It loses weight. It gradually gets smaller and smaller until it reaches one inch in diameter. If you don't feed it then, it dies."

"What does it eat?"

"Anything people can eat."

"Is it clean?"

"It's probably cleaner than you are," Smith says to the shopkeeper.

"What about its commercial possibilities? Is it edible?"

"I don't know. I never tried."

"What about its fur? Can that be used?"

"Probably."[12]

"I suppose that's the only one you have . . ."

---

[11]In particular, I was thinking of the ones that were being sold as key chains. How much could a few hundred of those cost? I was trying to think cheap again. The fuzzies had to be (a) believable, (b) easily made, and (c) a minimum of a special effects problem.

[12]Gene Coon didn't like this idea. Fuzzies were supposed to be cute. It wasn't exactly aesthetic to hint that people were skinning them for their fur—besides, in this particular future, women were beyond adorning themselves with the fur of animals.

"No . . . I have a few more in my ship. I never travel without a few fuzzies."

"What'll you take for them?"

Smith shakes his head. "I couldn't sell my family . . . unless the price were right."

The shopkeeper is insistent. He and Smith haggle for a bit. Eventually they agree on terms. Smith will sell the shopkeeper twenty-five small fuzzies, which he just happens to have, and the shopkeeper will pay Smith ten credits apiece.

As a sign of good will, Smith leaves the shopkeeper the first fuzzy. He will bring the rest in a few hours. He leaves, giving the shopkeeper a word of warning not to feed the fuzzy too much at first. "Give him a chance to get acclimated."

Kirk and Spock examine the animal on the counter top, then they follow Smith.

Smith is surprised when they follow him into another store, but he continues with his business. It becomes quickly apparent that he is setting up another shopkeeper just as he set up the first. He pulls another fuzzy out of his kit bag . . .

By the time Smith is through, he has contracted to sell almost five hundred fuzzies to various storekeepers at the trading post, for prices ranging from ten to twenty-five credits apiece.

Back on the *Enterprise,* Kirk and Spock discuss what they have seen.[13] Kirk had decided that Smith is harmless—just a clever rascal and a shrewd businessman. Spock, however, expresses his misgivings . . .

Meanwhile, they have to stay on watch for a possible attempt to get at the grain in the warehouse. (For some reason the warehouse looks strangely like the outside of a movie soundstage.)[14] Kirk orders the guard doubled.[15] Jones and his assistant inspect the grain and report that it is still safe. The assistant is a twitchy young man who makes frequent trips to check on the grain.

Meanwhile, Smith has delivered his five hundred fuzzies and they have become an instant craze. The original five

---

[13]If they discuss it, then we don't even have to show it. The discussion alone is enough to establish the fact.

[14]It is impossible to think much cheaper than this.

[15]See! I *had* thought to post a guard.

hundred have sold out amazingly fast. The shopkeepers clamor for more. Somehow, Smith is able to meet their demands, although at a slight rise in price.[16]

Within a day, it seems as if everybody has a fuzzy. Those who don't have one yet, have them on order. Smith, of course, continues to sell them wholesale. He also barters for food, fuel, water, etc. using fuzzies instead of cash.[17]

Fuzzies appear everywhere. Even Janice Rand[18] brings one onto the *Enterprise*. Other crew members start showing up with fuzzies on their shoulders, or in their pockets.[19] Everybody admits that they are cute, but Mr. Scott complains that they keep crawling into his machines, and Kirk has to issue an order to keep fuzzies off the bridge.

However, almost immediately it becomes apparent that the fuzzies are fantastically prolific. Janice Rand's fuzzy drops a litter of ten golden pups, each the size of a thumb. Soon, other fuzzy owners report that their fuzzies too have had litters.

McCoy dissects one and reports that the little beasts are asexual, reproducing at will. "Whenever one of the little creatures is fed enough . . . POW! He has pups. I mean, *she* has pups—er, *it* has pups."

Because the creatures are such simple organisms, a newborn fuzzy is as mature as a full-grown fuzzy. The only difference is size.

Kirk confronts Smith just as Smith is preparing to leave. "You knew about the fuzzies breeding so fast, didn't you?"

---

[16]On rereading this, I am amazed at how impossible it would have been to portray on film—at least, as it is written here, it would have been. That we were able to keep so much of the flavor of this in the final shooting script, although we had changed so many of the details, is a tribute to something or somebody. I think.

[17]*"Where does he get all the fuzzies from a one man ship?"* Gene had written, then crossed it out. Apparently he had thought it over and decided the answer was obvious.

[18]*"No."* Gene meant that the lovely Grace Lee Whitney who had played Janice Rand would not be back for the show's second season. When I asked him why, he said, "She transferred to another ship."

[19]*"No pockets."* Well, how was I to know? I hadn't been watching the show regularly.

Smith nods. "Of course. That's my job. I'm a fuzzy sales-man. It's a harmless enough business, Captain. It hurts no one. Besides, that's how I carry my stock. I keep a few for breeding, and when I get to a planet, I can manufacture as many as I need."

Kirk shakes his head. The fuzzies may be a pleasant enough animal, but Smith certainly isn't. His attitude towards business leaves much to be desired. Shortly thereafter, Smith leaves the trading post.

When Kirk and Spock return to the *Enterprise,* they dis-cover that Janice Rand's fuzzy has just dropped its second litter. Worse, the fuzzies of the first litter have had their first litters. Janice Rand is now the proud owner of 121 fuzzies. She goes to the galley to get some food for them . . . quite a bit.[20]

For the next few days, the story is the same all over. Every-body who has a fuzzy reports that the fuzzies are breeding as fast as they are being fed. There are fuzzies everywhere, you can't give them away. They are overrunning the *Enter-prise.*

Little balls of fluff sit patiently on desks, chairs, tables, in Kirk's coffee cup, on the floor, in corners, under beds, on bookshelves, in the galley . . .

The cook[21] complains that fuzzies have gotten into his flour stores and completely eaten them. Kirk inspects and sees that the fuzzies have gone through a large bin of white flour, and in its place have left only more fuzzies.

Kirk and Spock stare down into the flour bin at the seeth-ing mass of fuzzies[22] . . . and they are both thinking the same thing: the grain!

He and Spock race to the granary. They break the seal on the door and open it. The worst has definitely happened. There is no grain—just a solid, seething mass of fuzzies. (Per-haps they are mewling hungrily.) The fuzzies do not have to

---

[60]All right, Janice, but you'll be *sor-ree* . . .

[61]I know, I know. There's no cook on the *Enterprise,* just machines. We'll talk about this later. Maybe.

[62]If we had filmed this shot, the visual memory of it would have been enough so that we would not have had to show the interior of the warehouse, also seething. Some things are far more effective if they are left to the viewer's imagination.

be shown. The interior of the warehouse can be suggested by having a number of fuzzies roll out when the door is opened.

Aghast, they stare into the warehouse. Apparently, somehow the fuzzies have gotten into the grain. Perhaps it was through an air vent, or perhaps someone accidentally dropped one, or perhaps it is sabotage . . .

In any case, as was previously noted, a fuzzy reproduces as fast as it is fed. McCoy's experiments have shown that under optimum conditions, a fuzzy can reproduce every twelve hours.[23] The young are born mature and they are ready to reproduce within a few hours too. The faster you feed them, the faster they reproduce.

(Under normal conditions, on their home planet, fuzzies probably do not have optimum growth conditions. They probably have a great many natural enemies and food is probably more scarce. But people tend to overfeed their pets, and so . . .)

Fuzzies have an extremely fast metabolic rate. Their growth is inhibited only by the amount of food available. It is not important how old a fuzzy is, but how much it has been fed. These fuzzies have been able to eat to their hearts' content. There must be several hundred thousand of them in the warehouse.

"One million, seven hundred and seventy one thousand, five hundred and sixty one," comments Spock.[24]

Kirk looks at him.

---

[23]Originally, I had written: ". . . under optimum conditions, a fuzzy can drop a litter every eighteen hours. The young will mature and begin reproducing within another twenty-four hours." But I wanted to speed it up, and I figured if the audience would believe an eighteen-hour gestation period, they'd believe a twelve-hour one. By the way, did you know that opossums have gestation periods of only eleven days?

[24]This line is directly derived from a scene in "Return of the Archons." Kirk and Spock are chained to a wall in a deep dark dungeon and Kirk remarks, "I wonder how long we've been here." Spock replies, almost casually, "Seventeen minutes and ten seconds." Or something like that. The episode had been aired the same week I was rewriting this, and I had thought, "Hey, that's a funny thing for Spock to say—but it's logical." So I wrote a variation of it.

"That's assuming an average litter of ten every twelve hours, of course."[25]

"Oh."

Kirk makes an immediate decision. "First, close that door! Second, capture Cyrano Smith!"

It now becomes apparent to Kirk that the fuzzies were Smith's plot to destroy the grain.

The *Enterprise* takes after Smith's ship. With their bigger, more powerful engines they quickly catch up and overtake the ship. They beam Smith aboard and take his tiny ship in tow. Smith protests his innocence. He knew the fuzzies were fast breeders, but he knew nothing about the grain.

Kirk ignores his protestations of innocence. This is a matter for the Interstellar Commerce Commission[26]—tampering with interstellar shipments.

However, when they return to the trading post, there is another surprise for them. All the 1,771,561 fuzzies that have eaten the grain are dead. Indeed, many of the older ones (on the bottom of the pile) were already dead, but undiscovered.

McCoy performs a dissection on some of the dead fuzzies and discovers that they have been poisoned, yet the grain has tested out as being harmless. McCoy tests the grain again —that is, what is left of it.

This time he discovers a virus imbedded in the grain. Ordinarily, this virus tests out harmless, but it has the peculiar property that when it is taken into a living creature's body, it undergoes a change. It becomes an inert material. It is not a poison, but just as carbon monoxide can suffocate a person, the inert chemical in the bloodstream can cause a creature to die because it is not getting enough nourishment. No matter how much it eats, it will starve to death once the reaction is started.

The process is a delayed action one. A sufficient level of the virus is necessary in the bloodstream to generate a threshold level of inert material. Once that threshold is

---

[25]Of course. If you're going to tell a joke, tell it all.

[26]*"Federation."* There's no such thing as an Interstellar Commerce Commission.

achieved, death follows. Inadvertently, by destroying the grain, the fuzzies have saved the people of Barth.[27]

Further tests by McCoy show that if this grain had been used for seed, the virus would have been present in all of the crops raised.[28] Apparently someone had tampered with the grain long before Smith arrived at the trading post planet.

Strangely, it is Smith who fingers the villain.[29] Damon Jones' assistant is revealed to be an employee of the Barth Corporation. He is taken into custody. Jones will arrange for a new shipment of grain.

But what about Smith and the fuzzies? There is still a plague of the little fluff balls on the trading post.

Kirk decides on a punishment to fit the crime. Smith will have to stay on the trading post until he can get rid of every last fuzzy. In short, he has to be the dog catcher!

Smith protests, but Kirk asks him if he would rather be charged with violating Interstellar Customs by transporting animals from one planet to another.[30]

Smith decides to stay and catch fuzzies.

Back on the *Enterprise*, now strangely free of fuzzies, Spock congratulates Kirk on a remarkably logical solution to the whole problem. Kirk accepts the praise modestly. "It did seem to have a feeling of justice about it . . ."

Suddenly he stops. Janice Rand is holding two gold balls of fluff. "What are those?" he gasps, aghast.

"Earrings," she says and puts them on. They all have a good laugh, except Spock. He only looks bemused.

In the first version, the one that didn't get turned in, I had also written an afterthought. I include that here to show an alternate direction the episode might have gone.

---

[27] *"And many other planets."*

[28] This was necessary so that all future crops from this seed grain would be lethal. An ordinary poison wouldn't have been passed on and on, but a virus would continue to infect and grow with all future generations of the grain.

[29] *"How?"*

[30] *"Why didn't we bring this up before?"* asked Gene Coon, then in a different pen, he suggested changing it to *"Harmful animals."* It's illegal to transport animals that are proven harmful. Yeah, that made sense.

AFTERTHOUGHT

In this story I have pictured Smith as a colorful rogue who is well aware of what he is doing by spreading fuzzies throughout the galaxy. He knows that without natural enemies, fuzzies could eat a planet bare.

However, there is another way that Smith could be pictured. He could be a doddering old man who is unaware of the consequences of having too many fuzzies. He could come aboard the *Enterprise* or the trading post like a little old lady who lives with sixty-three cats—there can be no such thing as too many fuzzies for him.

When other people show an interest in the fuzzies, he gives them away. Love (and fuzzies) should be shared. Smith wants to spread love and fuzzies to every planet in the galaxy, unaware of the ecological damage he is doing in the process.

At first, Kirk thinks of the old man as just a harmless eccentric. After he discovers the fuzzies in the warehouse, he decides that maybe he is more than that. Maybe he is a cunning saboteur.

When Smith is brought back and shown the results of what he has caused, he is shocked. Never before has he stayed in one place long enough to see what happened when the fuzzies began multiplying rapidly.

For the first time, he realizes what he has done—there can be such a thing as too much love. He decides he must undo the damage. Fortunately, he knows just the way . . . the fuzzies have a natural enemy: a creature that is all mouth and teeth. It is extremely voracious and breeds just as fast as fuzzies—

Kirk stops him before he puts that plan into action. The

old man vows to help exterminate the fuzzies and undo the damage he has caused.

The first approach as detailed in the preceding twelve pages, can be played as a comic adventure with overtones of farce. The second interpretation can be played for whimsy shading into pathos as the old man breaks down and cries when he realizes what he has done. You can't help but feel sorry for the poor old man who loves people and fuzzies so much that he cannot conceive of two many or too much being a bad thing. (What a perfect role for Boris Karloff . . .)[31]

Either approach could be fun, or perhaps a combination of the two . . . the old man is a bit of a rogue, and a bit of an eccentric.

Of the five premises that I submitted to STAR TREK, the one that they thought showed the most promise was also the one that was going to be the hardest to turn into a usable TV script.

Why?

Very simple. It had no story.

It was a premise built around a gag—the gag is this: everybody runs around in circles, making a lot of noise and chasing a lot of red herrings, without noticing that the *real* danger is already underfoot and breeding rapidly. The prolific abilities of the fuzzies should seem to be only a minor subplot, a running gag, and secondary to what seemed to be the major conflict.

Only problem was, the story didn't *have* a major conflict. At best, it had a couple funny scenes. At worst, it was a transparent set-up for an obvious punch line—opening a door and being inundated by fuzzies.

Of the five stories, "The Fuzzies" was both the best and the worst that they could have chosen.

The worst because I didn't know how to do it. I had absolutely no idea of how to put the thing together to make it work on screen.

The best because it forced me to be a better writer than

---

[31] I do not know why I did not turn this Afterthought in with the rewritten premise. (Perhaps my agent didn't like it and advised me not to.) On rereading it now, I can only say, *Sigh*. Boris Karloff on STAR TREK . . . *Sigh*.

any of the other premises would have. The challenges in "The Fuzzies" were greater than the challenges in any of the other stories—but not quite big enough to look insurmountable.

Any of the other four stories would have required a simple straightforward telling of an action adventure plot—not that writing such a script is necessarily an *easy* task, but definitely easier than writing a script which provides the illusion of action and adventure while disguising the fact that it is really a shaggy-creature story.

Why Gene Coon chose "The Fuzzies" over the other four—well, actually, the other two ("The Cosmic Chess Game" was unusable and they were already doing "The Doomsday Machine")—is a question that someday I would like to have answered.

I mean, it would be nice to know.

Oh—if you're thinking that all of this happened overnight, let me put some dates in here to help you sort things out.

Those outlines were turned in to my agent in February, and he turned them in to STAR TREK almost immediately.

Gene Coon's office didn't reply until June.

They only had twelve or thirteen scripts by then that they thought were usable. I don't know, maybe they were getting a little desperate.*

---

*Actually, they were not getting desperate. Since I wrote this, I found out that they were actually overbought at the time; but they were so intrigued with the possibilities of the fuzzies that they were considering buying the story anyway. Which proves the point about writing a story so good that they just *had* to use it. And also proved my agent correct—they would throw away something they'd already bought if something better came in. In a memo to Gene Coon, D.C. Fontana, story editor, expressed the opinion that a script based on "The Fuzzies" would be preferable to some of the other ideas that were already in development. Their thinking was that they would buy the story alone and assign it to a writer of already proven ability. As it happened though, things developed quite differently.

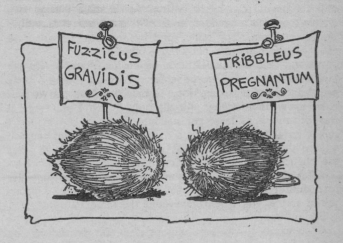

CHAPTER FIVE:

"A Fuzzy Thing Happened to Me . . . "

When Gene Coon called my agent in June and said, "I want to talk to Gerrold about his fuzzies," I quit my job at CBS. I'd had it exactly four days.

I'd been working down in the Black Hole of Calcutta at CBS Television City in Hollywood—that black and white Vehicle Assembly Building at Fairfax and Beverly. I'd been hired to type up scripts for various TV series—not write them, just type up the stencils for the mimeograph machines. And if you think that didn't *hurt*, you don't know the meaning of pain. I wanted to write my own stories, not someone else's.

That four days did prove one thing to me though—I *could* write better than some of the hacks who were actually being paid for it. For instance, the first fifty-three drafts of the pilot for *Hawaii Five-O* were worse than dreadful. They were crimes against humanity. The writers should have been shot for mental cruelty to typists. To this day, I have been unable to watch a single episode of that series. (It may have turned into something quite good by now, but I'm sorry—I can't get the bad taste out of my mind.)

Anyway, the promise—the mere chance that I might get into STAR TREK—was incentive enough for me to throw away a singularly unrewarding job. It paid terribly, and it was emotionally unsatisfying, and the only reason I had taken it was because it at least got me into a studio and maybe I might be able to move up someday. I hoped. But the job was so depressing that it was worth discarding to go after the chance of making my first professional sale.

After all, it was the opportunity to leap from shit-shoveler to Beautiful Person all in one jump. If you were as determined as me, you would have done the same.

So.

Once again I was carefully briefed and primed by my agent: Coon wasn't buying the story—he was only interested in it. This meeting was for him to tell me the kind of story I would have to write for him to buy. We were going to spend a half hour or so *talking* about my premise. I had to understand, my agent pointed out, that there was no commitment here. Of any kind. STAR TREK was doing me a favor by even noticing my existence. "So, don't get your hopes up yet—nobody's mentioned money."

There are too many people running around Hollywood, you've probably met the type, who can talk a polite rejection slip into an almost-contract. They always sound very good, but their deals are always "pending"—it's something for them to talk about on the unemployment line. My agent didn't want me to be one of those. (Hell, I didn't want me to be one of those.)*

---

*For some reason, STAR TREK attracted an inordinate number of these types. Later on I ran into a few of them. A few hundred of them.

So it was with a bit less fear, but not too much more expectation, that I met Gene Coon again.

Sure enough: "I'm not buying the story yet, David. I'm only interested in it. You haven't written the kind of outline that I'll buy; that's what we're going to talk about . . ."

Actually, we discussed all five of my premises and Gene explained his reasons for rejecting each of the first four. He felt "The Protracted Man" might be too expensive and too time-consuming because of the problems of editing the film and cutting the negatives to properly achieve the color-shattering effect. "Bandi" just didn't turn him on, and it didn't have the possibilities for humor that "The Fuzzies" did.

And along about this time the network sent down a memo that said they wanted more "planet" stories—i.e., episodes that took place on other worlds rather than solely aboard the *Enterprise*. Of course, that takes more money when you have to build the sets, so the network also included a paragraph or six about continuing to keep the overall costs down. Of course, the only way to keep costs down on STAR TREK is to do shipboard stories only . . .

And you wonder why producers get schizoid?

STAR TREK's production problems were more complex than any other TV series ever put on the air. And it will probably hold that record for years to come.

Any other continuing series—that is a TV show with the same continuing characters from week to week—can depend on certain factors to help them keep their costs down. *Gunsmoke* and *Bonanza* do not have to build a new western set every week; they already have their permanent sets, and if they want to shoot a new location, there are plenty of other western sets and locales that they can use; that is, most of their "world" already exists. Same with props and costumes. It isn't necessary for the production crew of *Marcus Welby* to design new costumes or hospital utensils week after week—and if it *were* necessary, they could probably order most of what they need from catalogues.

Same with *Ironside* and *Hawaii Five-O*. These shows use San Francisco and Honolulu as background sets. They didn't have to pay to build them, though, the cities were already there.

Not so with STAR TREK. Everything you see on the screen has to be built. From scratch. And that means that somebody has to think about what it will look like first—which is an additional problem, because you're creating a whole new culture. That means architecture, clothing styles, art, language patterns, hair styles, *everything*. And you can't look it up in *National Geographic*. They don't know what the sky city of Stratos looks like—so you have to make it up yourself.

The *Enterprise* itself is the only continuing set on STAR TREK. The props, the costumes and the hair styles are all fairly well standardized. Once built or established, they can be used for as many episodes as the network is willing to buy. If all your stories took place *only* on the *Enterprise,* you'd only have two variable costs: special effects and the number of speaking parts. Everything else could be kept within known parameters.

Unfortunately for the penny-counters, STAR TREK is about the *voyages* of the good ship *Enterprise*—and that means you have to *show* strange and exotic locales. Which means they have to be built. Which means money.

An episode of STAR TREK cost $185,000. Period. No more. Once in a while, you can go a weensy bit over budget—but even these "overages" are limited. You cannot spend more than the show will return in projected profits.

Each episode is worth so much money to the studio. Each time it is shown, the studio gets paid so much for that showing. The studio budgets the cost of the episode based on how much they will get back from it.

Which seems fairly simple, but there's a joker in the deck. It's called syndication. After a series goes off network television (and is out of production), the studio can package all the old episodes and sell them to the local markets in each city. Which is why STAR TREK started out on channel 4 and ended up on channel 13.

Naturally, syndication brings in more money to the studios. Lots more. In fact, syndication brings in so much money that the studios take that projected income into consideration when making their budgeting decisions on how much to allocate per episode.

If a series is successful—say, *I Love Lucy*—then it is worth a lot more than a series that is a flop. (Does anyone remember *The Ugliest Girl in Town*?) That's elementary, of course—but even a flop can be worth money on the syndication market—if you have enough episodes of it. With syndication, it's not quality that counts, it's quantity. In television the idea is to survive long enough to get as many episodes into the can as possible before the ratings catch up with you. Otherwise, you've got a disaster on your hands.

If STAR TREK had only gone for one season, there would have been only twenty-nine episodes of it. That's not enough for syndication. A syndicate market usually "strips" a show —that is, they run it five days a week, usually in the late afternoon or early evening. *Get Smart, I Dream of Jeannie, Wild Wild West*—you can usually still find these series in any major American city between the hours of four and seven o'clock. Twenty-nine episodes will last exactly five weeks and four days before you have to start over again. In three months, you're starting on your third go-round and your ratings are starting to droop. You've worn out the series and you have to find something else for that time slot. If you're a station manager, it's not worth the trouble to syndicate a one-season series.

Two seasons? Well, maybe . . . STAR TREK would have had a combined total of fifty-six episodes. That's not really enough, it's only eleven weeks and one day, but you might be able to place it in a few markets. Three seasons? Eighty episodes total. Sixteen weeks. Okay, STAR TREK had a very big and very faithful following. Let's try it. The demographics show that it was reaching the people it wanted to reach.

But you really haven't got enough to make it profitable unless you've got five years worth of episodes. That's the point at which the bookkeeper can throw away his bottle of red ink. From here on in, the show *can't* lose money. Every episode filmed is one more investment in the highly profitable syndication market. The investment gets larger and more valuable with every successful season a series enjoys. (Think about *Bonanza* and *Gunsmoke* for a while—how long have they been on the air? Almost too long. If those shows were "stripped," they could go for two or three years before they'd have to start repeating. And for the first five syndication reruns, that's income for the writers, the directors, the producers and the actors who made those shows. And after that it continues to be income for the studios. There are almost too many episodes of *Gunsmoke* and *Bonanza* for the syndication market. They could go into competition with themselves . . .)

Because of this, too much of television's production is keyed to eventual syndication needs and considerations of story quality, subliminal meanings and social responsibility get lost in the shuffle. There isn't time to worry about art.

Case in point: every time a successful series is renewed for another season, everybody lines up for a raise, particularly the stars. If they don't get it, they hold out. And sometimes they get fired and new stars are brought in to take their place. But most of the time they get their raises because they're the stars and much of the series' appeal is embodied in them. *Mission Impossible* survived without Barbara Bain and Martin Landau, but could *All In the Family* make it without Carroll O'Connor? Would they even try? I doubt it.

Within five years, it is possible for a series to double in cost.*

These costs are allowable only so long as they fall within the margin of projected income from future syndication. Costs cannot be allowed to go beyond a certain point. In STAR TREK'S second season, that point was $185,000.

The only way to get around that is to do a script or two that allow you to save some money so you can spend the extra on a "big" show. Only thing is, if you bring in an episode under budget, the studio is going to ask why you don't do that all the time.

It's the rare producer who thinks in terms of stories—the rest of them are making sausages, all identical, all uniform, and all of them with just the correct amount of fat and sawdust to be profitable to the packer. Ugh.

Which brings me back to Gene Coon's office.

When you choose one premise over another, you choose it not because you happen to like it better or because you think it'll make a better show—you choose it because (a) it fits into the overall concept of the series, (b) it can be produced within the show's budget, (c) it doesn't seem to

---

*D. C. Fontana suggests that this is overly pessimistic, but it *has* happened, especially with situation comedies.

present any problems which might run into time and cost overruns, (d) it's suitable for television, as non-offensive as vanilla pudding, and (e) *maybe* it'll be entertaining.

Considering the importance of (a), (b), (c), and (d), it's a wonder anyone ever gets to (e).

But it does happen—it happened in this case and there are two reasons why: I was determined to write the best possible STAR TREK script and Gene Coon wanted to give me my chance.

That afternoon we went over the premise carefully and he explained in detail what he meant by each of his notes. At the same time, I was trying to figure out how to write the story.

One of the major problems, and one that I was aware of from the very beginning, was the breeding rate of the fuzzies. A television show takes only an hour of real-time. Hence, the action in it is compressed. I had to stretch my story seemingly across three days without also seeming to slow down the pace of it. Every scene had to advance the plot.

I had to establish that the fuzzies were breeding rapidly; I needed certain key scenes to do it, and the incidents that I chose to portray those scenes had to be carefully handled not to give away the punch line—and to me, the punch line of the story seemed so obvious (1,771,561 fuzzies falling out the door) that I wanted to do everything I could to minimize the buildup.

Irwin Blacker had taught a technique which I found very useful now. Understand that every scene in a script is a confrontation (either direct or indirect) between two or more people; the story can be broken down into a series of one-line descriptions: "Spock tells Kirk to use a better mouthwash. Kirk slugs Spock." Put these on 3x5 cards and you have the whole story in front of you to shuffle around as you choose.

The technique is especially helpful when you have two or more subplots to juggle, trying to fit them into a major plot. You can develop each plot line independent of the others and then assemble them for maximum impact and pacing. In this case, I was trying to build a story around the scenes depicting the fuzzies breeding.

The first set of cards looked something like this:

Uhura is given fuzzy by Cyrano, implication that she will bring creature aboard ship.

In Rec Room, Uhura's fuzzy has kittens. Second generation, eleven fuzzies. McCoy takes one.

Third generation. 121 fuzzies. Establish that fuzzies are asexual—*all* of them can breed.

Scene showing that fuzzies are starting to get out of hand. Fourth or fifth generation.

Fuzzies in plague proportions. Kirk finds fuzzies in ship's stores, orders them off ship.

Kirk finds fuzzies in grain. 1,771,561.

Kirk makes Cyrano clean up fuzzies.

Notice how the action builds toward a climax?

Having those cards to start with, then it is necessary to make up cards for the other elements of the plot and fit them in to see if they work.

At this point, a second set of cards is added:

Teaser: *Enterprise* answers emergency distress call.

Distress call is false alarm. Kirk is annoyed at local official responsible. Start of a beautiful relationship.

Kirk and local official have argument to dramatize the fact that they don't like each other.

Kirk and local official have another argument, heightening tension between them.

Local official is embarrassed at having assistant exposed as spy.

This set of cards is shuffled into the pack and then perhaps a couple of extra scenes are written, scenes that are necessary to fill holes, smooth transitions, and provide necessary background material:

McCoy studies fuzzies, reports analysis of their biology.

McCoy studies grain, reveals that it is poisoned.

Tag. Uhura with fluff-ball earrings.

This technique can be called "Instant Story." I know of no better method for breaking down a story into its component parts to see why it works—or, more often, why it doesn't work.

At this particular point in space and time, I had two thirds of my story. I had my major plot and I had one subplot masquerading as a major plot. Putting them on cards enabled me to see that I needed another subplot. I wasn't sure what it was yet, but I could see that I needed it.

Later on, when I did realize what should go in the gaps, the cards would help me put them in the right places. But on June 13, when I turned in my first outline for "A Fuzzy Thing Happened to Me . . ." the concept was still kind of bleary-eyed. The story was still in fragments and we didn't have all of them yet.

For instance . . .

The Interstellar Trading Post is called Topsy. This is because it was never "borned," it just grew. Because of its favorable location close to several major star systems, the post is an important junction of the space lanes. It is a colorful marketplace for a variety of wares.

As used in this story, it can be pictured in either of two ways:

FIRST: it could be a small westernish town . . . anything that exists on the back lot that can be used to suggest a fairly young city.

SECOND: the trading post could be a space station hanging in deep space at a point midway between several star systems . . .[1]

TEASER: INT. SHIP'S GALLEY—KIRK is talking to COOKIE, the ship's cook, and a colorful character he is . . .[2]

A wall panel bleeps and Kirk is called to the bridge by Spock. The *Enterprise* is receiving an emergency call from the trading post.

---

[1] I felt I had the right to at least *suggest* a space station. If it was too expensive to produce, let Gene Coon tell me.

[2] No, he isn't. The *Enterprise* doesn't have a ship's cook, only a mess officer to program the automatic machinery. (Source: Gene Coon.) (Well, I didn't know . . .)

INT. MAYOR LURRY'S OFFICE—LURRY, BARIS, DARVIN, KIRK, SPOCK . . . The situation is quickly explained. Baris is a farmer turned businessman. He has just recently imported a new type of grain from Earth (or wherever.) The grain is called triticale. (tri-ti-cay-lee). . .[3]

Baris fears that his competitors are out to sabotage his grain shipment . . .[4]

EXT.—MAIN PROMENADE OF TRADING POST. A variety of costumes from many different planets can be seen. The street is lined with shops. SULU and UHURA meet KIRK and SPOCK. Spock is still carrying a sample of the triticale grain.
Sulu notices it . . . he asks for a sample . . .[5]

INT. SHOP—SULU AND UHURA, LOOKING AROUND —STOREKEEPER AND JAY DAMON CYRANO AT COUNTER. . . . Cyrano is trying to unload some of his souvenirs on the shopkeeper in exchange for supplies. The storekeeper sees a dozen "Cyranos" a month, so he is understandably nonchalant . . .

Cyrano produces a fuzzy from his kit bag. Uhura and Sulu are both intrigued by the unusual animal. The shopkeeper also shows interest:

"What about its fur? Can that be used?"
"Sir!! You are talking about a friend of mine."

. . . Cyrano presents this fuzzy to Uhura . . .

ELSEWHERE IN THE TRADING POST—KIRK, LURRY, BARIS . . . Kirk assures Baris that no harm will come to the grain.

---

[3]There really is such a grain. I had read about it in the *Saturday Evening Post*. Gene Coon's reaction was: *"Then let us invent a vastly superior improvement. This is obviously 300 years from today."*

[4]Again, no large corporations. Instead: *"Must be a force hostile to well being of Federation in this area."* Having just seen a rerun of "Errand of Mercy," I suggested that the Klingons as used in that episode might be a particularly apt set of villains. Coon agreed.

[5]In "The Salt Vampire," Sulu was shown to be an amateur botanist. It seemed likely that he would know about triticale, and it was a convenient way to show that fuzzies like triticale too.

Baris is generally offensive and Kirk is having trouble controlling his patience, but he is willing to post security guards. Baris feels that it is Kirk's responsibility:

"After all, my taxes pay your salary, I'm your boss."
Kirk just looks at him, "Then I'd like a raise."[6]

INT. ENTERPRISE RECREATION ROOM/GALLEY. Kirk and Spock enter. Seeing the crowd, Kirk goes over to see what they are looking at. Uhura shows him the fuzzy . . . Spock picks up the creature and examines it curiously while Kirk questions Uhura about Cyrano . . .
Kirk starts to leave. He looks at Spock. Spock is absent-mindedly stroking the fuzzy. Spock realizes what he is doing and hands the fuzzy back to Uhura . . .

That scene was the "act ending," that is, the last scene before the commercial. Gene Coon felt it was a weak act ending, so it was combined with the first scene immediately following.
That scene showed Uhura once again in the recreation room with her fuzzy, plus ten baby fuzzies. (They do not nurse. Fuzzies are not mammalian.)

INT. BRIDGE—Kirk receives an urgent message from Baris. Another ship has arrived at the trading post. Baris is upset because it is the private ship of his biggest competitor, JOSEPH MACKIE.[7] . . . Kirk agrees to pay a call on Mackie.

On the way over to the trading post, Kirk runs into McCoy who expresses misgivings about letting fuzzies aboard the *Enterprise:* "This creature is too harmless to be harmless."

. . . Mackie is pure villain-type, a real nasty. Kirk meets him and of course likes him even less than he likes Baris.
Kirk doesn't want any part of their quarrel, but where it interferes with the peaceful running of the galaxy, it is Kirk's business to get involved . . .

---

[6]This is a particularly *bad* joke, but it served to establish the relationship between Kirk and Baris.

[7]Once again, Coon reminded me in the margin that the threat must be from outside the Federation.

On the way back to the *Enterprise,* they pass through the trading post, establishing that fuzzies are for sale in all the shops. Many people are carrying them.

On the ship, we see that Uhura's fuzzy has multiplied again and so have the first litter. There are now 121 of them.

Because Scotty has been burying himself in his technical manuals, Kirk orders him to take shore leave.

Mackie calls to complain that he is being persecuted, he keeps stumbling over Kirk's security guards. Kirk replies, "My men are on shore leave."

Meanwhile . . .

INT. LOCAL BAR. Several local people and several crewmen of the Enterprise. Also the crew of Mackie's yacht . . . one of them starts making comments about Kirk's capability as a Captain and perhaps the crew of the Enterprise goes along with it at first, thinking that the man is joking. But it soon becomes apparent that there is real hostility in the man's demeanor.

A fight breaks out between the two crews . . .

Act III begins with Kirk disciplining his men for fighting. Then he orders Mackie to keep his men confined to their own ship.

We also establish in this act that the fuzzies are starting to get out of hand.

And Baris (again!) comes to see Kirk with the accusation that Cyrano is a saboteur. (Cyrano has been in and out of every scene on the trading post, constantly with the fuzzies, and he was a witness to the fight—perhaps he helped instigate it.)

Kirk investigates Cyrano. He asks Cyrano if he knew that the fuzzies were such fast breeders. Cyrano tells Kirk of course he knew. That's how he carries his stock from planet to planet . . .

ENTERPRISE AGAIN—There are fuzzies everywhere. Little balls of fluff sit patiently on desks, chairs, tables, in Kirk's coffee cup . . .

INT. AT THE WAREHOUSE—Kirk opens a door and a mass of fuzzies rolls out . . .

Kirk makes a decision. "First, close that door. Second, capture Cyrano."

From here, the story proceeds very much as it did in the original premise. The dead fuzzies reveal that the grain was tampered with and Cyrano fingers Darvin as the culprit. Mackie and his men are sent packing, and Uhura shows up with a pair of earrings.

As you can see, *something* is missing. There isn't the tension and excitement necessary to sustain an hour of television. The story fragments are still only fragments—there is nothing to unify them yet, some kind of overall threat was needed . . .

Gene Coon said that big business was never the villain. After all, this was *American* television. "The threat has to come from outside the Federation." And when he said that, something went twang in my mind, something I'd seen on a first-season rerun—

I opened my mouth, wondering what I was going to say, and said, "Klingons!" The Klingons, as first portrayed in "Errand of Mercy," were a perfect threat—an uglier set of professional nasties couldn't have been found. Perhaps the fact that I had just seen the episode the week before had something to do with it.

The alien Klingons were ruthless, vicious, contemptuous, and in every way worthy opponents for Captain Kirk. Coon agreed that they were perfect for this story. Besides, he was planning to use them in other upcoming episodes as well. This would fit in nicely with his overall plans for the series.

Purely from a story point of view, the Klingons—think of the Mongol Hordes with spaceships and ray guns—provide an external conflict in perfect counterpoint to the internal conflict Kirk has with Baris. The Captain of the *Enterprise* will be bounced between them like a ping-pong ball.

Going back to the 3x5 cards—remember them?—the following scenes are added:

Klingons arrive at space station.

Kirk confronts Klingon captain, Klingon insists his presence is peaceful.

Fight breaks out in bar between Klingons and *Enterprise* crew.

Kirk disciplines men and cancels shore leave for both ships.

Klingon commander protests treatment.

Darvin revealed as Klingon spy, Klingon captain is embarrassed and leaves.

Now, we have a story.

The *essence* of drama is conflict. Drama and conflict are synonymous. Conflict means: man against _____. (Fill in the blank.) Man against man, man against nature, man against god, man against himself, man against _____.

In this case, man against Klingon. Also, man against man, and man against nature. (Nature in the form of the fuzzies.)

With the addition of the Klingons, what had been a mildly amusing sequence of scenes now becomes a unified story. The villainy of the Klingons makes Kirk seem more heroic—the harder the problem he has to solve, the greater a man he is when he solves it—and with the tension their presence provides, it becomes possible to orchestrate the excitement for maximum impact. Every scene has to be a dramatization of the essential conflict—anything tangential, no matter how funny, must be trimmed out, because now it is obvious which scenes advance the plot and which hold it back.

Fortunately, for all their threat and bluster—or more likely, *because* of it—the Klingons make the story even funnier. By heightening the tension, they also heighten the release— the more you are frightened, the louder you will laugh. And because the Klingons are such perfect villains, the last laugh must be on them.

And Kirk now has *two* seemingly impossible problems to cope with: Baris. Klingons. He also has the perfect way to handle both of them—sarcasm. Because he is otherwise tied down by bureaucracy, there is no direct action that he can take upon either situation, he can only endure them. But at least he can still express an opinion, and that is the perfect way to relieve some of the tension and frustration that both he and the viewer will be feeling at the constraints that have been placed upon him.

That it was the Klingons we used was almost accidental.

Gene Coon used the right words to trigger the memory—but it was the most fortunate accident of the script.

This was the handle I needed. Now I knew how to tell it. In retrospect, I don't think a better choice of villains could have been made.

Yes. A touch of Klingon makes it a story.

A Fuzzy Thing Happened to Me . . .

(An Outline by David Gerrold, June 17, 1967.)

TEASER

FADE IN:

1. INT. SHIP'S GALLEY—KIRK is conducting a white glove inspection. As usual, the Enterprise is spotless. With him is SMITH,[1] a young crewman with a clipboard, making notes on anything that Kirk says needs special attention.

   In the galley, Kirk pauses to talk to the Enterprise's Mess Officer, JAY FOWLER. Fowler is eagerly looking forward to the time a few days hence when the Enterprise will put in at the trading post.[2] It will give him a chance to take on a wider variety of supplies and to re-program his food machines for new combinations.

   Suddenly a wall panel BLEEPS. SPOCK'S VOICE comes from the bridge, "Captain, we are receiving an emergency distress call from the trading post."

   "What's the matter? Are they being attacked by the Klingons?"

---

[1] Smith is a forerunner of Ensign Chekov. I felt the ship needed a younger crewman aboard, so I wrote one in. I didn't know it at the time, but I was paralleling Gene Roddenberry's thinking.

[2] Gene Coon liked the idea of the trading post being a space station. So much for my agent . . .

"They didn't say. They're broadcasting a maximum security request. Presence of the Enterprise is urgently needed in order to maintain the security of the trading post!"

To Kirk, his duty is clear. He orders, "All ahead, Mr. Spock. Go to Warp Factor Five!"

END OF TEASER

ACT ONE

2 PROCESS SHOT—THE ENTERPRISE ARRIVES AT THE TRADING POST.

3 INT. BRIDGE—The ship is in a condition of battle readiness. All crew members are at their posts, waiting for the signal to fight.

Kirk contacts the "Mayor" of the trading post, a man named JOHN LURRY.

"What's the emergency, John? I thought you were being attacked."

"Uh, well Jim—there is an emergency, of a sort, but we're not being attacked. Perhaps you'd better come to my office and I'll explain."

4 INT. LURRY'S OFFICE in the trading post—LURRY, KIRK, SPOCK, BARIS AND DARVIN are present.

John Lurry is the owner of the trading post. He is a congenial white-haired old man.

With him is a coarse, heavy-set man, Nil Baris, a raw-boned farmer turned businessman. Baris has an air of roughness about him that is very unpleasant.

Baris' assistant is Arne Darvis, a thoroughly unpleasant young man. He is a bit of a twitch and he projects the image of a vulture. He is always hovering at Baris' side.

Kirk and Spock arrive. Kirk demands to know what the emergency is.

BARIS
(imperiously)
I ordered the alert, Captain Kirk![3]

KIRK
(looking at him)
Who are you?

LURRY
(hurriedly making introductions)
Jim, this is Nil Baris. Nil Baris, Captain James Kirk
of the Enterprise. Jim, Mr. Baris is the developer of
quadro-triticale.

KIRK
What's quadro-triticale?

BARIS
(motioning to his assistant)
This is quadro-triticale!

KIRK
(also at the assistant)
Him?

BARIS
This is quadro-triticale.

The assistant pulls out some grain samples from his brief-
case. He hands them to Baris, who hands them to Kirk.
Kirk glances at it only briefly, then hands it to a curious
Spock.

---

[3]I realize that it is not standard technique to switch into script
format in an outline, but I did so for two reasons. First of all,
it was easier. Secondly, and much more important, I wanted
the story to be as much mine as possible—if they bought my outline, that did not necessarily imply that they would hire me to write
the script. There are a lot of other writers in Hollywood who
could have done a competent job. Besides, I wanted to show
them that I could handle the script format. If they did let me do
my own script, much of my work would already be done. Or so
I thought.

KIRK

Wheat. So what about it? Why did you call me here?
What's the emergency?

BARIS

Quadro-triticale is not wheat, Captain Kirk! It is a
newly developed form of regular triticale.

KIRK

Regular triticale . . .

BARIS

I wouldn't expect a spaceship Captain to know about
such things, but regular triticale is . . .

KIRK

Regular triticale is a high-yield per acre hybrid of
wheat and rye.

BARIS
(taken aback)
Uh— . . . yes, that's it. Well, quadro-triticale is an
improvement even on that.

KIRK

And that's your emergency?

BARIS
(puzzled that Kirk has not seen the danger)
Of course, it is. Captain, this is valuable grain.
There's a warehouse full of it, right here at the trading post. I want it protected.

KIRK
(incredulously)
You used a maximum security alert to call me here,
just to protect a warehouse full of wheat?

BARIS
(correcting him)
Quadro-triticale.

KIRK

I don't care what it is! I—

LURRY

Jim, let me explain. We're on the frontier, here.
We're only a few light years from the Klingon em-
pire. Nil Baris is shipping his grain to Barger's
Planet.

KIRK

Barger's Planet? Isn't that the one that the Klingons
have been claiming for years?

LURRY

That's the one! They say that we have no right to be
there, but so far they haven't done anything but bluster. A large scale shipment of grain like this will
prove to them that the Federation has every intention
of developing this planet. They'll do everything they
can to weaken our position.

BARIS

And that includes sabotaging my grain. I'm sure
they'll try something. My freighter won't be here for
at least another two weeks, so during that time, I
want you and your men to guard that ware'   ꞋꞋe
and—

KIRK

Just a moment, Mr. Baris. Let me explain something
to you. The Enterprise has been assigned to this
quadrant of the galaxy. It's our duty to prevent
armed conflicts, but we are not your private police
force!

BARIS

But, Captain, this whole section of the galaxy is depending on my grain—

KIRK

That does not excuse your misuse of the emergency
defense alert! Now, if you'll excuse me, Mr. Baris,
          (taking out his communicator)
I'll return to my ship.

LURRY

Jim . . .

Kirk stops.

LURRY
(continuing; tolerant)
Jim, couldn't you at least assign a couple of men to guard the warehouse?

Kirk pauses.

SPOCK
It would be a logical precaution, Captain.

At the moment, Kirk does not care about logic. But he is fair. He is always fair. At last:

KIRK
All right. I'll post a guard over the warehouse. Two men.

Kirk is chagrined at having been convinced to post a guard over the grain, but not quite as chagrined as Baris, who had hoped for more.

KIRK
(to the communicator)
Kirk to Enterprise. Kirk to Enterprise.

VOICE
Enterprise here.

KIRK
I want two security men to guard a warehouse here at the trading post.

VOICE
Two security men to guard a . . . ?

KIRK
Warehouse. Also, authorize shore leave for all off-duty personnel.

VOICE

Yes, sir.

DISSOLVE TO:

5   INT. TRANSPORT ROOM—UHURA, SULU, AND A FEW OTHER CREW MEMBERS are in the transport room, waiting to be beamed over to the trading post. They are eager to go on shore leave. There is a little bit of small talk. Sulu invites Uhura to accompany him on a window shopping expedition. They step into the transport booth and are beamed over.

6   MAIN PROMENADE OF THE TRADING POST

A variety of costumes from many different planets can be seen. Most of the costumes should suggest rough frontier worlds. Perhaps, they can be drawn from stock. The street itself is lined with shops and signs indicating that there are other corridors and other shops. SULU AND UHURA AND PERHAPS ONE OR TWO OTHER CREW MEMBERS materialize.

The other crew members go their way. Sulu and the beautiful lieutenant start walking down the street. They run into KIRK and SPOCK. Spock is still carrying the sample of the quadro-triticale.

Sulu notices the grain. Because he is back on his botany kick, he asks for a sample. Spock gives him the grain. He no longer needs it and it would be illogical to carry it any further.

They exchange pleasantries. Kirk and Spock are on their way to pick up the official mail. Sulu and Uhura wander on and into:

7   INT. OF A TRADING POST SHOP—SULU, UHURA, STOREKEEPER, AND CYRANO DAY JAYMIN[4]

The shop is a kind of shop-of-all-planets. All kinds of strange things can be seen on the counters and shelves. Per-

---

[4] I did not like this name at all when I wrote it, but I had not realized that the name Jones was once again available for this story.

haps somebody has cleaned out the prop room and scattered the resulting items around as merchandise.

The crew members of the Enterprise look around, examining items which catch their fancy, but not really in a buying mood.

Cyrano Day Jaymin enters the shop and goes straight to the storekeeper. Perhaps the storekeeper knows him and tries to hide his dismay at seeing him. Perhaps the storekeeper doesn't know Cyrano Day Jaymin, but is familiar with his type.

Cyrano Day Jaymin is a planetary scout. He locates planets for the Federation and is paid by the Federation according to the intrinsic value of each planet he reports. Most planets are gas giants like Jupiter, but still there are a great many Earth-type planets in the galaxy that need locating.

The situation is roughly akin to gold-mining in California in 1840. Cyrano's success as a locator is evidenced by the fact that his clothes have an air of well-used shabbiness about them—but they are still flamboyant and colorful. He is a sort of faded swashbuckler.

He immediately corners the storekeeper and tries to unload some of his more precious souvenirs on the man. The storekeeper protests that he is already overstocked with Rigellian Flame Stones, and he doesn't want any more Sirian Glow-Water.

Most of Cyrano's items are rather commonplace things like that, so naturally his success as a salesman seems to match his success as a planetary locator. Cyrano tries to trade some of his souvenirs for supplies, but as the storekeeper sees a dozen "Cyranos" a month, he is understandably nonchalant about Cyrano's merchandise.

Accidentally (on purpose), Cyrano drops something fuzzy on the counter. It is a fuzzy.

Quickly, he stuffs it back into his bag. By this time, Sulu and Uhura are watching, idly amused.

The storekeeper asks him:

STOREKEEPER
(curious)

What was that?

JAYMIN
(nonchalant and matter-of-factly)
Nothing. Just a fuzzy.

STOREKEEPER
A fuzzy? What's a fuzzy?

Jaymin shrugs and pulls the little creature back out of the bag. He puts it on the counter. Immediately it begins purring and throbbing. Perhaps it tries to move. It inches along the counter by flexing its body. (This can be done either by wires, or by an unseen puppeteer. The fuzzy could be a big furry mitten.)

STOREKEEPER
(continuing)
What is it?

A good question. It is a golden blob of fluff about the size of a coffee cup, or perhaps a little big bigger. The storekeeper takes it curiously. The creature throbs and purrs in his hand like a hedonistic kitten. It is soft and warm and colored a bright green-gold color. It has no legs and no eyes—just a small soft mouth.

JAYMIN
What is it? Why it's only the sweetest little creature known to man since the invention of the woman.
(confidingly)
In fact, in some ways, it's better. A fuzzy doesn't nag.

UHURA
(interested in the creature)
He's darling. May I hold him . . . ?

She takes the fuzzy from the storekeeper oohing and ahhing over it.

JAYMIN
(to Uhura)
That's the way to hold the little fellow. Stroke him —that's it—and he'll purr for you.

(to Storekeeper)
A fuzzy is the only love that money can buy.[5]

STOREKEEPER
You selling 'em?

SULU
(taking the fuzzy from Uhura)
It won't bite, will it?

JAYMIN
(ignoring the storekeeper for the moment)
Bite? Of course not! There's a law against transporting harmful animals from one planet to another.

Uhura takes the fuzzy back. She strokes it and it throbs and purrs. It loves being held, and it loves the warmth of the human hand. It moves by flexing its body or by rolling, depending on how fast or how far it wants to go. It is a simple life form with only two senses, a heat detection sense and a food detection sense. (For this scene, the fuzzy can be like a glove, or a beanbag, which is manipulated like a hand puppet by the actor who is holding the creature. The fuzzy is very much like those garish blobs of fluff that you see in novelty stores.)

UHURA
What do you feed it?

JAYMIN
Ah, feed it? That's the lovely part about the little creatures. They'll eat anything. They're not fussy. They'll eat anything that people will eat.

He tickles the fuzzy in Uhura's hand.

JAYMIN
(continuing, taking the fuzzy)
This little fellow hasn't been fed in a week, and he's not complaining.

---

[5]It is purely coincidence that I acquired a small shaggy puppy about this time, and that the veterinarian where I took him for his shots had a sign on the wall, "A dog is the only love that money can buy." Purely coincidence.

(to fuzzy)

Are you?

(to Uhura)

He's getting skinny, but he's not complaining.

The fuzzy throbs and purrs. Fuzzies never complain.

UHURA

Shouldn't you feed him?

JAYMIN
(shaking his head)

Why? You know what happens if you feed a fuzzy . . . ?

SULU

What?

JAYMIN

You get a fat fuzzy![6]

SULU

Won't he starve?

JAYMIN

Oh, not for a little while yet . . . but if you're that worried about the little fellow, here—let me have a little bit of that grain you're holding.[7]

He takes a few of the stalks of quadro-triticale from Sulu and puts it on the counter. He puts the fuzzy near it. The fuzzy creeps over and starts munching on it. Sulu does not like to lose his grain sample. As Cyrano reaches for more, Sulu pulls back. Jaymin shrugs.

STOREKEEPER
(eyeing the fuzzy on the counter)

Is he clean?

---

[6] Oh, no, you don't!—I decided later that Cyrano was not the right person to say this line. I didn't want him to be an outright liar, just a charming con man. *Inept*, but charming.

[7] This was a little too obvious . . .

JAYMIN
(eyeing the storekeeper)
He's as clean as you are . . .
(looks again)
Perhaps cleaner.

The storekeeper lets this pass by. He leans on his counter
and looks at the fuzzy closely.

STOREKEEPER
I wonder if a creature like this has any commercial
possibilities . . .

JAYMIN
Probably. You might want to sell them . . .

STOREKEEPER
No, no. I meant, I wonder if its fur is any good . . . ?

JAYMIN
(shrugging)
Maybe . . .

STOREKEEPER
Are these things edible?

He pokes at the fuzzy. Jaymin snatches it up, posses-
sively.

JAYMIN
Sir! You are talking about a member of my family.

UHURA
(taking the fuzzy)
Is this the only one you have? He's darling.

STOREKEEPER
What'll you take for him, Mister?

JAYMIN
I couldn't dream of selling him. I couldn't dream
of selling any of my fuzzies. I just couldn't bear
to . . .

STOREKEEPER

How much?

JAYMIN

Make me an offer.

STOREKEEPER

A credit for each one.

JAYMIN

A credit?!! Is that an offer or a joke?

STOREKEEPER

All right. Two credits.

JAYMIN

Twice nothing is still nothing.

STOREKEEPER

Four and that's as high as I'll go.

JAYMIN

Ten.

STOREKEEPER

Ridiculous! Five.

JAYMIN

Nine.

STOREKEEPER

Not a cent more than six.

JAYMIN

Eight and a half.

STOREKEEPER

Too much. No deal.

JAYMIN

Eight.

STOREKEEPER

Six and a half.

JAYMIN

Seven and a half.

(no response)

Seven?

(still no response)

All right, you shylock. Six and a half.

STOREKEEPER

It's a deal. How many have you got?

JAYMIN

How many do you want?

STOREKEEPER
(thinking)

Maybe ten . . . fifteen . . .

JAYMIN

Take more. They go fast.

STOREKEEPER

All right. I'll take twenty—on consignment.

JAYMIN

You'll take twenty-five, cash in advance.

UHURA
(to storekeeper)

I'd like to buy one of these—I'll buy this one. How much are you selling it for?

STOREKEEPER

. . . well, figure a ten per cent markup for a reasonable profit, I think ten credits would be fair.

JAYMIN
(under his breath)

Robber!

UHURA

I would like to have one, but . . .

JAYMIN

Well, then my pretty little lady, I'm going to give you this one as a gift.

And he does so, much to the chagrin of the storekeeper. She accepts it delightedly. For some reason, she asks

Sulu to hold it for a moment, while she powders her
nose, or etc. Sulu fails to notice that the fuzzy is munching on the rest of his grain.

8   ELSEWHERE IN THE TRADING POST—Kirk runs
into Sulu and Uhura with her fuzzy. He asks her about it
and she mentions the strangely colorful Cyrano Day Jaymin.
Kirk makes a mental note to check into this Cyrano character.

Sulu and Uhura are about to return to the ship. They ask
Kirk if he is going to join them. He says he will be along
shortly, but first he wants to check the guards at the warehouse.

9   ENTERPRISE RECREATION ROOM/GALLEY
VARIOUS MEMBERS OF THE CREW are in the room.
MR. SCOTT is at one of the tables reading. SMITH asks
Mr. Scott what he is reading. Scotty shows the cover of it
to him. It is a technical journal. Smith nods, "What else?"

UHURA and SULU enter. She is still carrying the fuzzy.
Sulu goes up to Scotty to see what he is reading. Perhaps he
grins and remarks that Scotty is the only one who reads
technical manuals for pleasure.

Uhura gets herself a cup of coffee from the wall and sits
down at a table. She puts the fuzzy down. Perhaps it had
been perched on her shoulder.

As the fuzzy creeps along the table top, a small crowd
gathers to see the curious creature.

Some of them remark that they had seen them at the
trading post earlier. Others ask where Uhura got it. Everyone wants to hold it. Some try feeding it. Some ask if she
saw the man who was selling them. A few discuss the strange
Cyrano.

As they examine it, KIRK and SPOCK enter. They are
looking for Mr. Scott to check with him about certain re-
placement parts that he ordered, and also several necessary
but minor repairs. Kirk pauses to ask Scott what he is reading. Scott gives up and puts away his manual.

Meanwhile, Spock goes over to examine the fuzzy, because
he has noticed the crowd. Kirk wanders over also.

Spock picks the creature up and examines it curiously,
while Kirk tells Uhura about the ship's regulations. The

beautiful lieutenant is already familiar with the regulations. No mascots without the Captain's permission. All other animals must be kept in the biology section, etc.

Finally, Kirk agrees to let her keep the fuzzy, as long as it will not be a problem.[8] He starts to leave. Then he notices that Spock is absent-mindedly stroking the little beast. He stares at Spock for a moment.

Spock puts the fuzzy down, or hands it back.

As Kirk starts to leave the room, a wall panel bleeps. A Klingon ship has been sighted. It has stopped at the trading post and Klingon men are being beamed over. Kirk leaves the room at a run.

END ACT ONE

ACT TWO

FADE IN:

10 INT. BRIDGE OF ENTERPRISE

Kirk radios the Klingon ship. He asks the Klingon commander what he is doing at a Federation Protectorate. The Klingon replies that he is only there to give his men a chance for shore leave and to take on supplies and fresh water.

The Klingon adds that he knows that the two governments

---

[8]This was a problem that had been puzzling me through every draft of the story—it just didn't seem logical that a starship captain or his crew would be naive about alien animals. Yet I had to get the fuzzies loose aboard the *Enterprise* somehow, and not locked up in McCoy's lab. Standard operating procedure should require that all unfamiliar animals be studied carefully. And it seems like a foolish idea to allow animals, even domestic ones, to have free run of a spaceship or space station. Finally, I had to realize that the story I was telling was basically a comedy—meaning I could stretch things a bit. In order to work, the story had to be presented in terms of its contemporary equivalents: fuzzies are just a different breed of cat. Besides, transporting harmful animals is against Federation law—ergo, fuzzies are not harmful.

are technically at peace, but if any violence is provoked against him, he will answer it with violence.

Kirk replies that if there is violence, the Enterprise will not be the one that starts it.

The Klingon answers, "Good, then if neither of us is going to start anything, there should be no problem."

The Klingon signs off. Kirk gives orders for security men to patrol the trading post. Also, all shore leave parties must consist of at least three persons.

11   PROCESS SHOT—ENTERPRISE—CAPTAIN'S LOG, VOICE OVER

KIRK

Captain's log, Stardate 4532.7: We are keeping the Klingons under surveillance, and all crew members have been warned to watch for any signs of sabotage to the grain. So far, all has been peaceful. End of entry.

(pause)

Correction: One additional entry. Lt. Uhura has become a godmother and the population of the Enterprise has increased by ten.

12   INT. BIOLOGY SECTION OR RECREATION ROOM CLOSE SHOT of one big fuzzy and ten little ones in a box. They can be made to move by a hidden air hose.

CAMERA PULLS BACK to show a knot of people standing around oohing and ahhing. UHURA and McCOY are in the foreground.

McCOY

How long have you had that thing?

UHURA

Only a day. If I had paid for it, I would have gotten quite a bargain.

McCOY

I don't understand it. That big one—is that the mother?

UHURA
(nodding)

It was smaller when I first got it, but everybody was feeding it. They're cute to watch.

McCOY
(grunts, reaching into the box)

You mind if I take one of these to the lab? I'd like to find out what makes it tick.
(he avoids any mention of dissection)

UHURA

Sure, Bones. Go ahead. But if you're planning to dissect it, don't tell me.

Bones leaves with a baby fuzzy. Others crowd around and ask if they too might have a fuzzy. Perhaps it is mentioned in passing that others aboard the ship have brought fuzzies back from the trading post.

13 TRADING POST—Kirk is checking to see that there has been no trouble from the Klingons. Lurry confirms that the Klingons have been peaceful, but Baris has not. Lurry does mention that a man named Cyrano Day Jaymin has also created a minor sensation on the post with his fuzzies.

ON THE MAIN PROMENADE nearly every store has a sign that says they are selling fuzzies. Fuzzies are quite a bit in evidence.

The two of them visit Cyrano as he is making his rounds, distributing fuzzies to eager storekeepers. Kirk warns him about transporting harmful animals. Jaymin assures him that the fuzzies are harmless, and gives Kirk one as a token of his esteem.

As Jaymin leaves, Baris arrives. Baris eyes the fuzzy in Kirk's hands with reluctant distaste. Kirk ignores it. Actually, he doesn't quite know what to do with the little creature, so he just holds it.

Baris complains about the Klingons and demands that Kirk do something, like ordering them off the post. Kirk says that is beyond his authority. Kirk does agree to double the guard around the warehouse, but that is all. As he leaves, he hands the fuzzy to Baris' twitchy assistant.[9]

14 BACK ON THE ENTERPRISE

Kirk visits McCoy in the sick bay to ask for something for a headache.

> McCoy
>
> Why? What's the matter?

> KIRK
>
> I've been over to the post again.

> McCoy
>
> Let me guess. The Klingons? Baris? Cyrano Day Jaymin?

> KIRK
>
> All three. Say, how did you know about Jaymin?

McCoy holds up the fuzzy. It is now slightly bigger.

> KIRK
> (continuing)
>
> Oh.

> McCoy
>
> Jim, are you serious about letting these creatures aboard this ship?

> KIRK
>
> I don't see any reason why not. They make nice pets. They're quiet. They're clean. They're . . .

> McCoy
>
> There's something about them I don't like. They're too darn innocent.

> KIRK
>
> Well, Bones. You're outvoted by the rest of the crew. But, if you find any concrete reason why they

---

[9]This would have been a lovely gag, but as the story turned out . . .

shouldn't be allowed on the Enterprise, I'll do something about it, all right?

15 AT THE TRADING POST

Smith is at a store with two other crewmen. Idly, he looks at a display case full of fuzzies. The storekeeper tries to sell him one. Smith declines. The sign on the case shows that the price has already been lowered once.

Smith asks where he got so many. The storekeeper says that he only started out with a few, but that they have had several litters already.

Smith has not noticed that the other men have left without him. A Klingon soldier enters and starts looking around. The Klingon asks the storekeeper about the fuzzies. The storekeeper says that they are selling very well. They are very popular with the men of the Enterprise.

The Klingon says loud enough for Smith to hear that that is because the men of the Enterprise are soft.

Smith answers that remark, and one thing leads to another, and Smith and the Klingon get into an argument. The Klingon makes it known that he considers all Earthmen to be little better than weaklings. The Klingon is considering taking Smith apart, but every Klingon soldier is being tailed by at least two Enterprise security men. The Klingon glares at them and leaves.

16 BACK ABOARD THE ENTERPRISE

Uhura's fuzzy and its offspring have each had a litter of ten. There are now at least 121 fuzzies aboard the Enterprise—actually there are more, because other people have bought fuzzies.

But the beautiful lieutenant[10] is a bit dismayed to find that she now has about 40 or 50 fuzzies in her possession. She had given away all but four of them and those four have reproduced like little sons of guns.

McCoy notes that the creatures are asexual. They reproduce at will, with an average litter of ten and a gestation period of anywhere from 12 to 24 hours. They have an ex-

---

[10]Two of my favorite subjects are science fiction and sex . . . I dig Lieutenant Uhura.

tremely fast metabolism in many respects, and all food goes to the production of new fuzzies. He warns against feeding them too much.

"You know what you get if you feed a fuzzy?" he asks.[11]

"A fat fuzzy?" Uhura guesses.

"No. More fuzzies. Lots of little fuzzies. Hundreds of little fuzzies."

"Oh."

"So, stop feeding them." McCoy turns to go. Uhura asks him one more question. "Bones."

He turns back. "Yes?"

"Do you know anyone who wants a fuzzy?"

17 INT. BRIDGE

The KLINGON COMMANDER calls Kirk to complain about the constant harassment of his men.

"I don't like having my men tailed."

Kirk doesn't say anything.

"And I don't like stumbling over security guards every time I blow my nose."

Kirk is noncommittal. "Why are you here?" he asks.

"My men are on shore leave," he answers.

Kirk replies quietly, "So are mine."

The Klingon switches off in disgust.

Kirk checks his security guards. So far, no Klingon has come near the grain, although one or two hungry fuzzies have been sighted.

Kirk is too preoccupied to really hear the last. He switches off.

18 TRANSPORT ROOM

Scott is at the transport console with an assistant as a group of men are leaving for the trading post. Kirk wanders in and sees him there.

---

[11]This is where McCoy proves Cyrano a liar. But having Cyrano turn out to be a fraud was too much of a plot complication. So I just cut Cyrano's earlier reference to feeding fuzzies and side-stepped the whole issue. Actually, the gag grew out of a reference to the Walt Disney movie, *Mary Poppins.* "Do you know what you get if you feed the birds?" "No, what?" "Fat birds."

"Mr. Scott. Don't you ever relax?"

"Yes sir, I do."

Well, then what are you doing at the transport console."

"Working, sir."

"Well, get someone to relieve you. You're going on shore leave. That's an order."

"Yes, sir but—"

"Mr. Scott," says Kirk. "Force yourself to relax."[12]

"Yes, sir."

19 INTERIOR OF LOCAL BAR AND GRILL

Several local people and several crewmen of the Enterprise. Also several Klingons. Smith, Scott and a few other crewmen are at a table. Some of the Klingons begin making remarks about the Earthmen. Naturally, the Earthmen resent this. Smith, being young and willing, wants to fight. Scott holds him back—until one of the Klingons calls the Enterprise a sagging old rust bucket.

A fight breaks out.

The bartender calls security and we

CUT TO:

ACT THREE

FADE IN:

20 INT. OF BAR

Security arrives in force, and breaks up the fight. Kirk and Spock and McCoy arrive to survey the damage. Also, the Klingon commander arrives. He and Kirk exchange a few heated, but very oh-so-polite words.

The Klingons leave.

Kirk starts to speak to his men and we

---

[12] I like this line. I'm sorry it wasn't in the final script.

CUT TO:

21 INT. OF ENTERPRISE

Where Kirk finishes disciplining the men. He confines them to quarters or restricts their shore leave, and assigns them to the modern equivalent of K.P. Perhaps Smith is assigned to assist the Mess Officer.

After they are dismissed, Kirk chides Mr. Scott who has one hell of a black eye.

> KIRK
>
> What caused the fight, Scotty?

> SCOTT
>
> They insulted us.

> KIRK
>
> And you fought over that?

> SCOTT
>
> No, sir. Smith wanted to, but I tried to hold him back.

> KIRK
>
> Why did Smith want to fight?

> SCOTT
>
> The Klingons called you a—

Scott pauses.

> KIRK
>
> This is off the record.

> SCOTT
> *(relaxing slightly)*
>
> Well, sir. They said you were an overbearing, tin-plated hero with delusions of godhood.

> KIRK
>
> And that's when you started the fight?

> SCOTT
>
> No, sir.

                        KIRK
When?

                        SCOTT
When they insulted my engines, sir.

Kirk reacts

                        KIRK
Mr. Scott, I'm surprised at you.
                      (pause)
That's all, Scotty.

Scott starts to go.

                        KIRK
                    (continuing)
Oh . . . and Scotty . . .

He pauses.

                        KIRK
                    (continuing)
Remind me not to order you to take shore leave
again.

                        SCOTT
Yes, sir.

Scott leaves. McCoy reports on the condition of the
men. From there the discussion goes into a mention of
the fuzzies, which, by now, are showing signs of getting
out of control.

                        McCoy
Jim, you've got to do something about these
creatures.

                        KIRK
Why?

                        McCoy
They're getting out of hand. Do you know what
these things are? They're deadly!

KIRK
(stiffening)

Deadly?

McCOY

Well, not in a physical sense, but the nature of the beast is such that—well, here, you hold one and see for yourself!

KIRK

I've held a fuzzy before, Bones.

McCoy gestures with it. Kirk takes it.

KIRK
(continuing)

So?

The fuzzy purrs contentedly in his hand. Absent-mindedly he strokes it.

McCOY

See! It's habit forming. The thing is a parasite!

KIRK
(self-consciously handing the fuzzy to Spock, just to be rid of it)

Oh, come now, Bones. I'll admit that love is distasteful—
(he glances at Spock)
but hardly harmful.

SPOCK

I, personally find such open displays of emotion very distasteful.

McCOY

Jim, these things are absolutely useless to the running of this ship. But they consume food . . . like . . . like . . .
(he is at a loss for a comparison)
. . . and once they start eating, they start producing more of them . . .

SPOCK

For once, I'm forced to agree with the Doctor. It seems as if he is finally learning to think in a logical manner.

McCOY
(eyeing Spock)
Even our computerized First Officer agrees, Jim.

SPOCK

They are consuming our supplies and returning nothing.

KIRK

Well, I wouldn't exactly say that love is a nothing . . .
(pause)
One must be tolerant, Mr. Spock,
(another pause)
But you are both correct. This morning I found four fuzzies on the bridge. I've already issued orders to keep all fuzzies off the bridge, and that no more food is to be issued for the purpose of feeding fuzzies.

(pause)
If they must eat, let them eat leftovers.

McCOY

Jim, it's a little more complicated than that. While you've been sparring with the Klingons, the fuzzies have taken over your ship . . .

Finally, they convince Kirk to make an inspection of the ship. By now, there are fuzzies everywhere. They are into the fifth, sixth and seventh generations. There are fuzzies on the bridge, in the galley, etc.

Scott reports that he has fuzzies in his engine room and they're disrupting the work. The noise of forty fuzzies purring is driving his crew crazy.

The inspection of the ship convinces Kirk. He hadn't realized that the fuzzies were getting out of hand. He tells McCoy to get a few men together to collect all fuzzies.

22　KIRK returns to the TRADING POST to look for Cyrano. He finds him and questions him about the fuzzies.

KIRK
You knew about their breeding rate, didn't you?

JAYMIN
Of course, Captain Kirk, of course. Fuzzies are my business. I discovered them on a charming little planet where they have so many natural enemies they have to breed as fast as they can just to insure the survival of the species.

KIRK
How do you carry them without being inundated?

JAYMIN
I don't feed my fuzzies, except maybe once a week, or less . . .
(pause)
Only when I need to sell a few . . . I must admit I am surprised at the ferocity with which they breed here, but maybe it's something in the air . . .
(pause)
Maybe you just fed them too much, that could be it, you know. I don't have that much food to spare, so I don't have that problem.

Jaymin refuses to be brow beaten by Kirk and he finally leaves Kirk. He is behind schedule as it is, and he must be going, so, "Goodbye, Captain, it was nice talking to you." Jayman's ship leaves the trading post.

23　BARIS comes up to KIRK to warn him about a strange character named Cyrano. Kirk sighs heavily. "I know. I know. I just saw him leave the trading post."
Baris is sure that Cyrano is a saboteur. Kirk starts to reassure Baris that nobody has been near the grain at all. Baris is insistent. Finally, Kirk gets mad and tells Baris off. He tells him that he has been a nuisance, and that he (Kirk) has enough problems without having to be an interstellar scarecrow.

24 KIRK returns to the Enterprise to find that the fuzzy situation is completely out of control. As he walks down the corridor, there are fuzzies everywhere.

25 IN THE GALLEY Kirk goes to the wall panel to get a sandwich and a cup of coffee and as the panel slides open, there is no food on the plate, but a fat and sassy fuzzy.

That is the last straw. Kirk gets mad. If we thought he was mad before, that was nothing compared to this.

He calls for the crew of men assigned to collect fuzzies. Smith was one of them. Smith said that they started in the galley. Kirk asks him to look around the galley and what do you see? Fuzzies! That's what you see!

The galley is literally crawling with the fuzz balls.

The Mess Officer steps in and asks Kirk to come and look at something. Kirk steps into an area where one of the food processing panels has been opened. There are fuzzies all over the machinery.

But that is not all. He opens a bin that is supposed to be full of white flour. Kirk stares into it, aghast. The bin is full of fuzzies, squirming and seething and mewling.

Kirk stares into it, aghast. *The grain in the warehouse!* If the fuzzies could do this . . .

He calls for Spock, "Meet me in the transport room."

END ACT THREE

ACT FOUR

26 IN THE TRANSPORT ROOM while he is waiting for Spock, Kirk issues orders for a general alert. Every crew member is to bring every fuzzy on the ship to the transport room where they will be transported into open space.

The fuzzies are now recognized as vermin that must be destroyed.[13]

---

[13]When you think about it, there really is nothing else you can do. Sorry about that, nature lovers.

27 AT THE TRADING POST Lurry meets Kirk and Spock. As they move through the trading post, there are more fuzzies here than we have seen throughout the whole show. Lurry says that it is a plague. The fuzzies are increasing geometrically. Every twelve hours there are ten times as many.

The proprietor of the store where Uhura bought the first fuzzy is near tears. He can't even sweep them out of his shop. There are just too many.

28 AT THE WAREHOUSE—Baris is with them now. He is complaining and whining. He is sure that his grain has been sabotaged. Kirk asks him if the warehouse is secure. Baris says that it has been locked and nobody or nothing could get in.

Kirk says, "Then you have nothing to worry about, but just to make sure . . ."

He orders the warehouse door opened. If the fuzzies have gotten to the grain, there should be thousands of them on the other side of that door.

They have and there are.

When the door swings open, as many fuzzies as there are in existence come stumbling out as if they have been stacked up on the other side.

The interior of the warehouse is never shown—but the huge number of fuzzies inside the warehouse is suggested by the great number of fuzzies that tumble out of the door.

                    BARIS
                   (aghast)
There must be thousands.

                    KIRK
Hundreds of thousands.

                    SPOCK
One million, seven hundred and seventy-one thousand, five hundred and sixty-one.

Kirk looks at him. ("Oh really?")

SPOCK
(continuing)

That's assuming one fuzzy with an average litter of ten, every twelve hours for a period of three days.

KIRK
(knowingly)

Oh.

Kirk looks back into the warehouse.

KIRK

There's how they got in . . .
(pointing)
That vent . . .

CLOSE SHOT OF VENT with fuzzies hanging out of it.
ANGLE

KIRK
(continuing)

Mr. Spock . . .
(Spock looks up.)
We have two things to do.
(pause)
First, capture Cyrano Day Jaymin . . .
(another pause)
and second . . . close that door.

29 INT. BRIDGE The Enterprise is chasing the ship of Cyrano. Because of their greater power, it is only a matter of time before they capture him and beam him aboard. They take his ship in tow.

30 BACK AT THE TRADING POST they find that there is a surprise for them. Cyrano is actually innocent of plotting to destroy the grain.

They find that the 1,771,561 fuzzies in the warehouse have died. Indeed, many of the olders ones (on the bottom of the pile) were already dead, but undiscovered.

McCOY takes a dead fuzzy and a sample of the grain that is left.

31   Almost immediately, McCoy reports that the fuzzies have been poisoned. There is a virus in the grain that tests out as harmless, but has the peculiar property of turning into an inert material when it is taken into a living body, such as a fuzzy. It is not a poison in itself, but rather—like carbon monoxide—it can kill by suffocation. That is what killed the fuzzies.

Further tests show that if this grain had been used for seed, the virus would have been present in all of the crops raised. Apparently, the grain had been tampered with before it reached the post. The fuzzies have inadvertently saved many human lives.

32   When Baris and Darvin arrive, Cyrano is able to point out Darvin as a Klingon agent. In fact, Darvin is the one who pointed out the fuzzies to Cyrano in the first place.
(If so, then it was another Klingon agent, at the source, who poisoned the grain. Perhaps a subspace message could notify them of this.)[14]

Kirk orders the Klingon Commander to get the hell off Federation property. The Klingons leave.

And finally, Kirk orders Cyrano to get every last fuzzy off of the trading post. Cyrano objects at first, but Kirk threatens to have him charged with transporting an animal that has been proven harmful.

Cyrano protests that the job will take forever. Kirk says that he should think of it as job security.

Cyrano submits.

END ACT FOUR

TAG

33   BACK ON THE ENTERPRISE BRIDGE, now strangely free of fuzzies, Kirk wonders aloud how they managed to

---

[14]I was still fumbling around for an appropriate punch line. Hence the clumsiness of this denouement. We were still thinking of Darvin as a renegade Earthman. It wasn't until later that we thought he might be a disguised Klingon.

get rid of them all so quickly. McCoy says that it was all Scotty's doing. Kirk asks how.

Mr. Scott says he used the transporter.

KIRK

But where did you transport them? You didn't just transport them into outer space, did you?

SCOTT

No, sir. That would be inhuman.

KIRK

Then where, Mr. Scott?

SCOTT

This is off the record, sir?

KIRK

Off the record? Why?

SCOTT

You wouldn't want to be a party to an act of war? Would you?

KIRK

Mr. Scott, would you kindly tell me what you did with the fuzzies?

SCOTT

I gave them to the Klingons, sir.

KIRK

You gave them to the . . .

SCOTT

Aye, sir. I transported them smack into the middle of their engine room.[15]

FADE OUT.

THE END

---

[15]Haven't you ever wondered what the Klingons did with all those fuzzies? I'll bet that they didn't let any thoughts of inhumanity trouble them . . .

CHAPTER SIX:

Aboard the Good Ship *Enterprise*

I finally worked up my courage and asked if I could visit the set. Gene was almost surprised that I had bothered to ask.

Ande, Gene's secretary, told me how to find soundstage 9. It was very close by. She told me if I had any questions to ask Charlie Washburn, the second assistant director. (I do not know what a second assistant director does, but Charlie always seemed very busy. A lot of paper passed through his hands; obviously, he was responsible for seeing that a lot of production information was in the right place at the right time.)

On this particular day, they were shooting an episode called "The Doomsday Machine," written by a fellow named Norman Spinrad. I'd been introduced to him earlier, so I was glad to recognize at least one person on the set who I could pretend I knew.

Norman is a quietly brilliant human being who has done much to overcome the handicap of a New York accent. He has a head of hair like an explosion of schizophrenic brillo, his taste in clothing is somewhere between Little Richard and Wally Cox, and his language suggests that he was one of the people who taught Norman Mailer how to cuss; but all of these things are virtues in Hollywood. The important thing is that Norman Spinrad is a good writer. "The Doomsday Machine," a modern-dress retelling of Ahab and the whale, was one of STAR TREK's best episodes. (In my humble opinion, of course.)

Norman would disagree with me. He felt his story had been ruined by interminable rewrites. Not having followed the progress of his script and not being experienced in the ways of television, I could only listen and nod and wonder what would happen to me and my story. Aside from a couple of feeble protestations that so far all of Gene Coon's suggestions to me had seemed correct, I kept my mouth shut and my eyes open.

William Shatner and William Windom were rehearsing a scene from the show. Windom, playing Commodore Decker, was trying to describe the giant planet-killing doomsday machine to Captain Kirk. Or rather, to William Shatner —who had this incredible grin across his face that suggested he was waiting for a straight line. Sure enough:

Windom: "Jim, it was huge! It had a maw—"

Shatner: "A maw? Did you see its paw?"

Groans from the crew. They were looking for things to throw.

And it got worse. Let it be know that William Shatner, when presented with the opportunity, will rattle off an unbelievable number of really putrid jokes, each worse than the last. And he will do this until forcibly stopped.

Later though, he did something that has stuck in my mind

ever since, something that suggests just how experienced an actor he actually is.

They were about to shoot the scene where Kirk witnesses Decker's death. Marc Daniels, the director for this episode, suggested that Kirk show his grief and pain by lowering his face. At the same time, Jerry Finnerman, the director of photography, was making adjustments on a key light—much of STAR TREK'S mood was set by his creative use of colors and shadows.

Shatner was sitting behind a control console while Daniels and Finnerman discussed the best way to throw a shadow across him. Abruptly Shatner suggested that the light be only across his eyes, so that when he lowered his head, his face would go into shadow, thus heightening the effect of his grief. Daniels and Finnerman exchanged a glance. "Well," said Daniels, "it seemed like a good idea at the time."

They tried it and it worked.

A little thing? Perhaps. But it proved to me that William Shatner was a professional's professional. His first concern was the story and the show.

I didn't meet William Shatner that day. He seemed awfully busy—and besides, what would I have said to him? Captain Kirk still inspired awe in me. It would have been too precocious for me to say, "Hi there, I'm going to put words in your mouth." Furthermore, I figured that these people were probably hounded by fans all day long, probably the politest thing I could do was leave them alone. Unless properly introduced, of course.

And in due time, I was introduced to DeForest Kelley, James Doohan, Nichelle Nichols, and most of the stand-ins and extras who populated the *Enterprise.*

Without exception, the cast members of STAR TREK were all good people and incredibly gracious. I saw this time and time again, whenever visitors came onto the set, the cast would invariably go out of their way to say hello and find out who they were. Which is how I finally met Leonard Nimoy.

We were on soundstage 10, which had magically become Gamma Trianguli VI. The episode was "The Apple," by Max Ehrlich, and it concerned a tribe of white-haired natives who served the great god Vaal. The set for this episode was an orange sky and a green jungle—not just a little jungle either. This jungle filled the soundstage, more than filled it—overflowed in every direction. Far off on the horizon, tall palms were waving in the wind, dark clouds scudded the sky. As far as the eye could see, green, green and more green. As far as the second season was concerned, the budget for greenery had been *blown*. After "The Apple" Kirk couldn't have afforded a daisy for his lapel—if he'd had a lapel.

I was sitting off to one side looking through a copy of the script, there were always copies lying around and I got to read half a season that way, when suddenly Leonard Nimoy was sitting next to me. There was an ugly black hole in his chest where a poisonous plant had attacked him only moments before, but it didn't seem to be bothering him much. "I've seen you around here for a few days," he said. "Who are you?"

"Uh—I'm David Gerrold," I managed to say. "I'm writing one of the scripts."

"Oh? Which one?"

"Urk—" I said. It isn't easy to tell an actor what you're going to make him do—and that Vulcan makeup was intimidating. Leonard Nimoy's very calm and stoic manner was all that was necessary to complete the illusion that he was all Vulcan all the way through. I'd been keeping my distance from him out of politeness and respect, and a healthy bit of trepidation, but now—well, this was the equivalent of a command performance.

"It's called 'A Fuzzy Thing Happened to Me . . .'" I blurted. "It's about these little fuzzies that breed like crazy until Captain Kirk is up to his hips in them."

"Sounds like a cute idea. I'll look forward to reading it."

And then I did a brave thing. I admitted that I was having a little trouble understanding the character of Spock—which was making it difficult to write dialogue for him. In response, he told me about a show they'd already filmed, called "Amok Time." It was about Mr. Spock's seven year urge to mate. The script had been done by Theodore Sturgeon.*

---

*I was impressed by that. If I had to pick ten science fiction writers as the all time *best*, Theodore Sturgeon would be three of them. Robert A. Heinlein would be another three. The other four would be Isaac Asimov and Arthur C. Clarke.

Leonard was quite enthusiastic about "Amok Time," and thought it might turn out to be one of STAR TREK's best shows. It gave quite a bit of background information about Vulcans in general, and it was climaxed by a fight to the death between Kirk and Spock.

We spoke for about twenty minutes or so, and then they needed him in front of the cameras again. (Dr. McCoy was waiting with a box of bandaids.)

But my day had been "made." After having Mr. Spock explained to me by Leonard Nimoy, anything else would have been anti-climactic. And it was nice to know that Mr. Spock was human after all.

My excuse for hanging around the set was logical.

When a writer is at his typewriter, he's mentally playing all the parts at once. He's Captain Kirk and Mr. Spock and Lt. Uhura and Mr. Scott and Dr. McCoy all in his own head. If he knows the actors who will be playing these parts, even a little bit, the job is both easier and harder. Easier because he knows what his characters will look like; harder because he has to write speeches that are not beyond the capabilities of those actors. And if the characters are part of a continuing series, the writer has to know as much of what has gone before as he can find out. He has to know what has been established as being possible for the *Enterprise,* the characters, and the format of the show.

Because I'd missed most of the first season, I was suddenly enrolled in the David Gerrold Earn-While-You-Learn school of television writing, with cram courses in Starship Technology, Alien Biology, Klingon Psychology, and Interstellar Law—not to mention additional classes in Television Limitations, The Care and Feeding of Precious Egos, and Soundstage Discipline.

I had to learn everything I could about STAR TREK in a hurry. Had I been able to watch the show regularly, I would not have made such simple—and obvious—errors as suggesting a ship's cook or mail stops or pockets on the uniforms.

With school finished (er, almost finished; I was only three units away from my degree) I was able to watch STAR TREK reruns every Thursday night. It was not enough. I needed more, so every time someone left a script lying around on the set, whether for a current or upcoming episode, I was there reading it. I went through thirteen episodes in two weeks. I nearly O.D.'d on STAR TREK.

I spent time talking to the actors—and a lot more time just listening to them, memorizing their facial expressions and their speech patterns, so that what I wrote would be as natural to them as their own selves.

And I watched the dailies. Daily.

The "dailies" are just that—a daily ritual involving producer, director, story editor, director of photography, and anyone else who feels concerned with the show. Dailies are run when a projection room is available, usually between 11:00 and 3:00. STAR TREK's dailies were run at one o'clock, right after lunch, and the usable footage that was shot on the preceding day was shown.

These are the actual "takes." They run in sequences of scenes, two or three usable takes of each one. Usually with sound, they begin with a quick flash of an identifying clapboard—the "clap" is for synchronizing sound and picture —the offscreen voice of the soundman yelling "speed" and the director calling for action. Then, the action.

On this particular day, one of the shots was a long closeup of Dr. McCoy listening to a conversation between Kirk and Spock as they discussed the nature of Vaal, the all-powerful god of Gamma Trianguli VI. He had no lines of his own, all he had to do was react. "Watch this," said someone goodnaturedly. "DeForest's got only four basic expressions. He counts them off like clockwork."

Sure enough: number one was a puzzled frown, number two was a raised eyebrow, number three was a *lowered* eyebrow, and number four was a skeptical stare.

And then De Kelley fooled us all. Number five was the raising of the *other* eyebrow, number six was the lowering of it, number seven was a sideways scowl, sliding into number eight, an impatient scowl. Number nine was a . . .

About that time, they ran out of film. I assume he could have gone on indefinitely.

On a good show, the dailies are almost always a lot of fun. Not just for the footage, but for the comments made about it. Once, during a closeup of an actor screaming in pain, Gene Coon remarked, "He just saw his paycheck."

And then there are the flubs: the takes that are good up to a certain point—and then someone blows a line, or a door fails to open, or a prop misbehaves. Most of these don't get printed (that costs money) but occasionally one will be part of a good take and will show up in the dailies—like the sequence of Kirk trying to flip his communicator open and having it bounce shut on him three times in a row. Or an actor breaking up in the middle of a long speech. Or—

The *Enterprise* is being attacked. The ship is struck three times. Each time the camera is suddenly tilted sideways and the director yells "Roll!" The actors and actresses throw themselves to the floor and hurl themselves across the set. And each time, we hear one of the actresses cursing, "Oh, shit!" "Oh, shit!" "Oh, shit!" It would have been hysterical if the director hadn't ended it by telling us she'd broken her arm.

STAR TREK's dailies were the most popular on the Desilu/Paramount lot. In fact, they became so popular, they had to be limited to just the production personnel. The size of the audience was getting out of hand. (Later on, I had to get special permission just to attend the dailies of my own script. That's how strict they were getting.) Apparently, the presence of so many people was inhibiting the producer's and director's willingness to speak freely about the footage they were seeing.

As the season progressed, all of the marvelous flubs were collected into one big reel called "The Goodie Reel." This is a filmmaking tradition—the outtakes are collected for the enjoyment of the cast and crew at the last party of the season. Goodie reels are expensive, and not every television show produces one; but if a show has good morale, a goodie reel is one of the reasons why. The existence of one indicates a whole special attitude on the part of the production crew.

I've only seen a few goodie reels other than STAR TREK's. I've never seen a bad one. By the sheer nature of the beast, a goodie reel can't help but be hysterical. There are more laughs per minute than are to be found even on *Laugh-In*. A really good goodie reel approaches the Marx Brothers in the level of its insanity.*

---

*If somebody were smart, they could put together one hell of a TV special just out of goodie reels—or even a whole TV series. Hmm . . . Except the actors' contracts wouldn't allow it. Pity.

Some of the funniest stuff, though, doesn't even get on film. On a happy set—and STAR TREK's was one of the happiest—it's like a twenty-six week costume party; the practical jokes, put-ons, put-downs and wisecracks are endless. William Shatner's penchant for bad puns and worse jokes was almost unbearable. (Only my high degree of respect for the man and his fine reputation as an actor prevents me from repeating any of them here.) And because of that, he was one of the most fun to watch—especially during rehearsal, when he refused to take *anything* seriously. I don't think anyone minded though—he always got it right for the cameras.

The other cast members weren't slouches either. One day, during a particularly intense confrontation between McCoy and Spock, DeForest Kelley leaned forward and kissed Leonard Nimoy on the nose. Leonard just stared at him, shocked, then realized what he had done and broke up.

But it didn't end there. They couldn't do a retake. Every time Leonard got close to DeForest and looked him in the eye, he broke up laughing again. And the effect was contagious. Pretty soon no one on the set could keep a straight face. Leonard and De were too conscious of their nose-to-nose position, they couldn't stay in character long enough to do the shot. Finally, Joe Pevney, the director, gave up. They had to move to another set and pick up some other shots.

During the first season, there had been an episode where Nichelle Nichols as Lieutenant Uhura had had to "open hailing frequencies" fourteen times in one episode. Finally, in frustration at never having anything else to do, she turned to the camera and said, "If I have to open hailing frequencies one more time, I'm going to blow up this goddamn panel." But the joke was on her. When they saw that in the screening room, they decided the line was so funny that they wrote it into the next script. Well, a variation of it anyway.

The set was a popular one. *Mission Impossible* was on the two soundstages right next door and Martin Landau and Greg Morris were occasional visitors to the *Enterprise*. And when Paramount and Desilu merged and the wall was knocked down between the two lots, Michael Landon of *Bonanza* showed up one day. In costume. You expect to see weird characters aboard a starship, of course: blue-skinned An-

dorians, snout-nosed Tellarites, pointy-eared Vulcans and Romulans—but cowboys?!!

Roger C. Carmel, the actor who played Harry Mudd in "Mudd's Women" (first season) and also in "I, Mudd" (second season) showed up the week before the filming of the latter episode. Seeing De Kelley, he bellowed across the set, "Hey, you galactic quack! How the hell are you?" That stopped business for a while.

The Desilu commissary was always a fascinating place to eat lunch—but with STAR TREK on the lot, it could be frightening as well. The other people who worked at the studio never knew when they'd be sitting next to a red-skinned, half-naked worshipper of Vaal, or a Klingon warrior in full battle armor—or worse, three sets of identical twin girls in *very* flimsy costumes.*

Lunch was invariably an adventure as week to week saw a never-repeated parade of exotic aliens and half-clad girls and half-clad aliens and exotic girls and half-clad exotic men and . . . The standard comment was a whispered, "What do you suppose *they're* up to *now* . . . ?"

---

*Bill Theiss, costume designer, worked on the principle of visual suspense: "will she or won't she fall out of that costume?" The girls never did, of course, but you never gave up hoping . . .

In the course of that first two or three weeks, I talked to as many people as I could and learned as much as they could teach. I got my hands slapped by Prop Man Irving Feinberger, for touching a hand phaser, and a dirty look from Director Marc Daniels as well. I heard Makeup Man Fred Phillips complain about the rate at which Mr. Spock used up ears, and occasionally I ran into old friends I'd gone to school with—one was a makeup man himself, called in to help paint the Vaal worshippers, another showed up one day as an extra.

All of the regular cast members, of course, were more than willing to spend a little time with me, explaining the natures of the characters they played and their respective relationships with the other characters on the *Enterprise*. William Shatner told me how he imagined Captain Kirk to be a strong and loyal kind of Captain—and don't forget, he's the *hero* of the show—and what kind of lines the Captain would or would not say. Leonard Nimoy told me about Spock's devotion to duty and logic and his suppression of emotion. De Kelley commented that Dr. McCoy should be treated with more respect and more like a real doctor, but don't forget the funny interplay between him and Spock. Nichelle Nichols was concerned that Lieutenant Uhura be more than just a token Negro on the bridge, and James Doohan felt that the character of Mr. Scott had not been explored enough in previous episodes.

Yes, they were concerned with their respective characters. That's what they were being paid for—to be the best possible Captain Kirk, the best possible Mr. Spock, the best possible Dr. McCoy and Lieutenant Uhura and Mr. Scott. They took great care and concern over keeping their characters consistent.

And that meant that helping a new writer understand who these characters were was part of the job too. These people were professionals; they had to watch out for what individual scriptwriters should know, but usually didn't.

Did it help to make them look better on the set and in front of the camera? Sure it did—but it wasn't glory-hogging. I never saw any of these people ever forget that they were an ensemble. The appeal of the *Enterprise* was in the interrelationships of its crew and not in any one particular character. That each member of the cast strove to make his character interesting and believable was his job in making the ensemble work.

I learned more of what I needed to know in just that few weeks of making a nuisance of myself on the lot than I'd been able to pick up from all the episodes I'd seen rerun on the tube. So when I say that my reason for hanging around the set was logical—it was.

But it was also a lot of fun.

Finally, Gene Coon bought my outline. He had been about to hand it back to me for one more rewrite, just on the last two pages, then changed his mind. "Hell, I'll buy it now and you can bring in the two pages tomorrow."*

Then came the important part—the decision about the script.

Now, let me explain something here. A story outline is worth only about $650. Not bad money for an afternoon's work (assuming you could sell every outline you wrote)—but it was nothing compared to the $3000 or so you could get for doing the script, too.

Which explains why a TV writer is unhappy if he sells *only* the outline.

TV writers are gamblers. An outline is only a stake with which to go after the big money of the script assignment. If he doesn't get the job, he's lost the bet. If all he gets is $650 for the story, well at least he's recouping part of his investment. But the big money is the script.

A script assignment is like a piece of a sweepstakes ticket —especially when you consider the additional income of residuals for re-use privileges; but if selling a script is a piece of a sweepstakes ticket, then selling only the outline is having your horse trip at the starting gate.

In TV talk, it's called "picking up the option." Standard

---

*This was not an unreasonable request for me. Unfortunately, I had spoiled Gene Coon by being too fast. He knew if he asked for something by next week, I would be back with it the next morning. All I needed was time enough to get home to my typewriter.

practice is to hand out the assignment on the basis of a premise or outline. If for any reason either the outline or the
writer proves unsuitable to the producer's needs, the option
is not picked up. The script is either forgotten, and the
show takes a loss on that story, or the choice script assignment is handed to some other writer, one who the producer
knows can deliver.

In my case, however, Gene Coon bought only the outline. He couldn't—just *couldn't*—bring himself to bet $3000*
on what was still mostly an unproven quantity. Me.

And yet, at the same time, he wanted to give me a chance
to write my own script.

To further complicate the situation, he could not ask me
to do it on speculation. That's a Writers' Guild Official
No-No. Professional writers do not work "on spec." If you
ask a writer to do any kind of work for you, you have to pay
him for it—and the Guild will even provide you with an
appropriate price list of basic minimums.

Both Gene Coon and I had had to keep that one thought
firmly in mind throughout all our early meetings. He was
not *asking* me for anything; he was only telling me what I
should do to make a usable story, one that he might buy if
I submitted it to him.

My agent had explained this to me too. Over and over
again, he'd stressed that I could neither ask for nor demand
a story contract. It was up to Gene Coon to offer. Were I
to presume one penny more than was fairly due me, I would
be shown the door and I would have destroyed all future opportunities for myself with STAR TREK. I would have established myself as being a leech, not a writer. And I would
also have made Gene Coon a lot more wary about helping
other new writers in the future.

So, my agent said to me, "David, Gene can't just give
you the script assignment. At best, he'll let you do it like
you did the outline. He'll tell you what he needs and it's up
to you to come up with something he can use. But he can't
ask you for it, else he has to pay you."

And within an hour of that, Gene Coon said: "David,

---

*This was minimum script and story money in 1967; tops was
$4500. These prices would be about $1000 higher now.

I can't give you a script assignment. I don't know that you can deliver—but I'll do this for you. I won't assign your story to anyone else for at least a month. That will give you a chance to see if you can do it yourself. If you can come up with a good script of this, I'd rather buy it from you. Now, I'm not *asking* you to do it, I'm just giving you the chance to submit your own draft."*

Yes, I know, the distinction here seems kind of slippery—and a good case can be made that STAR TREK was taking advantage of me.

Don't you believe it. This is the only way a new writer can start at the top.

What Gene did was not unfair. It was necessary. It would have been unfair if he had tried to do it to me a *second* time—because if he was buying a second script from me, that meant he knew I could deliver a finished product and was asking to see one "on spec." Only so long as I was *unproven* would I be required to prove myself this way—and that meant only *once*.

After the first script, you're a professional.

In the eyes of the studio, in the eyes of the producers, and in the eyes of the Writers' Guild, one sale qualifies you—you're a pro. (In fact, within a week, that latter organization was sending me a notice to join if I was planning to work in television again.) That first sale means that your days of writing "on spec" are over. You couldn't, even if you wanted to—the Guild will fine you for it, anything up to 100% of your income on that project. The theory here is that good writers always produce good words; if you're not getting paid for them, then you're working for free. And because the Guild gets paid out of the writers' incomes, its attitude is roughly the same as that of a pimp whose prostitutes are giving away their favors rather than charging for them. (In fact, I used to tell people I was a high-priced prostitute—but that led to too many misinterpretations.)

Anyway, I had a month to write the script.

I did it in two and a half days.

---

*I was beginning to pick up a pattern here. I suspect that somebody at the studio was priming my agent as carefully as he was priming me.

Well, the rough draft, that is. I was working directly from my outline, so most of the material remained the same. It was merely a matter of translating everything into script format, fleshing out what had previously only been suggested. And it was a great way to find out all the weaknesses in my story. When you stretch thirty pages into sixty, the holes get twice as big.

I took the rough draft down to the studio for Gene Coon to see. I was bothered by certain elements of its structure.

We had a story conference about it a week later. Gene said the structure was okay—but there were certain elements of detail that bothered him.

And then we went through the script page by page. Gene had scrawled notes profusely across every page of the manuscript and covered the title page as well with a few general notes:

> "Let us establish better that the quadro-triticale is of extreme importance to the Federation . . .
> "Let us somehow determine that Darvin is a Klingon agent. This will mean making something more of him . . .
> "Scene needed after discovery of poison in quadro-triticale. First, suspicion falls on Cyrano, but he is finally cleared . . . somehow get the goods on Darvin . . . Wrap up that Klingon ship is here just to verify the poisoning of the quadro-triticale. Build more in the ending. Flesh out considerably.
> "Suspect the entire script will be short. Generally thin . . . and skeletal. Explanations! Reasonings! Decisions! Make Kirk stronger, more in control. Importance of disaster when fuzzies eat it, later a big salvation . . ."

And then, he handed me a six page analysis by Bob Justman.

Bob Justman was the show's Associate Producer. (In the third season, he became Co-Producer. Later, after he left, he produced a show of his own, *Then Came Bronson*.) His duties, roughly, consisted of figuring out how much a script would cost to film. That he was very good at it is legend— but there is no truth at all to the rumor that he could judge a script to within ten cents of its final cost, including sandwiches for the extras, merely by weighing it in his hand. Usually, he flipped the pages first before making such a pronouncement. As a courtesy to the author.

Justman had owl eyes, wire-rimmed glasses that made

them look bigger, and a large, bushy-red mustache. He presented one of the friendliest demeanors on the lot—but don't let his looks fool you. Beneath that warm furry exterior, there lurked the heart of a miser. You would have thought he was spending his *own* money.

And vicious—? Well, no—not really, but anyone who would send a six-page, single-spaced, one-thousand-words-to-the-page memo to a new writer, listing in glaring detail *all* the faults in his first rough draft script, is the kind of man who would sacrifice naked girl scouts, cookie packages still clutched in their hands, before a giant statue of Mammon, the god of money, while cackling gleefully and muttering arcane verses from the *Wall Street Journal*. (In fact, the girl scouts were delivered to his office once a month, just before the full moon.)

Had I not had the biggest ego west of Harlan Ellison, I would have fled screaming back to my typewriter and walled it up in a dungeon for having been party to such an atrocity as Justman seemed to be accusing me of.

Fortunately, I came to my senses in time. If I was going to compete with the pros, then I should be required to meet *their* standards of professionalism. And that's what Justman—and Coon—were demanding of me.

All right—but all I had asked for was just a *little* help with a couple of minor problems—Coon and Justman between them had picked enough nits to leave the script a cratered, pock-marked mass of bleeding words and ichor-dripping scenes. They handed it back to me in a plastic bag.

—Oddly enough, most of their comments were correct.

For example:

> Justman: "I dislike the teaser very, very much. I consider it quite bad. There is no hook at the end of it. There is no jeopardy . . ."

I hadn't liked the teaser either, but my agent had forbidden me to change it—according to him, I had to stick *exactly* to what they had bought in the outline—so I turned in an alternate teaser with the script, one that started in Lurry's office with a confrontation between Kirk and Koloth, Koloth demanding shore leave rights for his men. Justman didn't like that either:

> "David's alternate teaser is a little better, but not much . . .
> "I like the idea of having this Trading Post within the

confines of a Space Station. We could probably get a Miniature Space Station built and photographed and we would have something for ourselves for future shows.

"Set construction costs for this show are liable to be very, very high due to construction of Trading Post sets. However, I feel that we can do something about this after this script is re-written and cleaned up . . .

"The Main Promenade of the Trading Post, as indicated on Page 12, is a swell thing, but who can afford it? . . .

"Cyrano . . . could stand some more development . . . Does he remind you of Harry Mudd? . .

"On Page 17, let's re-write so that Ensign Chekov has the Doggerty part. I feel that as long as the prices are equal, we should take as much advantage of our regulars as we possibly can . . .*

"We should do some further investigation with regard to the Fuzzies and what they are to look like. I think it is important not only to develop the Fuzzy which is visually interesting and which we can also make for peanuts, but it should be something that we would have a great interest in marketing as a promotional device . . .

"You are absolutely correct. Scott should just stand up on Page 34 and belt the Klingon right in the chops."

On Page 34, a Klingon warrior was trying to pick a fight with ~~Crewman Doggerty~~ Ensign Chekov and Mr. Scott. Mr. Scott says, "The Captain told us not to go looking for trouble, lad," but when the Klingon calls the *Enterprise* a sagging old rust-bucket, Mr. Scott replies, "The Captain didn't say a word about trouble looking for us, did he though?" And then he stands up and swings. Both Gene Coon and Bob Justman thought this latter line unnecessary.

Later on, Kirk decides to go after the missing Cyrano. He orders Scotty to fire up the engines. Scotty replies, "The little beasties love the warmth of my engines. But if I turn 'em on, I'll roast them."

Kirk glances around the fuzzy-bedecked engine room. "We wouldn't want that, would we, Mr. Scott?"

Scotty still has a black eye from the barroom brawl he started. He rubs it painfully. "No, sir. I have a very gentle nature."

---

*Smith in the outline became Doggerty in the rough draft. By now I was changing the names of the subsidiary characters as often as my underwear.

When he finally does activate the engines, there is a puff of smoke from one of them and we see a quick shot of Scotty pulling a charred fuzzy out of it.

Bob Justman's reaction was terse:

"On Page 41, if I read Scott's first speech in the Engine Room correctly, I have to come to the conclusion that the *Enterprise*'s engines are either coal burning or oil burning . . ."*

Additional comments concerned the problem of showing the fuzzies in the *Enterprise*'s stores. Justman again:

"On Page 46, we refer to 'cardboard cartons with holes chewed in them.' This is very old-fashioned for the *Enterprise*. I think we had best stay as far away from how food is stored and handled on our ship as we possibly can. I would go along with a redress of one of our sets in which the two long walls had sliding panels, which opened up on cue. Each panel could be a food storage compartment. We would only have to open up a few of the panels to discover piles of squirming fuzzies inside . . .

"Let's forge ahead to the bottom of page 57. I must make the statement that Darvin sure doesn't hold up under cross-examination. At least he answers all of Kirk's questions truthfully and to the best of his ability . . .*

"I have a suggestion for page 61. Scotty should confess that he gave poisoned grain to all the fuzzies. That is, he gave poisoned grain to all the fuzzies, except one. And that one fuzzy he transported into the Klingon engine room. And he should thereupon give Kirk an estimate of how long it will take those fuzzies to completely inundate the Klingon vessel.

---

*When I rewrote the scene, I merely changed Scotty's line to: "I cannot do it, Captain . . . They're into the heat exchangers. If I turn on the engines, the thermal emissions will roast them!" Apparently, this satisfied Bob Justman because no more was ever said about the matter. Besides, the whole sequence of chasing after Cyrano had to be dropped; there wasn't time for it.

But this still wasn't the end of the joke. At the end of the season, a shot showed up in the goodie reel of a crewman shoveling coal into the *Enterprise*'s engines as fast as he could. Hm, must have been warp speed 10. The "crewman" was Gregg Peters, Associate Producer and Production Manager.

*I still feel this way about the final draft. Even though we solved the problem enough to please Bob Justman, Darvin still didn't hold up well during questioning.

"Sorry about the shortness of this particular memo, but I feel that your own comments in the margins on my copy of the script take care of most of the problems. I would be interested to find out how many pages this script actually has. Since David typed the script using elite type face, I have the impression that it runs to more pages than are indicated. However, that too is no real indication, as the pace of this show should be rather rapid. I don't envision our pages averaging anything more than 45 seconds a page, due to the type of show it is. This sort of show, with strong comedic overtones, must necessarily move very rapidly. Therefore, I feel that we will need at least 66 full pages to enable us to get anything approaching sufficient footage."

I include that last comment because it touches on one of the elements that played a very large part in determining the final shape of the script.

My Selectric typewriter was a 12-pitch machine. That is, it typed twelve characters to the inch—as opposed to 10-pitch which typed only ten characters to the inch. The difference was an extra three words per line, or fifty words per page. It was the difference between *elite* type-spacing and *pica*, as Bob Justman had pointed out. TV scripts are typed in pica; I was using the wrong spacing. And I would pay for it later.

He was correct that we would need about 66 pages; it was that all-important page count that would determine how much of the story we would have time to tell. Despite my smaller type-face and my longer pages, both he and Gene Coon thought the script might run a little short. Just how short, though, we wouldn't know until it was sent to mimeo.

Gene's comments on the script took a different tack. He was concerned about preserving STAR TREK's internal consistency. Some of his notes were not only apt, but great fun to read.

For instance, in the much disliked teaser, Kirk asks the ship's computer for a projection of information. Getting it, he thanks the computer. The computer responds with a, "(Whirr-click) You're welcome."

Gene Coon simply noted, *"Don't humanize our computer."**

In the scene where Cyrano bargains with the storekeeper,

---

*To which I still disagree. If *I* were programming that computer, it would learn some manners.

he calls the man a "shylock." Gene wrote in the margin: *"David, you're a goy."* (Actually, I'm not—and I offered to show him my circumcision to prove it.)

In the scene leading up to the barroom brawl, the Klingon is making remarks about Kirk. ~~Doggerty~~ Chekov responds, "And your Captain is a cold-hearted war machine!" The Klingon only smiles. "In a Klingon, that's something to be proud of." Gene said, *"More nasty, please."* Otherwise, the joke isn't funny; the bigger the buildup, the bigger the release.

Later, when Kirk quizzes Scotty about who started the fight, Scotty reports exactly what the Klingon called Kirk, "A swaggering, tin-plated, over-bearing dictator with delusions of godhood." Gene liked this so much, he suggested we strengthen it—both in the fight scene and in Scotty's report to Kirk later on. *"Get some fun out of this,"* he wrote. *"Like every man's entitled to his own opinion, joke being he didn't get mad when Kirk was insulted, but he flipped when the ship was."*

Elsewhere, he noted a shortcut I had taken between two topics, a blatant attempt to change the subject in mid-scene. While Kirk was asking about injuries from the fight, McCoy is complaining about fuzzies. Gene pounced on it with a simple: *"Hell of a place to start talking about fuzzies."* I threw out the rest of that scene.

A couple of other scenes were crossed out too, with the simple notation: *"Save money!"* (Extra shots of the transporter room, things like that.)

All of these, however, were little things; they could easily be rewritten. Of more importance was a serious flaw in the structure of the script itself: it lacked unity. We were telling the fuzzy joke all right, but we weren't tying it in with the damn Klingons. And this was particularly obvious in the weakness of the ending.

In this first draft, it was Cyrano who fingered Darvin as the spy. This was a little contrived—hell, it was a *lot* contrived. It was very, very bad. After all, on a space station, they should have run into each other a lot earlier.

No, we needed *something* else . . . something to punch it up, some kind of impact, something to bring this all together and make the ending twice as exciting . . .

And as Gene was saying this to me, a thought was growing in my mind . . .

"Let's try this," I said excitedly. The thought was still taking shape even as I was talking, an incredible *Ah ha!!* of an idea—"It's trite, it's shtick, it's hokey, it's been done before," I said, jumping up and down with enthusiasm anyway. "But the fuzzies are *allergic* to Klingons. They like Earthmen, but they spit and hiss at Klingons. We see it first in the bar— then later on with Darvin; that's how we recognize him as a disguised Klingon!"

Gene looked at me. "You're right," he said. "It is trite. It is shtick. It is hokey. And it has been done before." Pause. A smile spread across his face. "But we'll do it."

From that moment, the basic idea was complete.

Oh, there was still a lot of work to be done, but now I *knew* the story I was telling. All of it. There weren't any holes any more.

Just one or two little things . . .

For instance, The *Enterprise* had a new regular character, a fellow named Chekov—

Back in 66, when STAR TREK was first presented, one of its most important aspects was the multi-national character of its crew. Scotty was obviously a Scot, Dr. McCoy was a deep southerner, Uhura was not only African, but her name translates into "freedom" in Swahili. Mr. Sulu, of course, was oriental, although his exact ancestry was never pinpointed. In the *Star Trek Guide*, he was identified as "Japanese in character." Throughout the first and second seasons, we continually met additional characters such as Reilly, an Irishman, and Kyle, an Englishman. By implication, other nationalities were represented as well.*

Not only other nationalities, but other races as well. Mr. Spock was half-Vulcan, but the *Star Trek Guide* suggested that members of other alien species might also appear as *Enterprise* crew members, a possibility that was unfortunately never explored.

However, one nationality had been overlooked—and Gene

---

*Somewhere aboard the *Enterprise* must be a fanatical German officer, a high-spirited Israeli, a soft-speaking Hindu who quotes continually from the prophet, a couple of Amerinds and an Eskimo . . .

Roddenberry himself later admitted that this was an error.

It took a pointed editorial in no less than *Pravda,* the Soviet newspaper, to bring home the fact that there was no Russian aboard the *Enterprise.* After all, throughout most of the sixties, the Soviet Union had been putting men into space with all the regularity of the Manhattan crosstown shuttle. And certainly, the Soviet Union was going to continue to be important in the future development and history of space travel. They felt—and justifiably so—that they had been slighted.

One of the underlying themes of the show was international cooperation. Not having a Russian aboard belied the "united" in "United Systems Starship."*

So Ensign Chekov was created.

He was to be young—Gene wanted a character for younger viewers to identify with, something I had been thinking about too. Smith-who-became-Doggerty could just as easily be Chekov. Had I known about Chekov sooner, he would have been.

In one sense, though, the joke was on the Russians.

Every STAR TREK character had to have one or two identifying characteristics, a handle with which the writers could approach them. For Mr. Spock, it was his devotion to logic and his pride in his Vulcan ancestry; for Dr. McCoy, it was his down-home approach to medicine: "I'm a doctor, not a fortune-teller." Mr. Sulu was a botanist as well as a skilled swordsman, and Mr. Scott (as pointed out in the *Guide*) was known to consider his engine room the highest form of relaxation known to man. Nurse Chapel had an unrequited crush on Spock and Lieutenant Uhura had a beautiful singing voice as well as being a generally sexy woman. Captain Kirk—well, he was too busy being Captain; besides, William Shatner had made the character too much a part of himself for him to be approached otherwise.

For Mr. Chekov, though, it was the Russian Joke. It worked like this:

SPOCK
Mr. Chekov, hand me the atom-emulsifier.

---

*Hm. There should have been a Chinese aboard too . . .

CHEKOV
Ah, yes. The atom-emulsifier. It vas inwented by
Ivan the Terrible.

Or:

KIRK
This planet is a paradise.

CHEKOV
Yes. It's almost as nice as Moscow.

And so on.

Whatever you were talking about, the Russians had done
it first, and better.

Pravda wanted a Russian on the *Enterprise?*

Okay—but he was going to be *fiercely* Russian:

SCOTTY
Are you still drinking that soda pop, lad? When are
you going to switch to something civilized, like
scotch?

CHEKOV
Vodka *is* civilized. In Moscow, they wouldn't drink
anything else."*

The actor they hired to play Ensign Chekov was Walter
Koenig. He fit into the STAR TREK ensemble as easily as if
he'd been there from the start.

I'd been around the set for some time before I met him.
Not all the cast members were on the set every day, just the
days they were needed. Thus, it was possible to go for several
days without seeing one of the stars, or even a couple weeks
if you wanted to meet all of the regulars.

Chekov was the only one I hadn't met yet. Oh, there was
this fellow on the set during the filming of "The Apple,"
always smiling, kind of a Beatle-ish haircut, and in an ensign

---

*This is from *my* version of the barroom scene. It wasn't used
in the shooting script, though. A pity, because I thought it was
better than the joke they did use, more subtle.

uniform, but I hadn't associated him with the still phantom Chekov. He smiled at me in passing and I smiled back, and both of us probably wondered who the other was.

This went on for several days—on a soundstage that's longer than real-time—with me too polite to speak until I was spoken to, and Walter not sure whether I was just a visitor or somebody he should get to know; at that time, he was still being hired on a show-by-show basis.

For some reason, actors—the ones who are good enough to get paid for it—scare me. If DeForest Kelley hadn't introduced us, I'd probably still be waiting to meet Walter Koenig.

All I remember was that I mumbled something polite and kicked myself for not realizing before. Meanwhile, De was telling Walter that I was writing one of the upcoming scripts. That's when I found out that actors are afraid of writers too.

I mean, think about it. Suppose I decided there wasn't room for Chekov in my story—that made me one of the people who determined whether or not he was going to work.

Thank God the crew of the *Enterprise* wasn't being paid by the spoken word. I would have felt guilty every line I cut.

Fortunately, though, most of those kind of heavy decisions are made by the front office, meaning the producers and the directors. Thus, it was possible for the cast and the writers to get along fairly well.

I was one of the few writers who was concerned enough about the show to want to spend so much time immersed in it. I didn't realize it, but the cast was flattered by that. Most TV writers just don't take that kind of interest in a show; they're just disembodied names on the credits. For a writer to show such an active interest means that the series is more to him than just a script assignment and a paycheck.

In some respects, writers are the stepchildren of the industry. They are not really considered a part of the show or the production team. In fact, there are some series where the writers are not even allowed on the set. Fortunately, STAR TREK was more progressive.

Oddly enough, the only other writers who made a point of visiting the STAR TREK set were also science fiction writers—Harlan Ellison, Theodore Sturgeon, Norman Spinrad and Robert Bloch. It wasn't enough that these men had done scripts for the show, they had to come by and look at the flashing lights and pretty girls too. There's something about science fiction that requires an intense involvement from the writer as well as the audience. It speaks well of the field that science fiction writers are so concerned about their stories, regardless of the medium in which they are presented. STAR TREK's best episodes were written by people who understood both science fiction and television.

I got a little bit of ego-boo* out of it too.

There were almost always fans on the set. Friends or friends of friends. People who knew somebody, or had written in and asked if they could *puh-lease* visit the set. Tourists from all over the country made the Desilu lot one of their stops in California—this despite the fact that it was Universal that was selling studio tours.

Shortly after Walter and I had been introduced and were standing around trying to think of something to say to each other, a couple of the show's fans, two young men, about sixteen or seventeen, came up. They weren't quite sure who Walter was, but anybody in a Starfleet uniform, even a stand-in, was someone worth talking to. When they found out he was going to be a semi-regular on the show, alternating appearances with Mr. Sulu—the budget couldn't afford both of them in the same episode*—they were doubly excited. They were talking to a *star*.

I politely faded away. This was Walter's moment.

Uh uh, not Walter. He dragged me back in: "And this is one of our writers. He's working on a script now."

"Oh, wow! Oh, wow!" Apparently, Walter hadn't realized that to a science fiction fan, writers are the very highest in the pantheon of possible gods. And these were typical, immerse-yourself-in-all-the-memorabilia, rabid-type fans.

The bigger of the two gushed at me, "Oh, wow! Can I shake your hand? I want to compliment you—you guys who write this show are geniuses!!" Etc., etc.

Frankly, I was embarrassed. Walter hadn't seen one word of what I had written, neither had anybody else outside of

---

*ego-boosting, or ego-massage. Praise.

*While George Takei was away, making *The Green Berets*, all of his parts went to Chekov, a fortunate break for Walter.

Gene Coon, Bob Justman, and Dorothy Fontana, the story editor. The episode I was working on might not even get filmed, it was still possible to shelve the story if it didn't work out, yet these two young fanatics were trying to praise me for something they hadn't seen.

And I tried to tell them that. They were wrong to flatter me without reason—and they were wrong to give me credit for other people's work.

But no, they wouldn't listen. They wanted to know that they were talking to one of the "special dreamers." Therefore, I was nominated. Just as I had spent my youth looking up at people like Ted Sturgeon and Isaac Asimov, so were these two teenagers looking up at me. It was an odd sensation.

"Look," I said. "Why don't you wait until after my script is telecast? Then you can write me a letter and tell me what you thought of it. But it's a mistake to compliment me until then."

"Look," said the fan. "This is our favorite TV show. It's always great. Just to be hired to work on a STAR TREK story means that you must have a lot of imagination. Let me compliment you for that."

"Well . . . all right." It was the last modest thing I said for three years.

Suddenly, these two vacationing schoolkids had shown me just how far I had come in the past year. I was no longer on the outside, nose pressed flat against the window, tongue hanging out—now I was part of the magic myself. A small part yes, but a part nonetheless and the show's fans would seek me out because of that part. As far as the public was concerned, I was now a part of the STAR TREK team. Like I said, it was a very odd sensation. But very pleasant.

Walter must have been feeling the same thing. By this time, he had been part of quite a few episodes, but none of them would be on the air yet for several months. There were fans visiting the set every day now and he was always friendly to them, but he must have been uncomfortable at being treated like a star before he felt he had earned that privilege.

Walter had been hired around April or May. The character of Chekov was starting to take shape on paper, and it was time to start looking around for an actor to play him. Of course, when the word went out that one of television's hottest new series was looking for a new "regular," enough prospective Chekovs showed up at the studio to crew three new starships.

Winnowing them down was a brutal process. In Hollywood's pre-television days, the goal of every young actor was to land the lead in a movie. After a few movies, he might begin to be thought of as an up-and-coming actor. Television changed all that—now the promised land meant being a regular character on a continuing series. It meant you worked regularly and you were a star within six months. You'd be touching more people in a year than you might hope to do in a lifetime of movies. There were a lot of fellows who wanted to be Chekov.

They besieged every secretary in the building. Gene Coon's secretary, Ande, reported that nearly all of them came in nervous and asking questions like, "What are they looking for? What can you tell me that will help me? What should I do to get on their good side? Is there a piece of spinach hanging from my teeth?"

Ande, who is as near to the perfect secretary as I've ever met, told them nothing.*

When Walter was interviewed, they made him read a scene from "Catspaw," an episode where the *Enterprise* is menaced by a sorcerer and his familiar. (The episode was written by Robert Bloch.) They wanted the prospective crewman to read a sample of dialogue consisting of: "Captain! Captain! The ship is burning up!" First serious, then funny. They only had that one script, but they needed to see if Walter could handle a wide variety of material.

While Roddenberry, Coon, and others who were party to this decision were debating the merits of the various actors, Walter was sent with Fred Phillips, the makeup man, over to Max Factor's in Hollywood. There, Walter tried on several wigs (including a blond one). They took several of them back to the studio and Walter modeled them for the producers.

---

*Ande had a sense of humor that was deadly. She could say things that few other people could get away with. One afternoon, to a fellow who had reacted negatively to her being black, she smiled sweetly and said, "Hi. I'm Gene L.'s Coon."

He was asked to wait outside again, while they spoke to another actor. Nobody told him anything.

After a while, they sent him over to the costume department so Bill Theiss could measure him. Finally, in frustration, Walter asked, "Listen, when do I find out if I get the part or not?"

"Huh?" said Bill Theiss. "Don't you know? You've already got it." And that's how Walter Koenig found out he was going to play Ensign Chekov.

As for the wig, that was used only once, in the episode, "Who Mourns for Adonis?" After that, Walter's own hair was long enough so that the wig was no longer needed.

That episode also provided one of the funniest shots for the goodie reel. Michael Forest, the actor who played the Greek God, Adonis, apparently felt that his costume was a bit fey. So he pranced up to his throne, daintily rearranged his skirt as he sat down, carefully crossed his legs and blew a kiss to the camera.

But of course, that kind of clowning went on all the time. In the episode, "Mirror, Mirror," there is a shot where William Shatner, DeForest Kelley, James Doohan and Nichelle Nichols move carefully down an *Enterprise* corridor. What the home viewer didn't see was that immediately after, they formed a conga line and came choo-chooing back across the set.

Ah, those long summer afternoons. After a while, the heat gets to you.

I had a script to write.

Actually, re-write.

Normally, a writer is expected to take two or three weeks per draft. I didn't know any better. I did it in one.

And at that, I thought I was taking too long. (Well, I was well motivated.) I averaged two scenes—about three or four pages each—per day, one in the morning and one in the afternoon. I needed sixty pages, one for each minute of film. (I still didn't realize my 12-pitch spacing was throwing that measurement off, but I'd learn soon enough.) Working directly from my first draft and Gene's notes, I found that I had just enough emotional energy per bout at the typewriter to do one complete "motivational unit" at a time. (*Scene* to the layman.) Its climax was my climax, and I needed to rest for a few hours to recharge my batteries.*

So I found excuses to run down to Hollywood and visit the set; I needed to know some obscure detail—uh, the dilithium crystals in the matter-antimatter generators, are they five-pointed or six-pointed?

As long as my work was fast, as long as it was *good,* and as long as I didn't make too much of a nuisance of myself, nobody seemed to mind.

On one of these visits, I ended up in Gene Coon's office.

"David," he said. "You can't call your creatures fuzzies."

"Why not?"

"H. Beam Piper wrote a book called *Little Fuzzy,*" he said.

"I know. I read it. So what? His creatures were nothing like mine."

"Just to be on the safe side, legal department wants us to change the name."

"Okay," I sighed. "I suppose that also rules out furries?"

He gave me a look. "Yes. That also rules out furries."

I sighed. Loudly. "Okay. I'll think up another name."

That evening, I sat down at my typewriter and starting making up a bunch of nonsense words.

I typed:

shagbies	charlies
shaggies	trippies
shappies	tribbies
gollawogs	tribbles
gollies	triblets
callahans	trippets
callies	willies
goonies	brazzies
goomies	triffles
gombahs	piffles
coombahs	puffies
roonies	poofies

And a whole lot of other silly words.

---

*To this day, my working habits have not changed. I write in the morning and I write in the afternoon, one motivational unit at a time. My evenings I keep for drinking.

There was no flash of *Ah ha!* inspiration. I didn't like any of them.

So I started crossing off the ones I hated the most and the ones that were obviously unusable. I couldn't use "willies" because Eric Frank Russell had already written a book called *The Space Willies*. I didn't like "triffles" because that was too reminiscent of John Wyndham's *Day of the Triffids*. (I wonder how he came up with that name?) In fact, I almost crossed off all the words starting with "tri-," but no, there was something about that kind of prefix that I wanted to keep.

I didn't like "charlies" or "roonies," and "shagbies" and "gollawogs" were just a bit too *cute*. So were "puffies" and "poofies." "Callahans" and "callies" were out, and "goonies" and "goomies" didn't make it either.

This process of elimination went on for a couple days. Until all I was left with was "triblets," "tribbles," "tribbies," and "trippies."

"Trippies" sounded like hippies, and "triblets" sounded like triplets with a post-nasal problem. "Tribbies" didn't sound too good either.

Tribbles.

Hmm.

I turned the word over on my tongue. I didn't like it.

I mean, I wasn't *in love* with it. I still wanted to use fuzzies.

But, on the other hand, "tribbles" had possibilities . . .

"Tribbles," I said, trying to get used to the word. "Tribbles. Yeah, I guess so . . ."

Besides, Gene had said we would need a new title. We couldn't use "A Fuzzy Thing Happened to Me . . ."

I considered it—and then inspiration did strike me! Yes, tribbles was perfect!

I could call the show: *"You Think You've Got Tribbles—?"*

Gene Coon hated it.

The title, that is; not the name "tribbles." I turned in to him a list of eight possible alternate names, but I told him that I liked tribbles best. He scanned the list quickly and handed it back to me. "Okay," he said. "Tribbles it is."

Frankly, I felt pretty sure of that choice. The other seven names on the list were not even my runners-up; they were the first losers. I'd weighted it in favor of tribbles.

Then I told him my new title. That's what he hated.

He raised an eyebrow at me and shook his head. "No. We won't call it that. We'll have to think of something else."

"All right," I said. But I was disappointed. Why call the creatures tribbles if you don't take advantage of at least one good pun?

Oh, yes. On the same day I turned in that list, July 17, I also turned in my "official" first draft.

(According to my notes, Gene Coon didn't even read this version, just skimmed it and bought it. I can understand the reasoning here. All they had to pay me was Guild minimum— $2000 for the script; there was enough in my script to make it worth buying and they still had enough left in the writing budget to hire someone else later on for a rewrite. If necessary. On the other hand, had I been a big name pro, the script might have cost them twice as much.)

Once again, Gene Coon and I went over the script. From this point on, it was a *legal* script assignment. I'd shown enough ability on my first two drafts to warrant purchase of my script; but now, I had to turn in a *filmable* version.

Just as the premise went through two versions, and the outline through three, so would the script go through a series of metamorphoses and changes. Each time, it would get a little bit closer to what we wanted it to be. Like the sculptor who carves away everything that doesn't look like an elephant, we would trim away everything that didn't look like STAR TREK.

But if I thought it was going to get easier as I got closer to the final draft, I was wrong.

How to make a tribble breathe.

How to make a tribble walk.

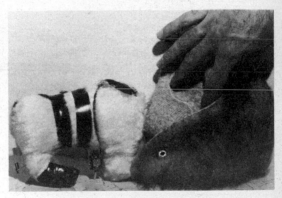

William Shatner
(photo by Stan Burns)

Captain James T. Kirk

Leonard Nimoy
(photo by Stan Burns)

Mr. Spock—First Officer

DeForest Kelley
(Dr. Leonard McCoy)
(photo by Stan Burns)

James Doohan
(Chief Engineer Montgomery Scott)
(photo by Stan Burns)

Nichelle Nichols
(Communications Officer Lt. Uhura)
(photo by Stan Burns)

Walter Koenig
(Ensign Chekov)
(photo by Stan Burns)

William Campbell
(Guest Star on "The Tribbles")

regular cast who did not appear in "The Tribbles"
—George Takei (Helmsman)
(photo by Stan Burns)

Majel Barrett (Nurse Christine Chapel)
(photo by Stan Burns)

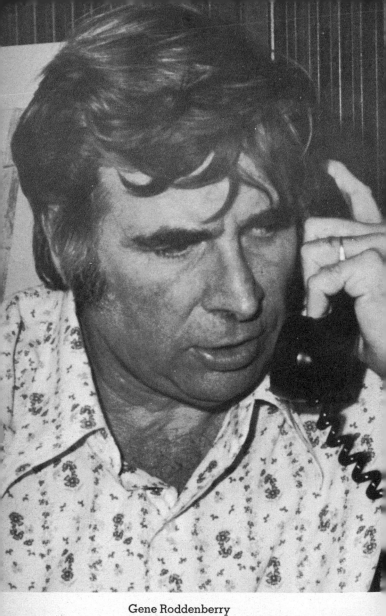

Gene Roddenberry
Producer
(photo by Stan Burns)

(Trading Post and Bar: Cyrano Jones and Barkeeper)

Uhura: "What is it?"
Cyrano: (offscreen) "Why, little darlin', it's a tribble."

Uhura: "Oh! It's purring!"

(Manager Lurry's office: Baris, Lurry, Kirk, Spock, Darvin)
Kirk: "Wheat? Wheat?"
Baris: "Quadro-triticale is not wheat, Captain."

Baris: "I want that grain protected!"
Kirk: "I have never questioned either the orders or the intelligence of any representative of the Federation ... until now."

(Koloth and Korax, the Klingons)
Koloth: "My dear Captain Kirk, let me assure you that my intentions are peaceful."

(Transporter Room: F. G. Crewman, Kirk, Freeman, Scott, Chekov)

Kirk: "Scotty, I want you to go on shore leave. I want you to make sure there is no trouble with the Klingons."

Scott: "But, Captain—"

Kirk: "Scotty, force yourself to relax."

(Interior—the Bar and Trading Post)

Scotty: "Scotch is for a real man."

(F. G. Freeman, Scotty and Chekov.)
B. G. Bartender, Korax, Cyrano.
Chekov: "Scotch? A little old lady in Leningrad invented it..."

(Korax, Cyrano)
Cyrano: "Friend Klingon...May I offer you a
charmin' little tribble...?"
Korax: "Get out of here with that parasite!"

(F. G. Freeman, Scott, Korax, Chekov.)
Korax bracing the *Enterprise* crew.
Scott: (to Chekov): "Don't do it, Mister. That's an order."

Chekov: "But you heard what he called the Captain!"

Cyrano leaves the scene, drink intact.

(F. G. Scotty, Chekov, Campbell, Kirk)
Kirk: "I want to know who threw the first punch."

(Sickbay: McCoy and Spock)
Spock: "There is something disquieting about these creatures."
McCoy: "Oh? Don't tell me you've got a feeling, Mr. Spock."
Spock: "Don't be insulting."

(Bridge: Spock, Kirk, McCoy, Uhura)
McCoy: "The nearest thing I can figure out is that they're born pregnant. It seems to be a great timesaver."

THE tribble in the Captain's chair.

In the Rec. room, the Captain and Spock
order a light lunch . . . but the tribbles
get there first. Scott enters with
an armful collected from the engine room.

The Captain and Spock hurriedly depart
the tribble-infested Rec. room, headed
for the quadro-triticale storehouse.

Kirk: "There must be hundreds of thousands of them."

Spock: "One million, seven hundred and seventy-one thousand, five hundred and sixty-one."

Spock: "Captain, this is most odd . . . this tribble is dead."

McCoy: "I still haven't figured out what keeps them alive . . ."

(McCoy, Kirk, Darvin)
Kirk: "Are you going to talk?"
Darvin: "I never want to see one of those furry things again!"

Captain Kirk sentences Cyrano Jones to cleaning the tribbles off the station. The ship is another matter.

Kirk: "Gentlemen, where are the tribbles?"

"Mr. Scott did the actual engineering..."

Kirk: "Mr. Scott! Where are the tribbles?"

Scotty: "I transported the whole kit and kaboodle into the
Klingon engine room where they'll be no tribble at all..."

David Gerrold before Tribbles

and after . . .

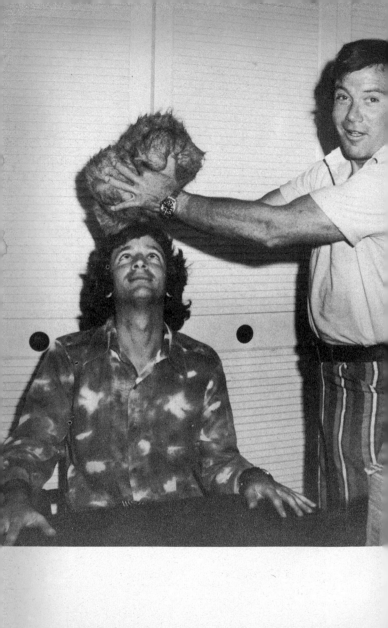

CHAPTER SEVEN:

"The City on the Edge of Forever"

If you're beginning to think that there is an awful lot of rewriting involved in the production of a television script, you're right. There is.

And I may be soundly thrashed by some of my more "artistic" colleagues in the Writers' Guild of America for saying this, but much of that rewriting is *necessary*.

It's not a matter of Art—this is television, forget the capital A—it's a matter of storytelling.

Assume for the moment that William Shakespeare has been reincarnated as a television writer—yes, I know; my gorge becomes buoyant at the thought too, but assume it anyway—and he turns out a beautiful piece of work for whatever series has been lucky enough to hire him.

No matter what it is, they can't use it.

No matter how *great* it is, no matter how *moving*, it may be another *Hamlet* or *Macbeth*, it may be the single most important playwriting effort of the twentieth century—they can't use it. At least not in its original form. Not on *series* television.

This may be television's greatest failing—that it cannot cope with quality—but it is the unfortunate nature of the beast.

Television puts special restrictions on the writer—especially series television—restrictions that have absolutely nothing at all to do with storytelling or Art or relevancy. For instance: a story must be broken into an equal number of 14-minute segments, each ending with a major climax. The story has to be structured to allow for commercials.

If the show is a series, the script has to fit into the overall format. The style of it has to be the show's style, not the writer's. The characters have to be consistent with what has been portrayed before, and the story has to be consistent with the producer's concept of the show. No matter how *good* a story it is, it can't be used if it damages the series's format or continuity.

Additionally, because of the time involved in television production—never enough—the process of analysis and correction has to be done hurriedly, and by a committee: director, producer, executive producer, story editor, sometimes a rewrite man or two, and frequently, the actors.

Admittedly, this is a lousy way to work. A committee is a notoriously inefficient device. The only time a committee accomplishes anything of note is when there is a strong boss in charge, one who knows what he wants to accomplish and how to delegate the responsibility to those best able to handle it. Then the committee becomes a team.

Good television is produced by good teams.

—But, here's the rub. The free-lance writer—that is, the average television writer—is *not* considered a member of the team. Not by fact, not by implication.

He is—as I said jokingly before—a prostitute. He sells his ideas, his words, a framework for the committee to build upon. Excuse me, the team. He sells it and is never heard from again. He doesn't show up on the set and he isn't invited to the cast parties. He's just some flunky they hired to do some typing. In Hollywood, you know yeu're going to get screwed—the time to complain is when you're not enjoying it.

The writer *should* be a member of the team, should not only be allowed to be on the set when they shoot his script, should be *required* to be there. Most writers would jump at the chance. If there was something that had to be corrected or changed, certainly the man whose name is going to be on the credits should have the first say so in the matter.

No writer likes having his words changed, they come out of his head, they are part of his identity. That's who he was when he wrote them. To change those words is to question the validity of that writer's *self*. So, if they have to be changed, isn't it his right first?

The good television writer is the one with a healthy awareness of the medium in which he is working. Most of all, he can think *visually*. And he demands as much from the medium as it is able to give—and more. If he can't do that, then he's not a good writer.

If the team is a good one, and if the writer understands what they want and how they work, then only a minimum of rewriting will be necessary, a line here, a word there, to fit the team's concept of the show. With a solidly established and comparatively simple format, like oh, say, *Gunsmoke*, the writer's only problem is keeping the relationships of the running characters correct as he tells his story. The background of the American West does not have to be explained —not to him, not to the audience—the writer knows exactly what he can or can't do.

With a more complex show, like STAR TREK, where the background changes every week, the writer is charged with the responsibility of inventing not just the story, but everything else that makes it believable: the characters, the planet, its history, the culture in which the characters are working, and even the physical laws of this part of the universe. The *Enterprise* did not come with a book of instructions. It had to be written as the concept of STAR TREK was developed.

Continuity was one of the biggest problems. If it is established that the phasers work one way, then the next week, they cannot be shown doing the opposite. Hence, one of the most important functions of the STAR TREK production team was to establish ground rules, to keep an over-view of the whole season and keep everything working within the same general background. The *Enterprise* works in this fashion, the relationship of the characters is such and such, the concept of the show is this and not that.

The free-lance writer who is writing only one episode cannot be expected to know the whole series. But the more he knows, the better he can work with the production team. If he knows the producer's concept of STAR TREK, he will not write a story that the producer can't use.

And if he doesn't know the producer's concept—well, then no matter how good a story it is, and no matter how good a writer he is, Shakespeare be damned—if it doesn't fit the series, it's going to have to be changed.

An example of this is an episode called, "The City on the Edge of Forever."

It was written by Harlan Ellison—who is a science fiction phenomenon.

Harlan Ellison is one of the nicest people you could meet —as long as you don't do it too often. He'll short out your brain circuits. He is funny and caustic and charming and aggressive and stylish and offensive and brilliant and opinionated and short. If he did not exist, it would be necessary to invent him. He climbs ladders, pulls the ladders up after him and keeps climbing. He is Lilliput's answer to King Kong. He is Munchkinland's answer to Godzilla. He is science fiction's answer to the world.

Harlan was one of the first writers to be hired to write for STAR TREK. He was also one of the best. But unfortunately, his script could not be produced as written.

According to Ellison, the network had been after Gene Roddenberry to keep the costs of the show down. Every time Ellison did a rewrite, the budget on his episode had been cut again, thus requiring another rewrite. (Harlan had made a deal with Roddenberry to do all of his own rewriting, rather than let anyone else touch his script.) "It was like a mad caucus race," says Ellison. "Every time I caught up with them, they were somewhere else."

Finally, a rewrite was done by one of the staff members; it was unsuitable too, but Harlan felt that he had been wronged: "I blew sky high. I went in there and literally threatened Roddenberry. I had been waiting in the secretary's anteroom and had gotten a rope and tied it in a hangman's noose and hung it over the water pipe, and when he came out I pointed to it and said, 'Tell me it's not true that somebody rewrote my words.'"

So. Once again, Harlan rewrote his script. Even though there was no money left in the budget to pay for the additional rewrite work, Harlan was willing to do the work *gratis* to protect his story. "They put me in the back room where the clothing designer, Bill Theiss, kept the spare costumes, there was a table back there, and I wrote on that script —rewrote, because they said they had to shoot it fast—I did four solid days' work, night and day, I slept on the floor in that back office, and wrote. In fact, the guards at Desilu used to come in at two in the morning with their guns drawn, they didn't know who the hell was in there, and they would see me sitting there with my eyes like a couple of poached eggs and they'd think, 'Oh, it's just the kook again with the story.' And I rewrote that thing from stem to stern and pruned it down . . . by that time, of course, the budget had dropped again. Gene Roddenberry promised me that he would rewrite it himself, that there were only minor changes and he would make them himself."

And Roddenberry did rewrite it. And he made several extensive changes. Changes that he felt were necessary.

Roddenberry recognized that Harlan's script was one of the strongest stories that STAR TREK might ever film. It concerned Captain Kirk, Mr. Spock and Dr. McCoy being catapulted back to the year 1930—where Kirk falls in love, but must allow the woman he loves to die in order for history to continue unchanged.

"Harlan's version was a great story," Roddenberry has said on innumerable occasions. "But it wasn't STAR TREK. He had one of our crewmen engaged in dope smuggling, the Captain forsaking the ship, the crew in mutiny, and our characters acting like other people entirely. It had to be changed to fit into the series continuity."

Harlan Ellison did not like Gene Roddenberry's rewrite any more than he had liked any of the previous attempts to rewrite his script, but STAR TREK was Gene Roddenberry's show. The buck stopped at his desk and the decisions had to be made by him. Whether the decisions were correct or not, Roddenberry was the one who had to make them.

Whether or not his rewrite was the best possible *story* is neither here nor there—art can never be independent of the context in which it is presented—it was the best possible "City on the Edge of Forever" for *Gene Roddenberry's* STAR TREK.

As long as it says, "Produced by Gene Roddenberry" on the credits, the responsibility and the decisions are Gene Roddenberry's.

The situation was an unfortunate one. Both men felt very strongly about their respective versions of the script, but only one could be produced. The result was ill feelings. This was one of those slippery instances where both individuals were right. Later on, *both* versions of the story won awards.

Harlan's version won the Writers' Guild Award, and Gene Roddenberry's version won the—But we'll talk about that later.

By the way, budget restrictions turned out to be one of the *least* important factors in the production of the episode. "City on the Edge of Forever" was slated to cost $191,000. But Gene Roddenberry insisted on doing it right—before he was through, they had spent $262,000 to make it an episode they could all be proud of.

Apparently it was money well spent. "City on the Edge of Forever" is recognized as one of STAR TREK's best episodes. The story was undeniably the most important incident that had ever happened to Captain Kirk. It was a definitive show.

CHAPTER EIGHT:

"The Trouble With Tribbles"

And yes, there was rewriting on my script too.

Far from creebing* about it, I'm grateful for it—I'm grateful that Gene Coon gave me the opportunity to do as much of that rewriting myself as I could handle.

---

*I was going to define "creebing" here, but on second thought, I won't. Creebing is one of those words whose meaning is obvious in context.

It taught me more about television in one month than I could have learned in any other way.

More than anything else, I needed guidance—personal tutelage, if you will—and Gene Coon worked closer with me on "The Trouble With Tribbles" than most collaborators would have. If it were up to me, Gene Coon would be entitled to half the credit for the episode—

Hell, it *is* up to me! I hereby declare to all the sundry that the final shape of "The Trouble With Tribbles" is as much Gene Coon's effort as it was mine.

This is not to say that Gene Coon was rewriting my work heavily—rather he was *un*writing. Or maybe the proper word is *editing*. Actually, there is no word to describe exactly what Gene Coon was doing—but to my mind the situation came as close to being the ideal writer-producer relationship as I have ever experienced.

Gene Coon never once told me what I *had* to do—instead, he kept telling me what I *couldn't* do, and it was up to me to come up with something that fit. "We need something here," he would say. And I would start spewing ideas at him until he heard one he liked.

Gene Coon was one of STAR TREK's two best producers—the other was Gene Roddenberry, of course—he knew science fiction and he knew television and he knew how to make the two of them work together.

Science fiction is primarily a literature of ideas. Television is a medium of action. It's difficult to make an idea exciting by itself—on film, it needs people in conflict to dramatize it. That Gene Coon was able to guide the writers, directors and actors in the successful achievement of this, that he was able to meld two such disparate elements into such a viable whole, was one of the major reasons for STAR TREK's success.

Like Gene Roddenberry, Gene Coon knew exactly how far he could go—and he was always willing to try to go just a little farther.

The viewers may not be aware of it, but the networks do exercise censorship over their programming.

At NBC, the policy is called "Broadcast Standards" or some such euphemism, but it's still censorship.

Anything that keeps an artist from telling his story honestly, and in the way that he feels is best, is censorship.

I remember once, overhearing Gene Coon on the phone to

Stanley Robertson, Manager of Film Programming at NBC, talking about an episode entitled "Wolf in the Fold." In the teaser of that show, Robert Bloch, the writer, had postulated a nine-layered drink; each layer of liquid caused the imbiber to experience a different emotion. Kirk, Spock, Scotty and McCoy were sitting in a pub on Argelius II and drinking these concoctions—and experiencing grief, joy, rage, love, envy, unhappiness, etc. in unison.

The network thought this bore an uncomfortable resemblance to a psychedelic drug or narcotic. NBC's Broadcast Standards said no. Gene Coon told them they were "full of horseshit." I'm sure he felt better for it—but the drink was excised from the script.

In "The Trouble With Tribbles," I know of only one reference that Broadcast Standards found objectionable. I had written *in description*—not as a line of dialogue: "To a Klingon, a tribble is as distasteful as a handful of excrement."

Gene Coon told me the comparison would have to be edited out—"The network is afraid it might film that way."

In the writing of the script, there were two other aspects that we had to be conscious of. First, do tribbles defecate? I suppose they did—but that's another of those subjects unsuitable for discussion in prime time.

The second aspect was even more delicate—do tribbles copulate? After all, we couldn't have tribbles fucking all over the ship, could we? We sidestepped the question by making tribbles asexual. (Later, a memo came back from Kellam-DeForest Research: "Asexual means reproducing by fission. Better make it bisexual, meaning the creature is both male and female." But to anyone with a dirty mind, this suggests even more exotic possibilities. *sigh*)

But perhaps, the most insane example of network doublethink is the following letter, sent to Gene Coon after he showed Broadcast Standards the outline for "A Fuzzy Thing Happened to Me . . ."

July 5, 1967

Dear Gene:

Confirming our recent telephone conversation, the above outline is approved with the following comments.

Excellent story! The writer has shown great imagination and grasp of our series. The touches of humor, with the underlying and very evident threat of jeopardy, are superbly played against one another. If the screenplay is as successful as the story outline, this should be one of the most visually exciting and provocative STAR TREK's ever put on film.

This does not constitute Broadcast Standards approval.

Regards,

I think I shall refrain from commenting on the above, and will just skip merrily on to the next topic.

I turned in my rewrite, expecting to have to do another rewrite.

I was wrong.

Gene Coon bought it and sent it down to be mimeographed before I'd even had a chance to talk to him about some of the things that were bothering me.

Oh, well—this was only the first draft. Surely, there'd be a chance to make a few *little* changes before it went in front of the cameras . . .

When it came back from mimeo, it was eighty pages long. Goddamn IBM 12-pitch spacing!

At a rate of one page per minute—and allowing for commercials—we had enough story to tell STAR TREK's first ninety-minute episode.

I showed up at Gene Coon's office the morning the scripts came back from mimeo department. Gene hadn't even had a chance to look at them yet. My copies were the first two that Ande, his secretary, handed out.

"It's going to need a little cutting," she said. (I do not believe she grinned; Ande was not a sadist.) "It's about twenty pages too long."

I walked out of the office in a daze. You do not tell a writer that he is going to have to gut his brainchild. You do not tell a writer that he is going to have to throw away one out of every four words that he has written. You just do not do it—unless you're working in television. Then you do it regularly.

I went over to the soundstage, found a place to sit down

and started working through the script. I figured it was my responsibility to cut it—besides, if I did it before someone else did, then at least I would have the chance to see that it was done right.

Cutting a script is not an easy job—when it is your *own* script, it is infinitely more difficult because you have fallen in love with certain scenes and have lost the ability to look at the whole story objectively.

But I had to. As far as I was concerned, I had to do as much of the work as possible because it was *my* story—I was going to give them a script that wouldn't *need* to be rewritten. At least, not too much. So I took a deep breath, a big mental step back and eyed my story as if I had never seen it before. Everything would have to be judged by whether it was necessary or not—did it advance the plot or hold it back? Was it important to the story? Was it essential?

If not, out.

Believe me, I was more brutal to the script than was necessary. I even cut most of the scene in the trading post where Cyrano haggles with the Trader about the price of tribbles on the open market.

Further complicating the task was the fact that I could not cut just *any* twenty pages at random. They had to come from specific sections in order to preserve the script structure. A television script is broken into four acts, each fifteen minutes long. This allows for lots of commercials, equally spaced, but it is a headache to the writer. For one thing, it means that he needs three major climaxes, each one bigger than the one before—the idea is to keep the viewer so hooked that he won't change stations during the commercial. So right there you have the whole structure of your story: Fifteen minutes and bang, a climax, (commercial), fifteen minutes and bang, another climax, (commercial, station break, another commercial), fifteen minutes and bang, a big climax, (commercial), and fifteen minutes in which to have the biggest climax of all, resolve the conflict and tie up all the loose ends. Did I say TV writers were prostitutes? Hell, we're crib girls, banging and climaxing every fifteen minutes.

Act I was twenty-one pages long, I had to cut at least five and a half. Act II was twenty-one pages too, another five and a half. Act III was only nineteen pages, and Act IV was a comfortable seventeen, four and two pages respectively. Act III ended on page 63 though, and for a while I was tempted just to throw away Act IV entirely. That would have solved everything in one swell foop.

But, no—

I started cutting. And cutting. And cutting. I had a black felt-tip pen and every time I came to something that could be considered superfluous, it disappeared under a thick black mark. I kept count of how many lines and pages I'd crossed out, I didn't want to overdo it.

After a while, DeForest Kelley came walking by and asked me what I was doing.

"My script came out a little long," I said. "I'm cutting it."

"Oh?" he said. "What parts are you cutting?" He stepped up for a closer look.

Right. I was cutting one of his scenes.

There was a pause.

"David," he said. "You're going about this all wrong. What you want to cut are some of the other characters. Some of the unnecessary ones." There was another pause . . . "Like Kirk. And Spock."

"Oh," I said. "Uh, well, I'll have to uh, think about it."

He raised his eyebrow at me and walked away.*

Later on, Walter Koenig wandered over. "Hi, what are you doing?"

"I'm cutting my script down."

"Anything of mine?" he asked—was that desperation edging his voice?

I couldn't resist. "All of it," I said.

He uttered a strangled scream. I think he was about to leap at me, but DeForest Kelley came passing by again. "It won't do any good, Walter—he won't listen to reason."

Actually, they were both pretty goodnatured about the whole thing. The yellow-covered scripts—that is, the first drafts—are never *final*. They're just to give the cast and crew something to start working with, a basic idea of the episode. It's not until the script gets put between gray covers that it's considered final—and even then, they keep making changes. So neither Walter nor DeForest were really upset. DeForest

---

*You have not been insulted until Dr. McCoy has raised his eyebrow at you.

even suggested a joke for one of the scenes, and later, Walter and I went over to the commissary together for lunch. (I was so lost in what I had been doing all morning, that for forty-five minutes I thought we were on a coffee break. I didn't realize that it was noon already.)

After lunch, I was called in to Gene Coon's office. He fixed me with his most penetrating, severe producer's stare. "David," he said, holding up a yellow-covered copy of "The Trouble With Tribbles." "Your script is too long. It's going to have to be cut."

"I know," I said, handing him one of my copies. "Here are my cuts."

"Now, I want you to—*what?*" He seemed a little flustered that I was so far ahead of him. After all, the scripts had only come back from mimeo that morning. Before he'd had a chance to tell me what was wrong, I'd already corrected it. Not only was that disconcerting, it almost bordered on the rude.

I mean, the least I could have done was wait to hear what he had to say . . .

Actually, I had a chance to do just a little more work on the script.

For instance, Matt Jefferies, set designer for STAR TREK, showed up at the dailies one afternoon. When I introduced myself, he said, "Oh, you're the one." And then, "We can't do your script. There's three miniatures and fourteen sets. Too expensive." And he frowned. Fiercely.

Actually, Matt is a very congenial person, but when he says a script is too expensive to build sets for, he knows what he's talking about. I replied, "There's only one miniature and five sets, and some corridors."

"Corridors?!!" he said. "Do you know how much a foot of corridor costs?!!"

No, I didn't.

He told me. (I would include it here, except I've forgotten.)

"Uh, well, maybe we don't need so much corridor," I said.

"Well, that's a start in the right direction. But you've got too many interiors. Interiors cost money. We can afford either a store or a bar. You can't have both."

"Oh," I said. And this was another one of those moments

when I was thinking faster than I realized. "How about if we make the store and the bar the same establishment. That'll also save money because we'll only need one actor instead of two."*

He thought about it. "Okay." And then he smiled for the first time. In fact, after that, he smiled almost every time we spoke. By giving him one less set to do, I had made a friend for life. I couldn't have done better if I'd taken a thorn out of his paw.

I also added DeForest Kelley's joke to the script. I hadn't really thought it fit in, at first, but it was too funny to ignore, and later on, as I kept cutting, I found the perfect place for it.

What I had was a scene with Captain Kirk up to his neck in tribbles; his immediate response is to go chasing after Cyrano, but when the space chase was cut because there wasn't time for it, I had to go directly to the next scene—the discovery that the tribbles are dying. I realized it would be much more dramatic if McCoy discovered it on screen, and this would allow even more tightening up of the plot. De Kelley's suggestion was the perfect entrance line: "Jim, I've got it—all we have to do is stop feeding them and they'll stop breeding!"

Captain Kirk, inundated in tribbles, sighs and rolls his eyes heavenward. *"Now* he tells me."

I'd been worried about the fourth act for some time. It seemed to me that the real punch line of the show came when Kirk opened the warehouse door and was inundated. That was the end of Act III. We still had a commercial and fifteen minutes to go. Everything seemed downhill from there.

Instead, Act IV was saved by combining those two scenes and one other, a confrontation with Baris, all into one—Captain Kirk is neck deep in tribbles, more and more tumbling down onto him at every moment, while the action of the story continues to swirl around him. The more we added to this scene, the funnier it became; the joke of the tumbling tribbles

---

*It also tightened up the story and made for a better series of gags.

became more and more outrageous—until Kirk's final, almost anguished, "Close that door!" is a perfect capper.

In structuring the show, I had wanted to make the tribbles seem almost an afterthought, you realize only subliminally that they are multiplying and multiplying—until suddenly, they are totally out of control and the grain has been eaten. But I had not thought there was any suspense in the show until James Doohan pointed it out to me. Captain Kirk has been placed in a steadily deteriorating situation—one that does not offer any possibility of resolution. Ultimately it could cost him his command. For fifty minutes, we watch Captain Kirk get more and more frustrated at his enforced inactivity. He's restricted from any kind of positive action and we become frustrated too. It isn't until the tribbles reveal Darvin as a Klingon agent that a course of action suggests itself. Our tension at not being able to act is relieved, and the climax of the show comes where it should, as close to the end as possible.

If realizing that the tribbles had to be Klingon-haters was the way to tie it all together—the handle I needed with which to tell the story—then the fact that I had to cut twenty extra pages was responsible for making it an *effective* story. Comedy must always move fast. A story is better compressed than padded.

Did I say, "Goddamn IBM 12-pitch spacing?"

I didn't mean it. It forced me to write a better script.

Now. How much of the actual shooting script was mine?

I mean, it's obvious that a lot of rewriting gets done after the script is turned in.

And that means, a lot of changes. A script can turn into a whole new story.

A gray-covered, final draft is mimeoed on white pages. Every time changes are made, the corrected pages are printed on a different color paper and copies are sent around to be inserted into everyone's script. The first changes come through on blue paper, the second ones on pink, then yellow, then green, then gold, then . . .

The final shooting version of "The Trouble With Tribbles," had pages in colors that had never been seen before by the eyes of man. Ultra-submarine brown, oyster-red, lavender strobe, feckless orange, unhappy purple . . .

But still, it was *my* script. It was my story and most of the words were mine.

Nichelle Nichols said it one afternoon, "I've never seen a script go through so many changes—and stay so much the same."

The changes were minor ones: the phrasing of a line, the structure of a scene, the addition of a word, or the cutting of a sentence. Through it all, the intent of the story remained unchanged.

There were a couple of scenes that were added and one that was cut; sure, my script needed "polishing." But even the producers of the show recognized that the story had been *mainly* the product of one person.

Proof? At the very beginning of the show, where the credits come on, where it says, "Written by," there is only one name on the screen.*

---

*And this was not merely some kind of "kindness." Credits policy was determined by long and serious haggling between the studios and the Writers' Guild. Residuals are paid *only* to the writer or writers whose names appear on the screen. Had anybody else done a significant amount of work on this script, not only would they have been entitled to credit and money, they would have fought fiercely for it. Residuals on a series television show, at that time, were worth 174% of minimum payment.

STAR TREK

"The Trouble With Tribbles"

Written by
David Gerrold

Prod. #5149-42
Series Created by
Gene Roddenberry
Desilu Productions, Inc.

REVISED FINAL DRAFT[1]
August 1, 1967

---

[1]This is the final draft shooting script, plus all changes that were mimeographed and sent around. Additional changes were made on the set, but do not appear here. Some of them are footnoted.

KIRK
SPOCK
McCOY
SCOTTY
CHEKOV
UHURA
ENSIGN FREEMAN

KOLOTH, A KLINGON CAPTAIN
KORAX, A KLINGON AIDE

COMMANDER LURRY
NILZ BARIS
ARNE DARVIN
CYRANO JONES
TRADER
ADMIRAL KOMACK
HELMSMAN'S VOICE
TWO GUARDS—CREWMEN OF THE ENTERPRISE
A SECURITY GUARD

AND KLINGONS AND CREWMEN
   AT LEAST FIVE OF EACH

SETS

INT. BRIDGE
INT. BRIEFING ROOM
INT. RECREATION ROOM
INT. SHIP'S CORRIDOR
INT. TRANSPORTER ROOM
INT. LAB

CORRIDOR OUTSIDE STORAGE COMPARTMENT—
   INCLUDING PANEL COMMANDER LURRY'S
   OFFICE
INT. BAR/STORE ON SPACE STATION

A MINIATURE OF THE SPACE STATION ITSELF

NOTE:
Please change Admiral Komack
to Admiral Fitzpatrick throughout
script.

THANK YOU

NOTE:
Please change Commander Lurry
to MR. LURRY, manager of the
Space Station.

THANK YOU

TEASER

FADE IN:

1 ENTERPRISE FLYBY (STOCK)   1

2 INT. BRIEFING ROOM   2

KIRK, SPOCK and CHEKOV are seated around the table Chekov is on the hot seat . . . as a young ensign, he is here to learn, and the Captain and the First Officer are now examining him to find out just how much he has learned. A lecture with questions, and it is obvious that Chekov hates it.

3 CLOSER ANGLE   3

as Spock consults tri-screen on table.

SPOCK

Deep space station K-7 is now in sensor range, Captain.

KIRK

Good. Mr. Chekov, this flight is supposed to give you both experience and knowledge. How close will we pass to the nearest Klingon outpost on our present course?

CHEKOV

One parsec, sir. Close enough to smell them.

SPOCK

That is not logical, Ensign. Odors cannot travel through the vacuum of space.

CHEKOV

I was making a little joke, sir.

SPOCK

It was extremely little, Ensign.

KIRK

Immediate past history of this quadrant, Mister Spock?

SPOCK

Under dispute between the two parties since initial contact. The battle of Donatu Five took place near here 23 solar years ago . . . inconclusive.

KIRK

Analysis of the disputed area.

SPOCK

Undeveloped. Sherman's Planet[2] claimed by both sides, our Federation and the Klingon Empire. Of course, we have the better claim.

CHEKOV

The area was first mapped by the famous Russian astronomer Ivan Burkoff almost two hun . . .

KIRK

John Burke, Ensign.

CHEKOV

Burke, sir? I don't think so. I'm sure it was . . .

SPOCK

John Burke was the chief astronomer at the Royal Academy in old Britain at the time.

---

[2]Sherman's Planet was named after my girl friend at the time, Miss Holly Sherman. As I mentioned before, she had been an Associate Bunny in *Winnie the Pooh.*

CHEKOV

Royal Academy? Oh. Oh, well!

KIRK

Is the rest of your history that faulty, Ensign? Key point of dispute.

CHEKOV

Under the terms of the Organian Peace Treaty, one side or the other must prove that they can develop the planet most efficiently.

KIRK

And unfortunately, the Klingons, though they are brutal and aggressive, are quite efficient.

CHEKOV

I remember once when Peter the Great had a problem like that. He . . .

UHURA'S VOICE
(interrupting)

Captain!

There is an urgency in her voice which causes Kirk to hammer on the intercom.

KIRK

Kirk here.

4   INSERT—VIEWING SCREEN—UHURA   4

UHURA

Captain, I'm picking up a subspace distress call— *priority channel!* It's from space station K-7!

5   WIDER ANGLE—KIRK, SPOCK, CHEKOV   5

CHEKOV
(to Spock)

Code one emergency? That's a disaster call.

SPOCK

Quite.

A flicker of light indicates the change.

KIRK
Go to Warp Factor Six.

UHURA'S VOICE
Aye aye, Captain.

Kirk snaps off the intercom, already half out of his chair and on his way to the door. Spock and Chekov follow immediately. As they go out:

UHURA'S VOICE
(amplified; loud speaker)
All hands . . . this is a red alert. Man your battle stations. Repeat . . . this is a red alert. Man your battle stations.

FADE OUT.

END TEASER[3]

---

[3]I did not write this teaser. Gene Coon did. My teaser had presented much the same information, but the dialogue was between Kirk and Spock already on the bridge. The main reason for rewriting the teaser was to make better use of Ensign Chekov and make him more important to the story. Gene's teaser has the added advantage of being shorter and funnier than mine.

ACT ONE

FADE IN:

6 OMITTED 6

7 SHOT OF SPACE STATION 7

It hangs against a backdrop of stars—slowly growing in size as the Enterprise approaches.

KIRK

Captain's log; Stardate 4523.3. Deep space station K-7 has issued a priority one call . . . more than an emergency, it signals near or total disaster. We can only assume the Klingons have attacked the station. We are going in armed for battle.

8 INT. BRIDGE—ANGLE ON FORWARD 8
SCREEN—SHOWING SPACE STATION

The space station rapidly grows in size as the Enterprise approaches.

9 ANOTHER ANGLE 9

as everyone on the bridge stares forward tensely. Chekov is in navigator's position.

CHEKOV

Main phasers armed and ready.

(looks up at Kirk)
There's nothing . . . Just the station, sir.

Kirk reacts. He steps down and peers over Chekov's shoulder. Perhaps he reaches past him and snaps a couple of switches.

KIRK
A priority one distress call . . . and they're sitting there absolutely peaceful . . . ?
(turning to Uhura)
Lieutenant Uhura, break subspace silence.

10   ANGLE ON UHURA   10

UHURA
Aye aye, captain.

11   ANGLE   11

Kirk gestures for her to put them on. He steps back to his chair.

KIRK
Space station K-7, this is Captain Kirk of the Enterprise. What is your emergency?

LURRY'S VOICE
Captain Kirk, this is Commander Lurry. I must apologize for the distress call. I—

KIRK
Commander Lurry, you have issued a priority one distress signal! State the nature of your emergency!

LURRY
Uh, perhaps you had better beam over, I—uh—I'll try to explain . . .

KIRK
. . . You'll try to explain . . . ? You'd better be prepared to do more than that. Kirk out.

He starts toward the door, issuing orders as he moves.

KIRK
(*continuing*)
Mr. Chekov, maintain battle readiness . . . Uhura, have the transporter room stand by . . . Mr. Spock, I'll need your help . . .

Kirk waits for Spock to join him at the elevator. They step into it as we:

CUT TO:

12   TRANSITION SHOT—SPACE STATION[4]   12

Enterprise hanging motionless nearby.

CUT TO:

13   INT. LURRY'S OFFICE ON THE SPACE   13
STATION[5]

LURRY, BARIS and DARVIN; Kirk and Spock materialize. Kirk is furious as he begins talking to Lurry as soon as materialization is complete.

KIRK
Commander Lurry, if there is no emergency, why did you order a priority one distress call?!

BARIS
(*stepping into shot*)
I ordered it, captain!

---

[4] The space station was shown to be rotating slowly—which is actually unnecessary if you have an artificial gravity.

[5] . . . and if the space station is rotating, then why was the *Enterprise* shown motionless through the window of Lurry's office? (Pick, pick, pick . . .) by the way, the *Enterprise* in the window was actually one of the plastic model kits that A-M-T was marketing at the time.

LURRY

Captain Kirk, this is Nilz Baris—he's out from Earth
to take charge of the Development Project for Sherman's Planet.

KIRK

And that gives you the authority to put a whole
quadrant on a defense alert . . . ?

DARVIN
(stiff and stuffy)

Mr. Baris is the Federation Under-Secretary in
Charge of Agricultural Affairs in this quadrant!

Kirk reacts—bureaucracy is still bureaucracy. He peers
at Darvin, curiously.

BARIS

This is my assistant, Arne Darvin.
(a beat)
Now, Captain, I want all available security guards.
I want them posted around the storage compartments.

KIRK
(angry, puzzled)[6]

Storage compartments? What storage compartments?

DARVIN

The storage compartments with the quadro-triticale.

KIRK

The what? What is . . .
(stumbling over the word*)
. . . quadro-triticale?

Darvin sniffs audibly at Kirk's ignorance. He pulls a
sample of the grain out of a container. He hands it to

[6]*Personal opinion:* Frankly, I thought William Shatner played
this line *too* angry, too puzzled.

*Pronounced quadro-tritti-cay-lee. [Footnote in script.—Ed.]

Baris who hands it to Kirk. Kirk glances at it only briefly, then hands it to a curious Spock. Spock examines it.

> KIRK
> *(continuing)*

Wheat. So what?

> BARIS

Quadro-triticale is not wheat, Captain! I wouldn't expect you—

> *(glancing at Spock)*

—or your First Officer—to know about such things, but—

Spock, who has been quietly watching all this:

> SPOCK

Quadro-triticale is a high-yield grain, a four-lobed hybrid of wheat and rye . . . a perennial, also, if I'm not mistaken . . . The root grain, triticale, can trace its ancestry all the way back to Twentieth Century Canada, when—

Kirk making no effort to conceal his amusement:

> KIRK

I think you've made your point, Mr. Spock.

Spock pauses and looks at Kirk. He gives Kirk the familiar Spock stare. He was just getting to the interesting part.

> LURRY
> *(interrupting)*

Captain, quadro-triticale is the only Earth grain that will grow on Sherman's Planet. We have several tons of it here on the station, and it's very important that that grain reach Sherman's Planet safely. Mr. Baris thinks that Klingon agents may try to sabotage it—

> KIRK
> *(irked—to Baris)*

You issued a priority one distress call because of a couple of tons of—wheat?!

DARVIN

Quadro-triticale.

Kirk starts to look at Darvin, but he is not worth it.

BARIS
(coming in fast—on top of Darvin's line)
Of course, I—

Kirk has the patience of a saint—unfortunately, Baris has exhausted it.

KIRK
Mr. Baris—you summoned the Enterprise here without an emergency! Now, you'll take responsibility for it! Misuse of the priority one channel is a Federation offense!

BARIS
I did not misuse the priority one channel! I want that grain protected!

LURRY
Captain Kirk, couldn't you at least post a couple of guards? . . . We do get a large number of ships passing through . . .

SPOCK
It would be a logical precaution, Captain. The Sherman's Planet affair is of extreme importance to the Federation . . .

Kirk looks at Spock as if to say "Blast your logic!" However, Spock is usually correct, so . . .

KIRK
(chagrined; taking out his communicator)
Kirk to Enterprise.

UHURA'S VOICE
Enterprise here.

KIRK
Secure from general quarters. Beam over *two* and

only two security guards. Have them report to Commander Lurry.
                    (*a beat*)
Also, authorize shore leave for all off-duty personnel.

                    UHURA
Yes, captain.

                    KIRK
Kirk out.

He puts away the communicator. Baris is upset because Kirk has only authorized two.

                    BARIS
Kirk! Starfleet Command is going to hear about *this* . . . A mere two men!

Kirk looks at Baris for a long moment.

                    KIRK
                    (*finally*)
I have never questioned either the orders, or the intelligence of any representative of the Federation . . .
                    (*pause, looking at Baris*)
. . . until now.

Leaving a speechless Baris and Darvin, Kirk exits, followed by Spock.

                                        CUT TO:

13A   13A
thru OMITTED[7]   thru
13C   13C

---

[7]Occasionally a scene is cut, but in order to keep the numbering of the shots correct, it still has to be noted in the script. Hence, the occasional "OMITTED."

13D   INT. BAR/STORE—ANGLE ON KIRK
         AND SPOCK   13D

> Like a Western general store, this is a combina-
> tion of two or more functions. Primarily it is a
> bar with a few tables and a bar against one wall,
> but a few extra props behind the bar should
> suggest that TRADER also runs a general store
> type of establishment. Kirk and Spock are at the
> bar, just putting down empty glasses. Kirk is shak-
> ing his head as he puts down the glass, looks at
> the wheat he holds in his hand.

KIRK
... summoned a starship on a priority A-1 channel
to guard some storage compartments.
                    (starts away)
Storage compartments of *wheat!*

SPOCK
Still, Captain, it is a logical precaution. The Klingons
would not like to see us successfully develop Sherman's Planet.

He and Spock are crossing toward the door on his last
line. Uhura and Chekov enter, followed separately by
CYRANO JONES. Uhura and Chekov wait to meet the
Captain, but Jones crosses past them to the bar beyond
where he will engage the Trader.

KIRK
(to Uhura and Chekov)
I see you didn't waste any time going off duty.

UHURA
How often do we get shore leave?

CHEKOV[8]
She wanted to shop ... and I wanted to help her.

_____

[8]Originally, Chekov's lines in this scene had been written for
Sulu, but George Takei was off in Georgia making *The Green*

KIRK

Mister Chekov.
(holds out wheat)
What do you make of this?

CHEKOV
(takes it eagerly)
Quadro-triticale! I've read about this, but I've never
seen any of it till now!

KIRK

Mister Spock, does everyone know about this grain,
but me?

CHEKOV

Not everyone, Captain. It's a Russian invention.

Kirk gives up . . . shot down in flames by nationalism
again. As he and Spock start to exit, Uhura and Chekov
move toward the bar.

14		14
thru	OMITTED	thru
16		16

17   ANGLE ON CYRANO   17

Cyrano Jones is arguing with the Trader. He has
a great amount of merchandise on the counter.
Obviously, he has been trying to sell it to the
Trader, and the Trader has obviously been very
stubborn.

TRADER

No! I don't want any. I told you before, and I'm telling you again.

Berets with John Wayne, so his lines were rewritten and given
to Walter Koenig. When James Blish wrote his short story adap-
tation of "The Trouble With Tribbles" for Bantam Books, apparently he was working from a first draft script because Sulu
was back again.

Chekov and Uhura approach and wait for the Trader's attention.

                    TRADER
                  (continuing)
I don't want any Spican Flame Gems. I already have
enough Spican Flame Gems to last me a lifetime.

Cyrano shrugs. He starts to open his carryall sack to
put them away.

                    CYRANO
                  (pityingly)
How sad for you, my friend . . .
                  (hopefully)
You won't find a finer stone anywhere . . .

The Trader is frowning.

                    CYRANO
            (continuing; hastily)
Ah, but I have something better . . .
          (picking a vial off the counter)
Surely, you want some Antarean Glow Water . . .

                    TRADER
              (deadly monotone)
I use it to polish the flame gems.

By this time Chekov and Uhura are watching interestedly. Cyrano sweeps most of his other stuff back into his
sack.

                    CYRANO
                   (sighing)
You are a most difficult man to reach . . .

Picking up something off the counter . . . it is a green-
gold ball of fluff, a tribble.

                    CYRANO
                  (continuing)
Surely, you want . . .

TRADER
(although he is interested)
... not at that price.

UHURA
(catching sight of the tribble)
Ooooh, what is it?. . . is it alive . . .?
(taking the tribble)
May I hold him? Oooh, he's adorable!
(to Cyrano)
What is it?

CYRANO
What is it? Why, little darlin', it's a tribble . . .

UHURA
(softly)
. . . a tribble?. . .

CYRANO
(continuing over)
It's only the sweetest little creature known to man—
exceptin' of course, yourself . . .

UHURA
(laughing; she is not taken in by the flattery)
Oh!. . . Oh! It's purring!

18 VERY CLOSE ANGLE ON TRIBBLE   18

The tribble in the lieutenant's hands purrs and
throbs. It is a ball of green-gold fluff about the size
of a large bean bag. Its purr is soft and high pitched
like a dove's cooing.

19 ANGLE   19

CYRANO
Ah, little lady, he's just sayin' that he likes you.

UHURA
He's adorable. Are you selling them?

TRADER

That's what we're trying to decide right now.
(*he glares at Cyrano*)

CYRANO
(*to Trader*)

My friend . . . ten credits apiece is a very reasonable price . . . You can see for yourself how much the lovely little lady here appreciates fine things . . .

TRADER
(*an offer*)

A credit a piece.

Chekov, asking Cyrano, as he takes the tribble from Uhura; he has put his grain on the counter: some spills out.

CHEKOV

He won't bite, will he?

Cyrano, making a great show out of ignoring the Storekeeper:

CYRANO

Sir! There is a law against transporting harmful animals from one planet to another, or weren't you aware of that . . . ? Besides, tribbles have no teeth.

TRADER
(*trying to attract Cyrano's attention*)

All right. I'll double my offer. Two credits.

Cyrano, taking the tribble from Chekov and plopping it on the counter in front of the Trader:

CYRANO

Twice nothing is still nothing . . .

The Trader looks down at the tribble . . . he looks at Cyrano.

TRADER
(eyeing the tribble)

Is he clean?

CYRANO
(eyeing the Trader)

He's as clean as you are.
(a second look)
I daresay a good deal cleaner . . .[9]

While they have been talking, the tribble has been inching along on the counter, toward the grain. It now reaches it.

UHURA

If you don't want him, I'll take him. I think he's cute.

Cyrano and the Trader both notice this. Trader is annoyed. Cyrano beams.

TRADER
(to Cyrano)

All right. Four.

CYRANO

Is that an offer or a joke?

And meanwhile, the tribble begins munching on Chekov's grain.

TRADER

That's my offer.

CYRANO
(starting to leave)[10]

Well, I can see that you're not interested . . .

---

[9]For some reason, this exchange of dialogue was cut from the final show, although it *was* shot. Pity about that . . .
[10]On film, Cyrano's reply was, "That's a joke."

He reaches for the tribble—the Trader stops him.

TRADER

All right . . . five . . .

Cyrano, returning quickly now that the Trader is talking money:

CYRANO

My friend—I'll tell you what I'll do for you. I can see that you're an honest man . . . I'll lower my price to eight and a half.

TRADER

You're talking yourself out of a deal. Six. Not a cent more.

CYRANO

Seven and a half.
            (no response)
Seven.
            (still no response)
All right, you robber. Six.

19A   INSERT—TRIBBLE   19A

happily munching on the grain; i.e., the grain is disappearing under it as the tribble throbs and croons contentedly.

19B   BACK TO SHOT   19B

TRADER

When can I have them?

CYRANO

Right away.

He starts pulling tribbles out of his sack.[11]

------

[11]No, he didn't. It was left unshown.

> UHURA
> *(to Trader)*
> How much are you selling them for?

> TRADER
> *(already counting his profits)*
> Well, let me see now . . . six credits . . . figure a rea-
> sonable markup for a reasonable profit . . . ten per
> cent markup . . . ten credits . . .

20   INSERT CYRANO   20

> CYRANO
> *(under his breath)*
> Thief!

21   ANGLE   21

> TRADER
> In fact, I'll sell you this one—

> CHEKOV
> Hey! He's eating my grain!

Quickly Chekov moves to rescue what is left of the
grain; fortunately tribbles are slow eaters.

> TRADER
> *(picking up the tribble)*
> That will be ten credits—

Cyrano, taking the tribble from the Trader, indignant-
ly:

> CYRANO
> Sir! ! ! That happens to be my sample. And it is mine
> to do with as *I* please . . . and I please to give it to
> the pretty little lady, here . . .

> UHURA
> Oh, I couldn't—

CYRANO

I insist.

TRADER

That's right. Ruin the market.

CYRANO

Hah! Once the pretty lady here starts to show this little precious around, you won't be able to keep up with 'em.

He gallantly hands the tribble to Uhura as we:[12]

DISSOLVE TO:

22   KIRK AND SPOCK IN BRIEFING ROOM— 22
     MED. ANGLE

Perhaps each has a cup of coffee, when a wall panel or desk panel BLEEPS.

KIRK

Kirk here.

UHURA'S VOICE

Message from Starfleet, captain. Priority channel. Admiral Komack speaking.

KIRK

Transfer it in here, Lieutenant.

A pause . . . then the screen on the table lights.

22A   INSERT—VIEW SCREEN   22A

---

[12]In the film version, Cyrano is shown beaming at Lieutenant Uhura. But actually, a better shot had been filmed, showing *both* the Trader and Cyrano beaming at her. It would have been a funnier capper to the scene. Occasionally, STAR TREK's cutting was very clumsy—but that was probably a result of the time pressure the cutters were under.

ADMIRAL KOMACK appears, seated at his desk.

KOMACK

Captain Kirk.

KIRK'S VOICE

Here, sir.

KOMACK

Captain, it is not necessary to remind you of the importance to the Federation of Sherman's Planet. The key to our winning of this planet is the grain, quadro-triticale. The shipment of it must be protected. Effective immediately you will render any aid and assistance which Under-Secretary Baris may require. The safety of the grain—and the project— is your responsibility. Starfleet out.[13]

22B   BACK TO TWO SHOT   22B

KIRK
(beat)

Now that's just lovely.

SPOCK

But not entirely unexpected.

The panel BLEEPS again.

UHURA'S VOICE

Captain Kirk! Captain Kirk!

KIRK

Kirk here. What's the matter, Lieutenant?

---

[13]This part was played by Ed Reimers, who used to do commercials for Allstate Insurance, concluding with the words: "You're in safe hands with Allstate," and a closeup of his hands holding a model house At the conclusion of this shot, they tossed him a tribble and he said, "Remember, Captain Kirk—you're in safe hands with tribbles," and held it out the same way. Naturally that little piece of film went straight into the goodie reel.

UHURA'S VOICE

Sensors are picking up a Klingon battle cruiser—
rapidly closing on the station!

23   TIGHT SHOT ON KIRK   23

as he reacts.

KIRK

Contact Commander Lurry. We're on our way.

24   ANGLE   24

as he and Spock race for the door, not even waiting
for Uhura's acknowledgment.

24A INT. CORRIDOR   24A

Kirk and Spock exit into corridor, run for an elevator.

CUT TO:

25   OMITTED   25

26   INT. ENTERPRISE—BRIDGE   26

as Kirk enters the bridge, followed by Spock.

KIRK
(to Chekov)
What's that Klingon ship doing now?

CHEKOV
Nothing, Captain. He's just sitting there . . . a hundred kilometers off K-7.

UHURA
I have Commander Lurry.

KIRK
Put him on visual, Lieutenant.

Kirk steps to his chair.

> KIRK
>
> Commander Lurry, there is a Klingon war ship hanging one hundred kilometers off your station . . .

26A　INSERT—VIEWSCREEN　　　26A

　　Past Chekov. Lurry is in his office.

> LURRY
>
> I do not think that the Klingons are planning to attack us.

26B　ANGLE ON KIRK　　　26B

> KIRK
>
> Why not?

26C　INSERT—VIEWSCREEN　　　26C

　　WIDENING ANGLE to reveal the Klingon Commander KOLOTH and his aide KORAX also in the office.

> LURRY
>
> Because at this moment, the Captain of the Klingon ship is sitting here in my office.

Kirk reacts, covering his shock.

> KIRK
>
> We're beaming over.

He and Spock start to leave the bridge as we:

　　　　　　　　　　　FADE OUT.

END OF ACT ONE

ACT TWO

FADE IN:

27 OMITTED   27

27A EXT. SPACE—SHOT OF SPACE STATION   27A

KIRK

Captain's log, Star date 4524.2. A Klingon warship
is hovering only a hundred kilometers of deep space
station K-7, while its Captain waits in the station
commander's office. Their intentions are unknown
. . .

28 INT. SPACE STATION—LURRY'S OFFICE 28
    —CLOSE SHOT ON KOLOTH

Koloth is the Klingon commander and, like the
last Klingon commander that we saw, he is an evil-
looking S.O.B.

KOLOTH

My dear Captain Kirk, let me assure you that my
intentions *are* peaceful.

CAMERA PULLS BACK to a FULL SHOT, revealing
Kirk, Spock, Lurry, and—if we can afford them—two
KLINGON AIDES.[14] Kirk and Spock are on one side
of the room. The Klingons are on the other. Lurry is
caught in the middle.

KOLOTH
(continuing)
As I have already told Commander Lurry, the pur-

---

[14]Apparently, we couldn't afford them. There was only one
Klingon aide. A fellow named Korax. Gene Coon thought the
names I used for the Klingons were deliciously evil-sounding.

pose of my presence here is to invoke shore leave rights.

Kirk and Spock exchange glances.

KIRK

Shore leave?

KOLOTH

Captain—Klingons are not as luxury-minded as Earthers. We do not equip *our* ships with non-essentials[15] . . . We have been in space for five months and what we choose as recreation is our own business.

(pause)

Under the terms of the Organian Peace Treaty, you cannot refuse us.

KIRK

The decision is not mine to make . . . Commander Lurry is in charge of the station.

LURRY

(aside to Kirk)

Kirk, I don't want them here—but I have no authority to refuse . . .

KIRK

I have some authority to act—and I'm going to use it.

(to Koloth)

All right—you can give your men shore leave—but no more than twelve at a time . . . and I promise you this, Koloth—for every one of your men on this station, I'll have at least one security guard . . . there won't be any trouble . . .

KOLOTH

Captain Kirk, no formal declaration of hostility has

---

[15]As he said this, his hands traced a feminine outline in the air. The gesture didn't show up too well on television due to some extraordinarily ill-timed cutting. Koloth was played by William Campbell.

been made between our two respective governments.
So, of course, the nature of our relationship *will* be a
peaceful one . . .

KIRK

Let us both take steps to make sure that it stays
that way . . .

The Klingon bows stiffly, politely. He turns on his heel
and exits. Korax follows. Kirk, Lurry and Spock exchange a worried glance.

DISSOLVE TO:

29   ENTERPRISE—HANGING MOTIONLESS   29
     IN SPACE

CUT TO:

30   INT. RECREATION ROOM OF SHIP   30

Kirk and Spock enter. There are a few crewmen
in the room. SCOTTY is at one table, reading. The
other people in the room are in a knot around the
other table. Kirk moves over to Scotty. Spock
moves towards the knot of people.

31   CLOSER ANGLE—KIRK AND SCOTTY   31

Kirk moves up and peers at the title of the tape
that Scotty is reading. It is a page reflected on a
screen.

KIRK

Another technical journal?

SCOTT

Aye, why shouldn't I?

KIRK

Mr. Scott, don't you ever relax?

                    SCOTT
                   (puzzled)
But I am relaxing . . .

Kirk nods—of course you are—he moves over towards
the group of people.

32   ANGLE   32

     McCOY and Uhura are in the f.g. of a knot of
     people. On the table is one larger tribble and at
     least ten smaller ones. They are playing with them.
     It is the quality of their playing that will make the
     tribbles seem alive.

                    McCOY
                   (to Uhura)
How long have you had that thing, Lieutenant?

                    UHURA
Only since yesterday. This morning, I found that he
—I mean *she* . . . had had babies.

                    McCOY
I'd say you got a bargain . . .

He picks up one of the tribbles and examines it curiously. Spock does likewise.

                    McCOY
                  (continuing)
. . . hmmmm . . .

                    SPOCK
Fascinating.

Kirk moves up to the group.

                    KIRK
Lieutenant Uhura, are you running a nursery?

UHURA

I hadn't intended to . . . but the tribble had other plans.

Spock absent-mindedly begins stroking his tribble. This is a bit of business which should be underplayed.

KIRK

You got this at the space station?

Uhura nods.

SPOCK

A most curious creature, Captain. Its trilling seems to have a tranquilizing effect on the human nervous system.

Kirk raises an eyebrow at Spock, who is absently stroking the tribble.

SPOCK
(continuing)

Fortunately, I am of course, immune to its effect.

Kirk grins at him, turns to leave. Spock comes out of it, realizing he is petting the tribble almost hypnotically, puts it down.[16] He follows Kirk out during:

McCOY
(to Uhura)

Lieutenant, do you mind if I take one of these things down to the lab to find out what makes it tick?

UHURA

It's all right with me, but if you're planning to dissect it, I don't want to hear about it.

McCOY

Lieutenant, I won't hurt a hair on his head. Where-ever that is.

---

[16]This was played up a lot more than the script suggests.

McCoy exits with a medium-sized tribble.

ENSIGN FREEMAN
Say, Lieutenant, if you're giving them away, could
I have one too?

UHURA
Sure, why not? They seem to be old enough.[17]

The crewman takes one eagerly—others also help
themselves.

CUT TO:

32A   INT. CORRIDOR—KIRK AND SPOCK   32A

Kirk and Spock round a bend, pause as:

CHEKOV'S VOICE
(filtered)
Bridge to Captain Kirk.

KIRK
(goes to button)
Kirk here.

CHEKOV'S VOICE
Mr. Baris is waiting on Channel E to speak to you,
sir.

KIRK
Pipe it down here, Mister Chekov.

CHEKOV'S VOICE
Aye, sir. Mr. Baris is coming on.

KIRK
Kirk here. What is it, Baris?

INTERCUT Baris in Lurry's office and Kirk in corridor.

----

[17]And then she said (to everyone else gathered around), "Well,
go on—go ahead." And they all helped themselves.

BARIS

Kirk! This station is swarming with Klingons!

KIRK

I was not aware that twelve Klingons were a 'swarm,' Mr. Baris.

BARIS
(quieter)

Captain Kirk. There are Klingon soldiers on this station. I want you to keep that grain safe.

KIRK

I have guards around your grain . . . I have guards on the Klingons! Those guards are there only because Starfleet wants them there! As for what *you* want . . .
(angry pause)
It has been noted and logged. Kirk out.

Kirk savagely slams off the button. He turns and starts away down the corridor.

SPOCK

Captain . . . may I ask where you'll be?

KIRK

Sickbay. With a headache!

He exits as we:

DISSOLVE TO:

33 INT. LAB   33

McCoy's lab. Bones is analyzing a sample of something as Kirk enters. In the f.g., is a box of tribbles.

KIRK

When you get a chance, Bones, I'd like something for a headache . . .

                              McCoy
                        (looking at Kirk)
Let me guess . . . the Klingons . . . Baris?

                              KIRK
Both . . .

McCoy nods as Kirk moves to look at the box of
tribbles.[18]

                              KIRK
                (continuing; looking at tribbles)
How many did Uhura give you?

                              McCoy
                   (taking pills from cabinet)
Just one.

                              KIRK
You've got eleven here.

                              McCoy
Oh, you noticed that.

He returns to Kirk with a couple of pills.

                              McCoy
               (continuing; handing Kirk tablets)
Here. This ought to take care of it.

Kirk, holding the tablets but concerned with the tribbles.

                              KIRK
Bones . . . ? Uh— . . . what . . . ? How . . . ?

---

[18]The continuity in this script—*mea culpa*—is atrocious. Only
a few minutes before, we saw McCoy taking one tribble. By
implication, not too much time has passed. Actually, what happened was that in the writing, all but the most necessary fragments of plot were omitted, and continuity was thrown to the
wind. Television employs a kind of visual shorthand and most
viewers are able to fill in the gaps in their own minds. Fortunately.

McCOY

I'm still trying to figure it out myself . . . I can tell
you this much—almost fifty percent of the creature's metabolism is geared to reproduction—Do
you know what you get if you feed a tribble too
much?

KIRK

A fat tribble?

McCOY
(slightly irked at being a straight man)
No. You get a whole bunch of hungry little tribbles.

Kirk swallows the headache pills.

KIRK
(starting to leave)
Well, Bones, I suggest you open a maternity ward.

Kirk exits. McCoy looks at the tribbles and grimaces
and we:[19]

DISSOLVE TO:

34 OMITTED   34

35 TRANSPORTER ROOM   35

Where a small knot of men are waiting to beam
over to the space station for shore leave. Chekov is
one of them. Mr. Scott is at the console with a
Technician. Kirk is speaking to him . . .

KIRK

I want all men who are going on shore leave to stay
in groups. Avoid any trouble with the Klingons.

---

[19]Right after this, I had written a scene with McCoy and Uhura
to show that the tribbles had bred again. Luckily some smart
soul realized it was unnecessary and cut it.

SCOTT
Aye, Captain, I'll tell them before they go.

KIRK
Mr. Scott, aren't you going on shore leave?

SCOTT
(puzzled slightly)
No, sir.

KIRK
Mr. Scott, I *want* you to go on shore leave. I want you to *make sure* there will be no trouble with the Klingons.

SCOTT
But, Captain—

Kirk stares Scott down.

SCOTT
(continuing, sad)
Aye, Captain.

KIRK
And Scotty . . .
(Scott looks up)
Enjoy yourself.

Scott moves to the transport platform, and we:

DISSOLVE TO:

36 INT. BAR/STORE ON SPACE STATION   36

As the three Earthmen—Scott, Chekov and Free-man—are sitting down, they notice a group of three or four Klingons at another table in the bar, but they make a point of ignoring them. Cyrano Jones enters the bar. Spotting the Earthmen at their table, he moves towards them . . .

CYRANO

Ah, friends, can I interest you in a tribble . . . ?

He is holding one at Mr. Scott's shoulder. Scotty turns
and looks straight into the tribble's absence of a face.
He shudders.

SCOTT

No, thank you.

CYRANO
(looking around)
Perhaps one of you other gents . . . ?

No response. Cyrano shrugs, walking away, cooing at
his tribble. In b.g., Waitress approaches Earthmen.

37　ANGLE ON KLINGON TABLE　　　　37

as Cyrano approaches. He goes to Korax, one
of the Klingon aides of Koloth.

CYRANO

. . . Friend Klingon . . . May I offer you a charmin'
little tribble . . .?

He offers the tribble. Korax stares at it.

38　CLOSE ANGLE—KORAX AND TRIBBLE　38

The tribble reacts to the Klingon.
It rears back with an angry spitting hiss. The
Klingon reacts just as violently to the tribble. They
hate and fear little fuzzy things.

39　ANGLE　　　　39

KORAX

Get it away from me!

> CYRANO
> *(to tribble)*

Stop that!

> *(to Korax)*

I can't understand—I apologize for his bad manners
. . . he's never done that before!

> KORAX

Take it away! Get out of here with that parasite.

> CYRANO

It's only a friendly little—

> KORAX
> *(loudly)*

Take it away!

40 ANGLE AT BAR   40

> Cyrano approaches Trader and puts the tribble on
> the counter. As the Waitress is taking down a
> pitcher, preparatory to using it:

> CYRANO

Sir . . .! Would you be willin' to engage in another
little transaction? One of my little tribbles in
exchange for a spot of . . .

As he says this, Trader looks at him, and turns the
pitcher upside down. Two or three tribbles tumble out
onto the counter in front of Cyrano. Cyrano looks at
them and his voice trails off. As the Trader moves
away, Cyrano shakes his head at the tribbles.

> CYRANO

Tsk, tsk, tsk.

We follow a Waitress now, as she moves across the room
to the Earthmen's table with a tray of drinks. She begins
setting them down. In front of Mr. Scott, she puts a
small bottle of Scotch and a glass.

In front of Chekov, she puts a small bottle of Vodka and a glass. The other crewmen get nondescript drinks.

41   TWO SHOT—SCOTT AND CHEKOV   41

Scott examines Chekov's drink, then looks up deadpan, but teasing.

SCOTT

When are you going off your milk diet, lad?

CHEKOV
(indignant)

This is vodka.

SCOTT

Where I come from, that's soda pop.
(indicates own glass)
Now this is a drink for a *man*.

CHEKOV

Scotch?

Scott nods.

CHEKOV
(continuing)

A little old lady from Leningrad invented it.

Mr. Scott raises an eyebrow at this. He watches as Chekov downs his drink in one quick gulp. He shudders and downs his Scotch.

42   ANGLE ON WHOLE BAR   42

The Klingons are laughing and joking amongst themselves. Korax suddenly rises and goes to Cyrano at the bar. Cyrano is contemplating an empty glass that the bartender has left on the bar. Korax steps up and pours something into it from his own bottle. Cyrano looks up. There are tribbles on the bar.

KORAX
(loudly)

The Earthers like those fuzzy things, don't they . . .?

He points at the tribbles on the bar, but they hiss and shrink away.

43　ANGLE　　　　　　　　　　　　　　　43

KORAX
(loud and obnoxious)

Frankly, I never liked Earthers . . . They remind me of Regulan Blood Worms . . .

44　ANGLE ON CHEKOV AND SCOTT　　　44

CHEKOV

That Cossack—

SCOTT

Easy, lad—you've got to learn to be forgiving . . .

45　ANGLE ON KORAX—CAMERA DOLLIES　45
　　WITH HIM

KORAX
(moving towards the Earthmen)

No—I just remembered—there is one Earthman who doesn't remind me of a Regulan Blood Worm— that's Kirk. A Regulan Blood Worm is soft and shapeless—but Kirk isn't soft . . .

Chekov is seething. Korax is being sarcastic.

KORAX
(continuing)

Kirk may be a swaggering, overbearing, tin-plated dictator with delusions of godhood, but he's not soft . . .

Chekov tries to stand, but Scott holds him down with a hand on his shoulder.

SCOTT
(gently)
Take it easy, lad. Everybody's entitled to an opinion . . .

KORAX
That's right . . . and if I think that Kirk is a Denebian Slime Devil . . . well, that's my opinion too . . .
(he smiles)

Chekov makes for the Klingon, only Scott has hold of Chekov's arm and jerks him quickly and awkwardly back down into his chair. As the Klingon laughs:

SCOTT
Don't do it, mister! That's an order!

CHEKOV
But you heard what he called the captain!

SCOTT
It's not worth it, lad! It's not worth fightin' for— We're big enough to take a few insults— Drink your drink.

He starts to pour Chekov another drink, but the vodka bottle is empty, so he pours the ensign a drink of Scotch instead. Chekov downs it without looking at it. His attention is still on Korax. After a bit, he does a take and looks at Scott with a peculiar expression on his face.

KORAX
(laughing)
Of course, I'd say that Captain Kirk deserves his ship . . .

Scott is listening now.

KORAX
(continuing)
We like the Enterprise—we really do . . .
(to Scott)
That sagging old rust bucket is designed like a
garbage scow! Half the quadrant knows it—that's
why they're learning to speak Klingonese!

He laughs as do his fellow Klingons.

CHEKOV
Mr. Scott!

SCOTT
(deceptively pleasant)
Laddy, don't you think you should re-phrase that?

KORAX[20]
You're right—I should . . . I didn't mean that the
Enterprise should be *hauling* garbage . . . I meant
that it should be *hauled away AS garbage* . . . !

Something snaps. Perhaps it is the swizzle stick in Scott's
hands. Without a word, Scott stands up and belts the
Klingon across the chops. The Klingon is hurled clear
across the room and onto the table of his friends. It
collapses onto the floor with him in the center of it.

46 SERIES OF SHOTS   46

as the Klingons rise and face the Earthmen. The
Earthmen face the Klingons. At the bar, Cyrano
looks up. The attendant starts to move to the wall
panel and:

ALL HELL BREAKS LOOSE! The Klingons and
the Earthmen attack each other with a ferocity
that is unparalleled in barroom brawls. Cyrano

---

[20]For the first few words of this line, Korax actually imitated
Mr. Scott's accent. A nice touch that.

watches calmly. Trader is at the wall panel yammering into it, but the noise of the fight keeps us from hearing what he has to say. Casually, Cyrano helps himself to a bottle and pours himself a drink.

As the fight continues, the violence and ferocity of it should be very great. Cyrano watches calmly as World War III rages about him. The punch line of this whole sequence is that he is able to walk out of the bar untouched.

Perhaps, as he walks out, we can see that he has also managed to appropriate a few bottles.

47   ANGLE ON WALL   47

As Cyrano strolls out of the bar, a squad of security men tear past him, running towards it. Cyrano watches them, toasts them with a bottle, and then strolls gaily off . . .[21]

                                        FADE OUT.

                    END OF ACT TWO

                      ACT THREE

FADE IN:

48   EXT. SPACE—ENTERPRISE   48

---

[21]As you can see, I wrote a minimum of description of the fight. I assumed—and correctly—that whatever I wrote, the director would have ideas of his own. Therefore, all I wanted to do was suggest the impact of the scene and leave him to choreograph it. And choreograph it he did. It was a marvelous fight, simply marvelous!

KIRK'S VOICE

Captain's log, Star date 4525.6. A small disturbance
between the Klingon crew and members of the
Enterprise crew . . .

49   INT. BAR   49

as the fight is being broken up by the squad of
security men. The bar is pretty well broken up too.
The combatants are being separated into their two
respective groups.

KIRK'S VOICE

. . . has broken out aboard Space Station K-7 . . .
I am forced to cancel shore leave for both ships.

50   OMITTED   50

51   INT. ENTERPRISE—BRIEFING ROOM   51

Or any place where Kirk can address the whole
line of transgressors. A few tribbles in evidence.

KIRK
(continuing the same sentence)
I want to know who started it . . .
(there is no response)
I'm waiting . . .
(he waits)
Freeman, who started it?

FREEMAN[22]
. . . Uh . . . I don't know, sir.

---

[22]Ensign Freeman is in this script for one reason only. Remember, I was a Theatre Arts major. I wrote this part intending
it as a walk-on for myself. Gene Coon had no objection at first,
but after a while he decided I was too skinny to be an *Enterprise* crewman, so a fellow named Paul Bradley (who worked for
STAR TREK regularly as an extra) got himself some speaking lines.
And some extra money. Lucky fellow.

KIRK

All right . . . Chekov . . .

Chekov stares resolutely ahead. He is not in the best
of condition . . . the effect of the fight and the vodka.

KIRK
(continuing)

. . . Chekov, I know you . . . you started it, didn't
you . . . ?

CHEKOV

No, sir. I didn't.

KIRK

Who did?

Chekov glances at Scott.

CHEKOV

Uh . . . I don't know, sir.

KIRK

You don't know.

Kirk, stepping back and surveying all of the men.
Scott is at the end of the line, next to Chekov.

KIRK
(continuing)

I want to know who threw the first punch? . . .
(he waits)
All right . . . you are all confined to quarters until
I find out who started it. That's all. Dismissed.
(the men start to file out)
Not you, Mr. Scott.

Scott pauses. Kirk steps closer to him as the last man
exits.

52   CLOSER ANGLE—KIRK AND SCOTT   52

KIRK

Mr. Scott, you were supposed to prevent trouble . . .

SCOTT

Aye, Captain . . .

KIRK

Who threw the first punch, Scotty?
                    (Scott hesitates)
Scotty . . .

SCOTT

Uh . . . I did, Captain.

KIRK
                    (momentarily startled)
You did? Mr. Scott . . . ?
                    (a beat)
What caused it, Scotty?

SCOTT
                    (stiffly)
They insulted us, sir.

KIRK

It must have been some insult, Mr. Scott.

SCOTT

Aye, it was . . .

KIRK

You threw the first punch . . .

SCOTT

Aye—Chekov wanted to, but I held him back.

KIRK

Why did Chekov want to fight . . . ?

SCOTT

Uh—the Klingons . . . is this off the record, Captain?

KIRK
                    (stiff)
No, this is not off the record.

SCOTT

Well, Captain, the Klingons called you a . . .
                (*pause to remember*)
. . . tin-plated, overbearing, swaggering dictator
with delusions of godhood.

Kirk reacts, intrigued in spite of himself.

KIRK

Was that all?

SCOTT

No, sir. They also compared you to a Denebian
Slime Devil . . .

KIRK

I see.

SCOTT

And then they said that you were a—

KIRK

I get the picture, Mr. Scott.

SCOTT

Yes, sir.

KIRK

And after they said all this, that's when you started
the fight . . . ?

SCOTT

No, sir.

Kirk reacts to this.

KIRK

No . . . ?

SCOTT

No, sir—I didn't. You told us to avoid trouble.

KIRK

Oh.

                    SCOTT
And I didn't see that it was worth fightin' about.
After all, we're big enough to take a few insults . . .
aren't we?

Slowly, Kirk nods . . .

                    KIRK
Mr. Scott, just what was it they said that made the
fight break out?

                    SCOTT
They called the Enterprise a garbage scow.
            (pause, then remembering to add)
. . . sir.

                    KIRK
I see. And that's when you hit the Klingon?

                    SCOTT
Yes, sir.

                (of course)

                    KIRK
            (comparing the two insults)
You hit the Klingon because he insulted the Enterprise . . . ? Not because he . . . ?

                    SCOTT
Well, Captain—this was a matter of pride!

Kirk reacts.

                    KIRK
                (pause)
That's all, Scotty . . .
                (Scott starts to go)
Oh—and Scotty . . .
                (Scott pauses)
You're restricted until further notice.

                    SCOTT
Yes, sir . . . Thank you, sir . . .

(pause)
It'll give me a chance to catch up on my technical journals.

Scott exits. Kirk stares after him regretfully. Scott is a good officer. Kirk does not like to have to discipline him. Kirk is also slightly amused at the whole incident.[23]

CUT TO:

52A INT. McCOY'S LAB—SPOCK AND McCOY[24] 52A

There are a number of tribbles in evidence on the counter, some of them feeding at a small dish. McCoy is examining one. Spock is regarding them with a jaundiced eye. McCoy glances sharply at him.

McCOY
What's the matter, Spock?

SPOCK
There is something disquieting about these creatures.

McCOY
Oh? Don't tell me you've got a feeling, Spock?

SPOCK
Of course not, Doctor. They remind me somewhat of the lilies of the field. They toil not, neither do they spin . . .[25] but they seem to eat a great deal. I see no practical use for them.

---

[23]This whole scene was one of the nicest in the show—it's my favorite because of the interplay between Kirk and Scotty. Later on, somebody in the front office remarked that it very possibly was one of the best scenes of the whole season. (Flattery will get you nowhere, but keep talking . . .)
[24]This scene was also written by Gene Coon. An excellent scene and it incorporates some necessary exposition which had previously been cut.
[25]On the other hand, I've always been a little startled at a bible-quoting Spock . . .

McCoy

Does everything have to have a practical use for you? They're . . . nice. They're furry and soft. They make a pleasant sound.

Spock

So would an ermine violin, Doctor, but I see no advantage in one.

McCoy

It is a human characteristic to be fond of lower animals . . . especially if they are attractive in some way.

Spock

I am aware of human characteristics, Doctor. I am frequently inundated by them. However, I have trained myself to put up with practically anything.

McCoy

Spock, I don't know much about tribbles, yet, but I've found out one thing about them. I like them better than I do you.[26]

Spock

They do, indeed, have at least one redeeming factor.

(pointed, at McCoy)

They do not talk too much. If you will excuse me, sir.

Spock leaves. McCoy glares after him.

DISSOLVE:

53   INT. BRIDGE—ON KIRK   53

stepping out of bridge elevator. He is gently kicking some tribbles out of the way. He goes to his

---

[26]And this was unnecessarily rude of McCoy. Tsk. (After viewing the episode, my sister asked me if the characters on STAR TREK were always that sarcastic.)

chair, still preoccupied with something. Almost without noticing it, he has to scoop three or four tribbles off of his chair before he can sit down.

He sits in the chair, absent-mindedly stroking a tribble that is perched on the chair arm. Suddenly he realizes, there are tribbles all over the bridge.

Kirk brushes the tribble away, and activates his intercom:

KIRK

Dr. McCoy, get up here, right away.

Kirk gets out of his chair and makes a circuit of the bridge . . . starting with Lieutenant Uhura and circling around counter-clockwise. He brushes tribbles off of consoles, out of chairs, down from shelves, etc.

KIRK
(continuing)
Lieutenant Uhura, how did all of these tribbles get into the bridge?

UHURA
I don't know, Captain. They seem to be all over the ship.

Kirk steps down into the center of the bridge and moves over to the central console. He brushes a tribble off of it. He crosses to the other side, as Bones ENTERS.

McCoy
You wanted to see me, Jim?

KIRK
Yes, I did.
(he holds up a tribble)

McCoy
Don't look at *me*. It's the tribbles who are breeding . . . If we don't get them off the ship we'll be hip deep in them!

KIRK

Explain yourself, Doctor.

MCCOY

The nearest thing I can figure out is that they're born pregnant. It seems to be a great timesaver . . .

KIRK
(sourly)

Really?

MCCOY

From all I can find out, they seem to be bi-sexual, reproducing at will.
(glancing around)
And they have a lot of will.

Spock comes over.

SPOCK

Captain, for once I am forced to agree with Doctor McCoy, though his way of putting it is most imprecise. They are consuming our supplies and returning nothing. I am running computations on their rate of reproduction, and although all of the figures are not yet in, I must confess I am somewhat alarmed by the direction they are taking.

UHURA

They do give us something, Mr. Spock. Their love.
(on Spock's raised eyebrows)
Cyrano Jones says that a tribble is the only love money can buy.

Spock gives her the stare. Kirk, amused, steps in.

KIRK

Lieutenant . . . too much of anything . . .
(eyeing Spock)
. . . even love . . . is not necessarily a good thing.
(pause)
Have a maintenance crew start clearing the whole

ship . . . Then contact Commander Lurry. Tell him I'm beaming over. Ask him to find Cyrano Jones.

Uhura nods and turns to her console . . . Kirk and Spock start for the elevator, but pause long enough to remove some of the tribbles that have crawled back up onto the consoles.

DISSOLVE TO:

54   SPACE STATION SHOT   54

Enterprise nearby.

55   INT. LURRY'S OFFICE   55

Lurry is standing. Cyrano Jones is sitting in a chair. Kirk is staring at him. Spock is standing thoughtfully.

CYRANO

Captain Kirk, I am mystified at your tone of voice. I have done nothing to warrant such severe treatment.

KIRK

Really?

SPOCK

Surely you realized what would happen if you transferred the tribbles from their predator-filled environment into an environment in which their natural multiplicative proclivities would have no restraining factors.

CYRANO

Yes, I . . .

(take)

Would you mind trying that on me again?

SPOCK

By removing them from their natural habitat, you

have, so to speak, removed the cork and let the genie escape.

CYRANO

If you mean do I know they breed fast, of course I do. That's how I maintain my stock. But breeding animals is not against regulations . . . only breeding dangerous ones. Tribbles are not dangerous.

KIRK

Just incredibly prolific.

CYRANO

Precisely. And at six credits a head . . . that is, a body . . . it mounts up. I'm a businessman, after all.

(beat)

Now, if you'll excuse me . . .

He rises—absent-mindedly he hands Kirk the tribble.

KIRK

You ought to sell a manual of instructions with these things.

CYRANO

If I did, Captain . . . what would happen to the search for knowledge? Pardon me. I must be tending to my ship.[27]

As he does so, Baris and Darvin enter.

KIRK
(under his breath)

Oh, fine.

DARVIN

Go ahead, sir. Tell him.

BARIS

Captain Kirk, I consider your security measures

---

[27]Joe Pevney, the director, added a beautiful bit here. Cyrano's parting line is a cheery "Au revoir."

a disgrace. In my opinion, you have taken this
entire . . . very . . . important . . . project . . . far
too lightly.

KIRK

I regard the project as extremely important, Mr.
Baris. It is you I regard lightly.

BARIS
(beat; dangerous)
I shall report fully to the proper authorities that
you have given free and complete access to this
station to a man who is quite probably a Klingon
agent.

Kirk stares hard at him.

KIRK

That is a very serious charge, Mr. Baris. To whom
do you refer?

BARIS

That man who just walked out of here. Cyrano
Jones!

KIRK
(amused)
A Klingon agent?

BARIS

You heard me.

KIRK

Oh. I heard you all right.

SPOCK
(to Baris)
He just couldn't believe his ears.

KIRK
(a pause, a take; then to Baris)
What evidence do you have against Cyrano Jones?

Baris draws himself up to his full height . . .

BARIS

My assistant here spent some time keeping Mr.
Jones under surveillance. His actions have been
. . . ah, most suspicious. I believe he was involved
in that little altercation between your men and the—

KIRK

Go on. What else do you have?

DARVIN

Captain, I checked his ship's log. He was within the
Klingon sphere of influence less than four months
ago.

BARIS

The man is an independent scout. It's quite possible
that he's also a Klingon spy.

Kirk glances at Spock.

SPOCK

We have checked on the background of Mr. Jones.
He is a licensed asteroid locater and prospector. He
has never broken the law . . . at least not severely
. . . and he has, for the past seven years, obtained
a marginal living by engaging in the buying and selling of rare merchandise . . . including, unfortunately, tribbles.

BARIS

He's after my grain! He's out to sabotage the entire
project.

KIRK

You have no proof of that.

DARVIN

You can't deny he has disrupted this station!

KIRK

People have disrupted Space Stations before without being Klingons . . .
                 (*meaningful look at the two*)

They need only have some influence. Unfortunately disrupting a space station is not an offense. If you'll excuse me . . . I have a ship to take care of . . . Mister Spock?[28]

Kirk starts to leave, realizes that he is still holding Cyrano's tribble. He shrugs, looks around and puts it in an ash tray or on a piece of sculpture—anywhere, just to get rid of it. They exit.

                                           DISSOLVE TO:

56   ENTERPRISE HANGING IN SPACE   56

                                           DISSOLVE TO:

57   INT. RECREATION ROOM   57

Kirk goes to a wall panel. Spock and Scott are also there.

                        KIRK
. . . Chicken sandwich, coffee.

Almost immediately, the wall panel BEEPS. Kirk goes over to the wall. A panel slides open. He stares.

58   CLOSE ANGLE ON PANEL   58

Kirk's sandwich is covered with tribbles, throbbing and purring.

59   ANGLE   59

                        KIRK
Mister Spock . . .

Spock approaches—he peers at it curiously.

---

[28]—and then Kirk exits just like Cyrano a few moments before. "I have a ship to tend to." And a cheery "Au revoir."

SPOCK

Most interesting . . .

Kirk reacts. Up till now, they have only been a nuisance —this scene should show that they are definitely out of hand.

KIRK

Mister Spock, I want these creatures off my ship. I don't care if it takes every man we've got. I want them off!

Scott approaches, takes a look.[29]

SCOTT

Aye, they've gotten into the machinery all right. They've probably gotten into all of the other food processors, too . . .

KIRK

How?

SCOTT

Probably through one of the air vents.
(*points to a duct*)

SPOCK
(*alarmed*)

Captain, there are vents like that in the space station . . .

KIRK

And the storage compartments . . .
(*stepping to a wall panel*)
This is Kirk. Contact Commander Lurry . . . and Nilz Baris. Have them meet us near the warehouse. We're beaming over.

---

[29]At this point, Scotty enters, his arms laden with tribbles. This obviates the need to show any food processing equipment at all— it's implied by Scotty's entrance.

Kirk and Spock exchange a glance. They run out of scene.

60		60
thru	OMITTED	thru
65		65

66 INT. TRANSPORTER ROOM   66

    Kirk and Spock enter, dash up the platform kicking tribbles out of the way.[30]

KIRK

Energize.

67 ANGLE ON Console   67

    as the crewman slides the lever upwards.

CUT TO:

68 SPACE STATION CORRIDOR—STORAGE
    COMPARTMENT   68

    CLOSE on Kirk's and Spock's feet as they . . . and a half dozen tribbles . . . materialize. CAMERA ANGLE WIDENS as Lurry and Baris, but not Darvin, come running to meet them.

LURRY

What's wrong?

KIRK
(glancing around)
Plenty—if what I think has happened, has happened.

Kirk turns to the storage compartment door. There are two guards standing by it. There are lots of tribbles in the corridor.

---

[30]For some reason, William Shatner picked up a tribble at this point and was carrying it with him for the rest of the act.

SPOCK
Guard, is this door secure?

GUARD
Yes, sir. Nothing could get in!

KIRK
I hope so. Open the door.

The Guard moves to the wall panel and touches a magnetic key to a panel. At first the door doesn't open . . .

KIRK
(continuing; impatient)
Open it!

The Guard fiddles with the key. Kirk watches, waits: finally he steps up and pushes the Guard aside and pushes the door.

GUARD
It's not working, sir. It seems to be—

What it seems to be, we will never know, because at that moment, the door slides open with a WHOOSH! ! ! This is immediately followed by a silent FWOMP! !

Hundreds and hundreds and hundreds (or at least as many as we can afford) of tribbles come tumbling out of the door, cascading down around Kirk, tumbling and seething and mewling and writhing and throbbing and trilling and purring and . . .

What we can see of Kirk, reacts.[31]

FADE OUT.

END OF ACT THREE

---

[31]D. C. Fontana later pointed out to me that it was bad script writing to just say, "Kirk reacts." I should indicate *how* he reacts. A very good point.

ACT FOUR

FADE IN:

69   INT. SPACE STATION—CORRIDOR   69
     OUTSIDE STORAGE COMPARTMENT—
     INCLUDING DOOR

Kirk is standing in the middle of a mountain of tribbles. More and more keep tumbling out, fat and sassy and lethargic.

70   ANGLE   70

SPOCK
(examining a tribble)
It seems to be gorged . . .

BARIS
Gorged! On my grain! Kirk! I'll hold you responsible! . . .
(despairingly at the grain)
There must be thousands.

KIRK
(peering into the storage compartment)
Hundreds of thousands . . .

SPOCK
One million, seven hundred and seventy-one thousand, five hundred and sixty-one.

Kirk looks at him ("Oh really?").

SPOCK
(continuing)
That's assuming one tribble multiplying with an average litter of ten, producing a new generation every twelve hours over a period of three days . . .

KIRK

That's assuming that one got in here three days ago . . .

SPOCK

Also allowing for the amount of grain consumed and the volume of the storage compartment . . .

BARIS

Kirk! You should have known!—You're responsible for turning the Development Project into a total disaster!

KIRK
(*slowly*)

Mr. Baris—

BARIS

Kirk, I'm through being intimidated! You've insulted me—ignored me—walked all over me! You've abused your authority and rejected my requests! And this . . . this . . .
(*indicating the tribbles*)
. . . is the result!! I'm going to hold you responsible.

Kirk, thoroughly angry, but thoroughly cool, reaches out, grabs Baris by the coat front.

KIRK

Baris, shut up. Or *I* will hold *you* in irons.

71 ANOTHER ANGLE   71

as McCoy approaches. Kirk releases Baris, who hauls himself together.

McCOY

Jim, I think I've got it. All we have to do is stop feeding them. Once they stop eating, they'll stop breeding.

Kirk looks at him.

> KIRK
> Now he tells me . . .

And McCoy looks at the tribbles on the corridor floor and realizes that his advice is a little late.

Spock is also looking at the tribbles on the floor—he is kneeling curiously.

> SPOCK
> Captain, this is most odd . . . this tribble is dead . . .
> *(he begins examining others)*
> . . . so are these . . .

McCoy and the others begin examining the tribbles more carefully. McCoy uses his Feinberger.[32]

> McCOY
> This one is alive—a lot of them are still alive . . . but they won't be for long . . .

72   ANGLE   72

> SPOCK
> A logical assumption is that there is something in the grain.

> KIRK
> Bones, I want a complete analysis of the tribbles, the grain, everything. I want to know what killed them.

> McCOY
> I still haven't figured out what keeps them alive.

---

[32]Named after Irving Feinberg, the propman. Irving used to slap people's hands for touching the props. During the filming of this episode, he actually took a tribble away from a little girl who was visiting the set. She only wanted to pet it . . .

Kirk just glares at him.

McCoy
(continuing)
I'll let you know as soon as I find anything.

McCoy, his arms laden with tribbles and etc., moves off.

BARIS
Kirk, that won't do you any good— The project is ruined . . . Starfleet will hear of this disaster . . . There'll be a board of inquiry, and they'll roast you alive, Kirk . . . I'm going to be there to enjoy every minute of it.

KIRK
All right. But until that board of inquiry convenes, I'm still a Captain.
We have two things to do . . . First, find Cyrano Jones.
(pause, glance at door)
Second, close that door.

CUT TO:

73 TRANSITION SHOT—SPACE STATION 73

CUT TO:

74 LURRY'S OFFICE 74

as the last few preparations are being made. Two crewmen escort Cyrano Jones into the room, then begin removing excess tribbles. Kirk and Spock and Lurry are discussing something. Baris is waiting at the door, looking for Darvin. Koloth enters, followed by Korax.

KIRK
What do you want?

KOLOTH

An official apology, Kirk, addressed to the High
Klingon Command. I want you to take responsibility
for your persecution of Klingon nationals in this
quadrant.

KIRK

An apology . . . ?

KOLOTH

You have harassed my men . . . treated us like
criminals. You have been most uncourteous,
Kirk . . . and if you wish to avoid a diplomatic
crisis . . .

BARIS

You can't let him, Kirk! That'll give them the wedge
they need to claim Sherman's Planet!

SPOCK

I believe more than the word of an aggrieved
Klingon commander will be necessary for that, Mr.
Baris.

Koloth glares at Spock.

KOLOTH

As far as Sherman's Planet is concerned . . .
Captain Kirk has just given it to us.

KIRK

We'll see about that, Captain. But before any
official action is taken, I want to find out just
what happened here. Who put the tribbles in the
quadro-triticale, and what was in the grain that
killed them?

Kirk starts to go on, but Koloth interrupts.

KOLOTH

Captain Kirk, before you go on, I have a request . . . ?

(a beat, as Kirk waits expectantly)
Can you get those thing out of here?

Koloth points uncomfortably at the tribbles that Cyrano
is holding in his lap and stroking. Kirk gestures to a
crewman. The man takes the tribbles and moves to the
door—just as Darvin enters.

75   CLOSER ANGLE—AT THE DOOR   75

    as the tribbles hiss and spit at Darvin. We must
    love them for the enemies they make.

76   ANOTHER ANGLE   76

    Cyrano looks surprised. Kirk and Spock react.
    Spock's eyebrows shooting up.

SPOCK
Remarkable.

KIRK
Jones . . . I thought tribbles liked everybody.

JONES
Why . . . they do, Captain. I can't understand it.
Last time I saw them act like that was in the bar.

KIRK
What was in the bar?

JONES
Klingons, sir. Him, for one.

He points at Korax. Kirk steps over, picks up a nice
big fat tribble. He moves to Korax, extends the tribble.
The tribble hisses and reacts.

KIRK
You're right, Jones . . .

He repeats the act with Koloth, who shrinks away . . .
they obviously hate the tribbles . . . and the tribble rears

back and hisses. Bones enters with a tricorder in time to hear:

> KIRK
> (*continuing*)
> They don't like Klingons.

He moves to Spock. The tribble purrs loudly.

> KIRK
> (*continuing*)
> They do like Vulcans. I never thought you had it in you, Spock.

> SPOCK
> Obviously the tribble is an extremely perceptive creature.

Kirk takes the tribble to Baris . . . the tribble purrs loudly.

> KIRK
> He even likes you, Baris. I guess there's no accounting for taste.

He moves back to Darvin, extends the tribble. Darvin shrinks, the tribble rears back and hisses violently.

> KIRK
> (*continuing*)
> But he doesn't like, you, Darvin. I wonder why. Bones . . .
> (*gestures to McCoy*)

Bones, curious, unbuckles his medical tri-corder. He runs a sensor over Darvin . . . looks at the reading, looks again . . . runs the sensor over Darvin again. He is puzzled. He repeats the performance.

> McCOY
> Jim . . .
> (*checking a reading*)

His heartbeat is all wrong . . . his body temperature is . . . Jim, this man is a Klingon!

BARIS

Klingon!?

Kirk looks at Baris. Two crewmen move up on either side of Darvin . . .

KIRK

What do you think Starfleet will have to say about this, Mr. Baris . . . ?
(to Bones)
What did you find out about the grain?

MCCOY

Oh. It was poisoned.

BARIS

Poisoned?!!

MCCOY

It's been impregnated with a virus . . . the virus turns into an inert material in the bloodstream. The more the organism eats, the more inert matter is built up. After two or three days, it would reach a point where they couldn't take in enough nourishment to survive.

KIRK

You mean they starved to death . . . ? A whole storage compartment full of grain and they starved to death?

MCCOY

That's essentially it.

Kirk looks at Darvin . . .

KIRK

You going to talk . . . ?

DARVIN

I have nothing to say.

Kirk picks up a couple of tribbles. He walks up to Darvin about to shove them in his face . . . The tribbles hiss.

DARVIN
(continuing)

All right. I poisoned the grain. Take it away![33]

KIRK

Then the tribbles didn't have anything to do with it . . . ?

DARVIN

I don't know—I never saw one before in my life!! I hope I never see one of those horrible fuzzy things again!

Kirk gestures. The two crewmen drag Darvin away. Kirk catches sight of Koloth, who has been standing rather quietly, for a Klingon.

KIRK

Captain Koloth—about that apology . . .

(pause)

You have six hours to get your ship out of Federation territory!

Koloth says nothing, leaves stiffly. The tribbles hiss at him.

KIRK
(continuing)

You know, I could almost learn to like tribbles.

77	77
& OMITTED	&
78	78

79   ANOTHER ANGLE   79

---

[33]Darvin still does not stand up very well to questioning . . .

CYRANO

. . . Ah, then Captain Kirk, I suppose that I may be free to go—

KIRK

Not yet. First I've got something to show you.

They exit, followed by Spock.

80   INT. STORE/BAR   80

Kirk, Spock and Jones enter. Trader is sitting in the door in the middle of a pile of tribbles. There are tribbles galore. It looks like a snowfall of fur. He has been inundated. He is close to tears, because there are too many even to try sweeping them out of his store. He sits there with his head in his hand.

81   ANGLE   81

CYRANO

Uh . . .

KIRK

Mr. Jones, do you know what the penalty is for transporting an animal that is proven harmful to human life . . . ?

CYRANO

But one little tribble isn't harmful . . . ?
        (Kirk stares at him)
Gentlemen, you wouldn't do a thing like that to me, now would you . . . ?

SPOCK

The penalty is twenty years in a rehabilitation colony.

CYRANO

. . . Ah now, Captain Kirk—*Friend* Kirk—surely we can come to some form of mutual understanding . . . After all, my little tribbles did put you wise to the poisoned grain—and they did help you to find the Klingon agent . . . we must have saved a lot of lives that way . . .

                    KIRK
Perhaps, there is one thing . . .

                    CYRANO
                    (eagerly)
Yes?!

                    KIRK
If you can remove every tribble from the space station, I'll have Commander Lurry return your ship to you . . .

                    CYRANO
                    (gasping)
Remove every tribble . . . ? That'll take years . . .

                    SPOCK
Seventeen point nine, to be exact.

                    CYRANO
Seventeen point nine years . . . ?

                    KIRK
Think of it as job security.

                    CYRANO
. . . Ahh, Captain, you are a hard man . . .
                    (looks at a tribble)
I'll do it.
                    (he sighs)

And Cyrano Jones begins picking up tribbles.

                              DISSOLVE TO:

82 ENTERPRISE FLYBY   82

83 INT. BRIDGE   83

     Kirk and Spock enter.

KIRK

I'm glad Starfleet was able to divert that freighter.
Sherman's Planet will get their quadro-triticale only
a few weeks late . . .

Kirk steps down and takes his place in his chair. He
glances around. The bridge is strangely free of tribbles.
Scott and McCoy are on the bridge, and Kirk is speaking to them when he says:

KIRK
(continuing)
I don't see any tribbles in here . . .

McCoy
You won't find a tribble on the whole ship.

KIRK
How did you do that, Bones?

McCoy
(suddenly modest)
I can't take the credit for another man's work.
Scotty did it.

KIRK
Where are they, Mr. Scott?

SCOTT
Oh, but Captain . . . it was Mr. Spock's recom-
mendation.

SPOCK
Based on computer analysis, of course, taking into
consideration the elements of . . .

KIRK
Gentlemen, if I may be so bold as to interrupt this
meeting of your mutual admiration society, I'd like
to know just what you did with the tribbles.

McCoy
Tell him, Spock.

SPOCK
It *was* Mr. Scott who did the actual engineering . . .

KIRK
(*firmly*)
Scott, how did you get rid of the tribbles?

SCOTT
I used the transporter, Captain.

KIRK
You used the transporter . . . ?

SCOTT
Aye.

KIRK
(*curious*)
Where did you transport them to, Scotty?

Scott coughs into his hand. McCoy looks off into the distance. Spock blinks and manages a patently blank, innocent stare.

KIRK
(*continuing*)
Scotty, you didn't just transport them out into space, did you?

SCOTT
(*slightly offended*)
Sir! That'd be inhuman!

KIRK
Mr. Scott . . . what did you do with them?

Well, he is going to have to tell it sooner or later:

SCOTT
I gave them a good home, sir.

KIRK
Where??

SCOTT

I gave them to the Klingons, sir . . .

KIRK
(reacting)

You gave them to the . . .

SCOTT

Aye, sir. Just before they went into warp I transported the whole kit and kaboodle into their engine room . . . where they'll be no tribble at all.[34]

All react as the joke sinks in . . .

84 FLY AWAY—ENTERPRISE   84

FADE OUT.

THE END

---

[34]I haven't the slightest idea who is responsible for this pun. I'm not. You can't pin this one on me.

CHAPTER NINE:

Tribble-Making

A lot of things happened between the writing of the script and the filming of the episode. After copies of the script had been sent around, and the planning of the episode was moving into higher gear, the first tribble jokes began to appear.

Irving Feinberg, the show's propman, was designated an "official tribble-maker," although actually, all he had to do was just keep tabs on them all.

The tribbles were really made by a fellow named Wah Chang—he did much of STAR TREK's special effects work, but he's also well known for his work in films like *Jack the Giant Killer, The Seven Faces of Dr. Lao,* and other fantasies requiring unusual effects or animation.

And Wah Chang himself didn't actually do the hard job of sewing the tribbles, he just designed them. The actual sewing was done by a lady named Jacqueline Cumeré—and if memory serves me correct, she was paid three hundred and fifty dollars to make five hundred of the beasties.

How do you make a tribble? Well, first you get a piece of synthetic fur. (Do *not* kill a real animal or use real animal fur! To do so violates the first commandment of the Universe: *Thou Shalt Not Waste!*)

Now, cut a double-oval out of cloth, something like this:

It's a figure-eight lying on its side. The two ovals should be joined along one side, and each one should be about as big in diameter as you want the whole tribble. Now, fold the ovals over, so the furry surface is on the inside and start sewing around the edges to make a bag—but don't sew all the way. Leave a couple inches of seam unsewn so you have an open-ended bag.

Turn the bag inside out so the fur is on the outside now, and stuff it with bits of foam rubber. When your tribble is thoroughly stuffed, sew up the hole, being careful to keep the edges of the cloth from showing at the seam.

If you've done it right, you'll have an "authentic" STAR TREK tribble, and if your stitches are small enough and if you've combed the fur properly, the seams won't even show.

You can make as many as you want for your own enjoyment and edification—but, unfortunately, you are *not* allowed to sell any. To do so would be an infringement on the copyright—yes, tribbles are copyrighted—and you would be liable to lawsuit.*

---

*On the other hand, if you're too lazy to make your own and want to *buy* an "Official David Gerrold Tribble,"—about as

Most of the tribbles used were made out of brown or white fur. Some of these were dappled with lighter or darker paint to give them additional color. There were a few tribbles, however, of a softer, fluffier fur; apparently, they had been an experiment. There weren't many of them, but they were used anyway. They made a nice contrast to the rest.

There were six "walking" tribbles made. Jim Rugg, STAR TREK's regular special effects man, made them out of little Japanese toy dogs. He cut off the heads of the dogs and attached a tribble skin to the neck; it covered the whole body, but was open at the bottom so the legs could have traction on the ground. When the batteries were put in and the thing was switched on, the tribble walked across tables, counters, chairs, floors, and railings on the *Enterprise*'s bridge.

Needless to say, they were quite noisy. The scenes using the moving tribbles had to have the dialogue "looped" in later.

There were also a few "beanbag" tribbles, filled with plastic beads or something. These were used when a tribble had to be shown perched on the edge of a desk or in a person's hand. They *sagged* like a real creature would.

And there were "breathing" tribbles. These were hollow, except for a small surgical balloon. A plastic tube led to a rubber squeeze bulb which controlled the tribble's inhaling and exhaling.

What was the reaction of the cast and crew to the script?

In general, they liked it. They thought it would be one of the better episodes—and usually, despite all the ballyhoo and backslapping that goes on around a movie set, a crew knows whether the script is a dog or not. You can tell by the mood of the cast and crew if the script is any good, and "Tribbles" was fun for them to work on.

Nichelle Nichols particularly liked the script. I finally met her during the filming of "Mirror, Mirror." While she ate her lunch one afternoon, we sat and chatted.

For some time, she had been complaining that Lieutenant Uhura wasn't being used properly—all she was doing was "opening the hailing frequencies, ho hum." She was delighted that this script finally got her off the bridge and enabled her

---

identical to the ones used on the show as can be made—write to: "Tribbles," Box 526, Hollywood, Calif. 90028, and ask for a catalogue and price list. (Tell them I said it's okay.)

to do something important to the plot, something which let her be a *woman*.

And as she said this, she dropped some cottage cheese into the cleavage of her skimpy costume.

Which didn't embarrass her a bit— *I* was the one who blushed.

A few weeks before that, *Newsweek* had published a major article about "The Negro in Television," pointing out the increased use of Blacks in major speaking roles. At that time, a Black who didn't shuffle was still a novelty on the boob tube—STAR TREK was one of the pleasant exceptions.

And at one point, I'd found myself thinking, "Now, let's see—can I write in a part for a Negro . . ." And immediately after, the other half of my brain had answered, "Dummy, you've already got a Negro in the script—Lieutenant Uhura." To which the first half of me replied, "No, Lieutenant Uhura isn't a Negro—she's just a human being."

At which point, I made the transition into realizing that sitting down and writing a part *specifically* for a Black would have been a major mistake. Thinking of a character as any kind of a classification reduces him from a human being to an object. A character cannot be: *a* Jew, *a* Negro, *a* homosexual, *a* Communist. Those are stereotypes, they're made out of cardboard for lazy writers and hacks to push around. A *real* character—the kind that lives and breathes and sweats and bleeds when you cut him—*is* Jewish, *is* Negro, *is* homosexual, *is* communist.

These words are *adjectives,* not *nouns.* An adjective describes a person, but a noun reduces him to an object. A noun purports to explain him; if you want to hate someone, you call him a name. A name says it all: "You Cossack!"

Nichelle probably didn't realize it—but that conversation taught me a lot about writing real characters.

One day, I showed up at the set and William Shatner said, "Hi, kid. What're you writing now?"

Kid—? (All right, so I still looked like an eighteen-year-old; did he have to rub it in?) I said, "I'm doing a story where you lose your voice in the teaser and don't get it back till the tag."

His reply wasn't unprintable—just deadly. I won't repeat it here. Suffice it to say, plowboys should never pull on number-one guns.

Later on, it was his turn to have fun at my expense. He decided he didn't like a line of the scene he was doing ("Mirror, Mirror,") and started calling, "I need a writer! Where's David Gerrold?!! Where's David Gerrold?!!"

Fortunately, I'd already left for the day.

But I got the last laugh on him. A couple of weeks later, when "The Trouble With Tribbles" went before the cameras, one of the most difficult scenes was the shot where Captain Kirk opens the storage compartment and is inundated with tribbles.

They had to shoot it eight times. They just couldn't get it right. The first time the tribbles didn't fall properly; the second time, someone missed a cue; the third time, they jammed in the hatchway again; the fourth time—

If William Shatner looks just a little harried in that shot, it isn't accidental. Having five hundred tribbles dropped on you eight times in a row, is *not* a happy experience.

I was beginning to feel like a real writer. I had joined the Writers' Guild, and I was attending private film screenings—and I got my second assignment.

STAR TREK was having some trouble with a script called "I, Mudd." It was about a fellow named Harry Mudd who'd taken over a planet of androids.

Gene Coon handed me a copy of it one afternoon, sat me down in his office and told me to read it while he went to see the dailies. When he got back, we would talk about it. He wanted to know what I thought of it.

It was a yellow-covered draft. I finished it before Gene got back, so I wandered out of his office to talk to Ande, his secretary. There was a tall fellow there, going through some papers. He was a big man, a genial-looking person with gray-brown hair. He had the kind of smile that wins elections and charms old ladies and reassures children who are being taken to the doctor for a shot. He was *impressive*. If you were casting the part of God and couldn't get Charlton Heston, this was the fellow.

No—better than that—he looked like a TV Producer. What a TV Producer *should* look like.

Ande said, "David, this is Gene Roddenberry."

"Oh—!" I said. And then, *"Oh!"*

We shook hands. (Mine shook without any help.) He said, "Hey, you wrote a good script there. Very nice." He handed the papers back to Ande and disappeared back into his own office. Obviously, he was very busy.

I stood there feeling like I'd had an audience with the Pope and forgotten to kiss the ring.*

Later that afternoon, I was called into see Bob Justman, Gene Coon and Gene Roddenberry— (And thinking, "Oh, God—what have I done now?") But all they wanted to do was talk about "I, Mudd." They wanted the script rewritten.

Huh—? Suddenly, I had been hired to *rewrite* someone else's script!

I guess that's a compliment when they figure you know enough to second-guess another writer.

—Actually, because they had only paid me Guild minimum for "The Trouble With Tribbles" they had an extra $1500 or so in the writing budget. If an established pro had done that episode, it would have cost them $4500 or so—they had gotten a real bargain. So they really weren't risking anything. They needed a rewrite and they wanted to know if I was fast enough and good enough to work for the show regularly. This way, I got the extra money, they got a rewrite and everybody came out ahead.

Seemed like a good idea to me.

Gene Coon and I went over the script in detail that afternoon and he wanted to know what I thought of it. I said, "If it's about Harry Mudd, we should meet him at the end of Act I, not Act II; we should meet him as soon as possible."

"What else is wrong?"

"Well, you have a robot imitating Kirk's voice and ordering the whole crew to beam down—" I was thinking on my feet again. "—Scotty didn't believe it in last season's 'Balance of Terror.' He won't believe it this season."

"Okay—so what do we do instead?" Gene was not only

---

*Dorothy Fontana says that it is only recently that they have gotten Gene to stop walking around on the ocean.

testing me, this was a serious script problem that had to be resolved.

"Isn't it obvious? If the androids can take over the ship, they can just as easily overpower the crew and beam them down by force. Why not?"

Gene accepted it—that's how a script is rewritten. You sit and pick at it and look for better ways to get there. In television, the writers who are most in demand are the ones who can think the fastest.

Okay, he handed me the script and told me to go to work. This was a Wednesday.

Monday morning, I was back in Gene's office.

"What are you doing here? You're supposed to be home working."

"I'm finished. Here it is." I had done it in four days.

I'd had an idea Friday afternoon and hadn't been able to talk to Gene about it, so I just wrote it in anyway—if they didn't like it, I could always take it out.

They had been planning to hire a set of twins to play two identical robots. I'd started thinking that with some clever editing and a couple of special effects matte shots, those twins could be made to look like six or eight robots. Or more. If each time they appeared, they wore a different number, they could be used to suggest five hundred identical androids.

So, I wrote it that way.

Gene raised his eyebrow at the idea and said, "I think you underestimate the problems involved . . . but the rest of the rewrite is good."

I wanted to do more work on the script, I had only brought it in to talk to Gene about it—but once again, he took it out of my hands, and my part of it was through. Thirteen hundred and fifty dollars for four days' work, eh? Well, I'm not proud—I took it.

By the time the script was filmed though—by the time that everybody else was finished working it over—not one line of mine remained. No, I take that back. One line of mine did remain in the shooting draft. Only one—everything else had been changed.

The only thing of mine that they did keep was the five hundred identical androids all in the shape of beautiful girls.

Yep, not only was I beginning to feel like a real writer—I was even being treated like one.

Sigh.

It wasn't that Ande liked to startle me—it's just that I startle so well.

One morning I walked into her office and she handed me a copy of my script—it was on blue pages by now, first set of corrections—"Here, autograph this."

"Huh? What for?"

"So we can send it to Heinlein."

"Urk—" I said. "Heinlein as in Robert A. Heinlein? Heinlein as in *Stranger in a Strange Land*? Heinlein as in Hugo Award? That Heinlein?"

"Uh huh," she said nonchalantly. "That's the one."

"Oh," I managed to say. With trembling hand and uneven pen, I fumbled something onto the paper like, "For Robert A. Heinlein, I hope you enjoy this as much as I have enjoyed all of your work."

But why did Heinlein want a copy of my script—?

Well, a couple of decades ago, this same Heinlein, the Dean of Science Fiction, wrote a book called *The Rolling Stones*. It was about the Stone Family, a high-spirited clan which bought its own spaceship and went roaming around the solar system. While on Mars, they picked up an animal called a Martian Flat Cat. It was flat and furry, colored a golden-brown, buzzed when it was happy, had two bright beady eyes, and reproduced like crazy, eight pups to a litter, a litter every sixty-four days. Pretty soon the flat cats overran the spaceship . . .

The similarity between tribbles and flat cats was unmistakable.

Coincidence? Or what?

Dare I breathe the word—*plagiarism?*—the worst possible sin a writer can commit, the theft of another man's work!

Believe me—I spent some uncomfortable moments with my head that morning. Because I'd read *The Rolling Stones* fifteen years before—and forgotten it completely. Or had I?

If I were a plagiarist, I'd picked the wrong work to steal from—too many other people would recognize it.

Where did my tribbles come from—? Where did the idea begin? Had I been original, or had I been inadvertently imitating something that had been implanted in my memory so deeply I was not aware that it was there?

Look—I thought I was telling the "rabbits in Australia" story. When rabbits were first introduced to Australia, they multiplied at an incredible rate because there were no predators or natural enemies to keep them in control. It was an ecology story—and a spaceship is the perfect setting for it because a spaceship *must be* a balanced ecology.

When it came to designing the creatures though, I had to be simple—they had to be easy to build; they had to be cheap, and they had to be believable. We wouldn't want to use rabbits for the story—we wanted something . . . well, *gimmicky*. We needed a science fiction animal.

If we used living Earth creatures, we would have three big problems—any one of which would be enough to keep the show from being filmed—first, what do you use and how do you make them look alien? Green mice? Gerbils? Hamsters? Where do you get five hundred of them on short notice? Who's going to do the makeup on them? Second problem: Who takes care of them for six days of filming? How do you keep them in control so they don't run loose all over the studio? How do you keep them from being the pests that you are portraying them as? Third: how do you keep the humane society off your neck the eighth time you have to drop all five hundred of them on William Shatner? And how do you convince William Shatner to stand still for it? And how do you show them dead without actually killing them? Drug them? Five hundred of them? Sure . . .

It was obvious that tribbles couldn't be played by living creatures, and I had never considered it seriously in my initial premise. I knew we were going to have to build something, and the building of it should be simple, cheap and fast. So, I had to think—what would be easy?

Holly (you remember her, don't you? I gave her a planet) Sherman had a key ring attached to a ball of pink fuzz. The more I looked at it, the more obvious it became. Pink and green and blue were colors too garish to use—and perhaps a little too effete—but the ease with which a fluff ball could be manufactured made it a natural candidate. A fluff ball is a perfect pet: it exists only for your affection. You take care of it—and it purrs at you; what more do you want from a pet? A pet is a substitute infant—but multiply it by one million and it's a parasite. Sure, fluff balls would be fun— and you could drop them on Shatner without hurting either them or him.

So, fluff balls it was.

From fluff balls to fuzzies to tribbles . . . as the script was written, the creatures remained basically the same, but the plot around them evolved, developed and tightened into its final form.

I admit—yes, the *gimmick* of my story was the same as the gimmick of Heinlein's, but the plot—and the plot is the *important part* of the story—was totally different. There were unavoidable echoes of Heinlein in one or two scenes—echoes that were not there in the initial premise, but that developed as the story was bludgeoned into shape. For instance: the scene where Cyrano barters with the Trader over the first tribble.

Many of STAR TREK's fans are also Heinlein fans. And one of the most frequent questions that crops up among them is: "Were you influenced by Heinlein's Flat Cats when you wrote the Tribbles? Is that where you got the idea?"

In all honesty, I must admit that if I was, it was a sub-conscious influence. Had I realized what I was doing, I either would not have done the story or would have worked to minimize the similarities.

The first ones to catch the resemblance were Kellam-DeForest Research. They noted almost offhandedly in their regular research report on the script that several chapters in Heinlein's book revolved around the same premise. They suggested that Heinlein could conceivably make a good case that the future value of his book as a film property would be damaged by STAR TREK's use of the gag, and it might be a good idea to purchase the rights from him. (Kellam-DeForest also noticed the similarity between our barroom brawl and the pie fight in *The Great Race*. Just as Tony Curtis walked through that one untouched, so did Cyrano Jones walk through ours.)

The problem was solved with a phone call. Either Gene Coon or Gene Roddenberry, I'm not sure which, called

Robert A. Heinlein and told him about the script. "We have a young kid here who's just done his first script. It's a very good one and we want to use it, but it's a lot like part of *The Rolling Stones* and we want to clear up any hassles *before* they start . . ."

Heinlein was very gracious about the whole thing. (I suppose he could have asked for money or credit. He didn't.) He simply said that he didn't see that there was any kind of a problem at all. But he would appreciate a copy of the script.

And that was why Ande startled me that morning.

Later, after the episode was aired, he sent a note to me, thanking me for the script and commenting that he thought it would probably film well—he didn't have TV reception in his area. He also said, and this I quote: "Let me add that I felt that the analogy to my flat cats was mild enough to be of no importance—and we both owe something to Ellis Parker Butler . . . and possibly to Noah."*

Other people, mostly hardcore fans, have commented more strongly on the resemblance—they have read more meanings into it than are really there. One fan even demanded to know why Heinlein didn't receive screen credit.

Look, ideas are common. What counts is what different writers do with them. "The Trouble With Tribbles" is NOT *The Rolling Stones.*

If the legal department of Desilu (now Paramount) Studios, a department that specializes in avoiding plagiarism suits, says that it's okay to film the episode, they'd better know what they're talking about. Every script is checked before it goes on the air. When a studio is investing that much money into a piece of film, they can't afford to leave anything to chance. Had there been even the slightest question of similarity or infringement, Heinlein would have been paid for his rights or the story would not have been filmed.

----

*Ellis Parker Butler wrote a story called "Pigs Is Pigs," about a postal inspector who refused to turn over a pair of guinea pigs to a fellow until the livestock tax was paid. The fellow claimed that guinea pigs were rodents and therefore exempt. The postal worker said, "Pigs is pigs." The man refused to pay. The Post Office had to take care of the guinea pigs. The guinea pigs began to breed. And breed. And breed . . . "Pigs is pigs."

As far as the studio was concerned, what I had written was *significantly* different from Heinlein's book.

—But as far as I'm concerned, the coincidence was just a little too close for me. I am very proud of my script, "The Trouble With Tribbles," but I would like it to be totally my own—and recognizably so. Coincidence or influence, there is no great honor in repeating another writer's ideas, no matter how well you do them.

The moral here is simple: if you know you're imitating another man's work, *don't*. And if you don't know, but the idea came too easily, then check to make sure. Double-check the books of your favorite authors, or check with an authority in the field. In the long run, it's the best thing to do.

After "The Apple," they filmed "Mirror, Mirror," and then "The Deadly Years," and "I, Mudd."

And then it was my turn. The second week in August 1967, they began shooting "The Trouble With Tribbles."

At last, the magic was real.

All the people I had imagined, made up from my own head, were suddenly alive and standing before me—doing what I had imagined them doing: Cyrano Jones, Nilz Baris, Arne Darvin, Trader, Mister Lurry, Captain Koloth, Korax.

Cyrano Jones was played—and sometimes overplayed—by Stanley Adams, a writer as well as an actor. Nilz Baris was William Schallert. He's played the mayor in *In the Heat of the Night*, but was probably more recognizable as Patty Duke's father. Arne Darvin was Charlie Brill—he did a short stint on *Laugh-In* the following year.

Mr. Lurry was Whit Bissell, a soft-spoken, white-haired gentleman who has been in countless movies and TV shows; he's the kind of character actor you always recognize, even if you don't remember his name. Captain Koloth was William Campbell—he'd been on STAR TREK before as Trelane in "The Squire of Gothos."

In that episode, he'd played a spoiled brat who took over the *Enterprise*. He teased Captain Kirk, Spock, Uhura, Sulu, McCoy and the rest of the crew until his parents showed up and told him he'd have to play nice or not at all.

That episode made considerable impact on the fans. It also allowed Campbell to show his versatility as an actor. So when the part of Captain Koloth came along—i.e. a dastardly gentleman—he was a logical choice.

An interesting sidelight to this is that Gene Roddenberry had been thinking that Kirk should have a Klingon counterpart. Just as the *Enterprise* is assigned to a specific quadrant of the galaxy, so would a specific Klingon ship be assigned by the Klingon High Command to the same quadrant. Thus the two Captains would continually find themselves confronting each other. Roddenberry had thought William Campbell as Captain Koloth might be perfect for this role. Campbell would then have become a semi-regular, appearing in every story where Kirk confronted Klingons.

Unfortunately, Campbell was not available the next time a Klingon episode was to be filmed, so another actor was hired. Later on, the idea of a continuing set of nasties was dropped or forgotten.

Koloth's aide, Korax, was played by Michael Pataki—a most vicious fellow indeed. Quite mean. He looked like a member of the Interstellar Hell's Angels. Admiral Komack was played by Ed Reimers, most famous for his All State Insurance commercials; and one of STAR TREK's regular extras, Paul Bradley, spoke Ensign Freeman's one line. The Trader was a fellow named Guy Raymond—he'd been doing some beer commercials as a bemused bartender while crazy things happened in his bar. So he was *perfect* for the Trader.

The interiors of the Trading Post were built on Soundstage 10. Almost all of STAR TREK's non-permanent interiors were constructed there. For this show, there were only three. Or three and a half:

There was Lurry's office—quite a big set, actually; it comprised a small transporter booth, an open area in front of a door, and the office proper with a large window in back, through which the *Enterprise* could be seen hanging in space.

The second set was the entrance to the storage compartments. This was a small, almost utilitarian corridor with angled walls. A couple of hatchways were set into them.

The third set was the trading post. (The half-set was the corridor outside of it.) This was also a very large set. There was a bar proper, behind which was a shelf of odd merchandise and an electronic drink mixer. Then there was a large open area of tables and booths.

The tables had been built by John Dwyer, the show's set

decorator, but the chairs had been scrounged from all over the city. It is very difficult to find twenty-four matching chairs—especially chairs that can be used on STAR TREK. Folding chairs from Abby Rents just wouldn't have made it.

Finally Dwyer found a company that had the chairs he wanted—but they didn't stock them in such large quantities. The chairs had to be pulled out of showrooms all over Los Angeles County.

When Joe Pevney, the director for "Tribbles," began planning the big fight scene, he came to Dwyer and asked, "What can I break?" Dwyer replied, "The tables. Not the chairs. The chairs we have to pay for."

The fight scene in "The Trouble With Tribbles" was one of the most fun to film. One whole end of Soundstage 10 was filled by (my nickname) The Bottom Half of Infinity, Bar, Grill and Trading Post—The Interstellar Stuckey's. It was filled with Earthmen, Klingons and assorted other Starfleet personnel. They were sitting and chatting amiably, drinking and boozing—

—abruptly a fight breaks out. The whole set erupts into an explosion of hurtling bodies and crashing furniture! The violence seems horrendous! Flailing fists and flying Earthmen! Clattering Klingons, noise and destruction!

—And a guy with a hand-held Arriflex scuttling sideways across the floor, tracking with Cyrano Jones, oblivious to anything behind him—

"Oh, hell, cut!" said the director. He eyed the mobile cameraman warily. "You got in the way of the big camera."

Sure enough, the fellow looked up, and there was the dolly-mounted Cyclops peering over his shoulder. "Sorry about that."

"All right," said Pevney. "Dress the set and let's do it again."

—And they did.

The scene had been so carefully choreographed that the second take was identical to the first. (Except that this time there was no errant cameraman wandering in front of the second camera.) The same tables went crashing, the same chairs went flying (gently), the same stunt men went tumbling. This fight had been so thoroughly planned that they could have taken it on the road.

Only a few feet away, a group of tourists stood and quietly watched.

Ho hum. Hollywood's best stuntmen demolish interstellar pubs routinely.

I was perched on a ladder, watching all this from a vantage point like a gawky vulture—and proud as a new parent. While the crew was setting up for closeups of specific sections of the fight, Walter Koenig came over to talk to a couple of the girls. Pointing at me, he said, "And this is the writer of the episode."

I puffed up my feathers, prepared to preen, readied myself for a little ego-boo. After all, this was *my* script. This would be honestly deserved. I checked to see if I had my pen for signing autographs.

"Oh," said the fans. And then, "Do you think Leonard Nimoy will be here today?"

So much for ego-boo.

CHAPTER TEN:

Author! Author!

"The Trouble With Tribbles" was telecast on December 29, 1967. I bought my first color TV so I could see the show in color, and I invited the immediate city to a party that evening so my friends could see the show too.

It was also a graduation party. I'd needed three units of *anything* to count as a senior project at Valley State College (now Cal State at Northridge) so I could get my degree. I turned in a copy of the shooting script and all the notes and outlines that led up to it. They didn't really have an instructor in the Theatre Arts department qualified to judge it, there weren't any writing classes, so they just gave it an A.

That, and the party, was the only response I got on "The Trouble With Tribbles" for a long time.

No, that's not entirely correct—about a week or so after the episode was telecast, there was a "Save STAR TREK" rally at NBC in Burbank. (Several of the cast and crew attended, but the word was out to be "incognito." We didn't want it to look like the rally was anything but spontaneous.)

Toward the end of the evening though, Mr. Scott's cover was blown and the fans flocked eagerly around James Doohan. For some reason, a kid about fourteen asked me if I worked for STAR TREK. I admitted (modestly) that I had written "The Trouble With Tribbles."

"Oh," he said. "I didn't like it. It wasn't like what they usually do. It wasn't exciting enough."

I wanted to punch him. Instead, I said, "Well, you're entitled to your opinion."

The rally broke up then anyway. The police were just discovering that someone had put "Mr. Spock for President" bumper stickers all over their cars and motorcycles.

Aside from that one comment, I might have dropped a stone down a well. For six months I stood there waiting for the splash.

I simply had no idea of what reaction my episode had gotten—just an occasional comment from a friend or relative who knew I had written it. Oh, and an article in a newspaper —some local paper in the east had a question and answer column, and one little girl had written in wanting to know what STAR TREK had used for the tribbles. The reporter who wrote the column had answered, "A lot of imagination."

Later on, I found out that the fan mail response had been tremendous—but none of that fan mail had been directed toward the writer. Most of it had been from eager young fans asking for tribbles. "You have so many, I saw all the millions on TV, surely you can spare just one . . ."

Some people even thought the tribbles were alive and one man was sure that they had been mistreated by being locked up in a cramped, hot storage compartment. A girl named Joanne Tribble wrote in saying that she was definitely *not* round and fuzzy. She included her measurements to prove it.

It wasn't until June that I found out just what kind of effect my script had had on STAR TREK fans . . .

There's a group in Los Angeles called the Los Angeles Science Fantasy Society. It is a science fiction and fantasy fan club. It is the oldest science fiction and fantasy fan club in the United States, probably the known universe. It is one aspect of a phenomenon called "fandom."

Fandom—which I must explain before I can go any farther —is a unique conglomeration of writers, artists, readers, editors, publishers, critics, designers, adolescents, cartoonists, pretty girls, misfits, geniuses, and just plain appreciators who like things out of the ordinary and each other. Ostensibly the phenomenon rotates around science fiction. Actually, it focuses on *anything* out of the ordinary: *2001: A Space Odyssey*, Tolkien's *Lord of the Rings*, *Tarzan*, Apollo 11, Sherlock Holmes, Georgette Heyer books, Chuck Jones cartoons, Ray Harryhausen movies, *Dark Shadows* TV series, *Fantastic Four* comic books, and a lot of other things too.

Not everybody likes everything that fandom has to offer, but there's something for everybody. Fans get together to exchange information, to gossip, to trade fanzines, to write fanzines, to do critical analyses, to attend conventions, to attend club meetings, to drink beer, to play poker—and sometimes even to talk about science fiction and fantasy.

Out of curiosity, I attended a meeting of the LASFS.* I was asked to introduce myself. I said, "My name is David Gerrold, and I wrote a script for STAR TREK," and sat down.

"Which one?" someone called.

"Uh—" (*Really,* for a moment there, I *was* trying to be modest.) "—it'll be rerun next week. You can see it then."

"What's the title?"

"Uh—" (It didn't work.) "—'The Trouble With Tribbles.' "

Applause. Yes, they applauded.

I was startled. But not as startled as I would be in a moment. Bruce Pelz, then Director of the club, eyed me from the

---

*If you are curious too, write to: LASFS, Box 3004, Santa Monica, Calif. 90403. Last I heard, meetings were on Thursdays at 8:00.

podium. "You know, don't you, that you've been nominated for a Hugo?"

And I said, *"Huh?"*

Now, maybe you don't know what a Hugo is—I did, and I was *startled*. I wouldn't have been more startled if Bruce Pelz had told me I had been awarded the Nobel Peace Prize. (Well, *maybe* the Nobel Peace Prize . . .)

The Hugo award is named after Hugo Gernsback, the father of modern science fiction. It is the field's equivalent to an Oscar. It is the highest honor that a science fiction writer can receive from the fans of science fiction. It is an international award and represents the opinions of fans from England, Japan, Australia, Ireland, Germany, France, Spain, Argentina, and anywhere else they read science fiction. To win a Hugo is to be told that you have written the *best* piece of science fiction in that category for that year. It is not an honor to be taken lightly.

Even for me to be nominated was a shock—and a piece of praise that I had not expected to be eligible to win for a long time—if ever. I had known about the existence of the Hugo. I had not yet considered it in terms of something that I might be able to achieve.

Yet, here I was *nominated* for one.

Think of it this way—what is your fondest dream?

What would you like to achieve more than anything else? If it's recognition that you are the very very best at something —anything—you begin to understand how I was starting to feel.

It was the first time that a writer's *first* sale had ever been nominated. And that nomination alone was enough to distort my sense of reality for a good long time to come. It is very difficult to maintain any kind of objectivity when abruptly you are being told that your words are as good as Theodore Sturgeon's Harlan Ellison's, Norman Spinrad's, and Jerome Bixby's—those were the four other writers on the ballot for the Best Dramatic Presentation.

Four other names in science fiction that I recognized—and admired; even to be classed with them was an honor. I'd been reading the stories and novels of these men for years—these were the most special of the special dreamers. And my inclusion on the ballot said to me that I had made it too.

The Hugos were awarded in August of 1968 at the 26th annual World Science Fiction Convention.

I lost. And a good thing too. Else I would have been unbearable for years. (Losing didn't teach me humility—but it did teach me I didn't have any. I lost badly.)

The winner was—ready?—Harlan Ellison, for his episode, "City on the Edge of Forever." Or maybe it was Gene Roddenberry who won—because the Hugo was awarded on the basis of what was seen on the air, and it was Gene Roddenberry's version that was filmed.

"The Trouble With Tribbles" came in a close second though. Six votes. I found it very easy to empathize with Hubert Humphrey two months later. Ah, well . . .

At that same convention, by the way, they had an auction. They auctioned off an hour of my time for twenty-two dollars. They auctioned off one of my tribbles for twenty-two dollars and fifty cents.

One thing about fans—they let you know how much you are worth.

CHAPTER ELEVEN:

The *Very Best* Tribble Story Ever Told . . .

Sometimes I wonder about that *other* STAR TREK episode.
You know, the one they didn't film because they made "The
Trouble With Tribbles" instead.

I wonder what they would have shown if they hadn't bought
my story.

It's worth thinking about . . .

—but not too much. Because "The Trouble With Tribbles"
did something that no other episode of a TV series has ever
done—it saved a life.

A lady named Bjo Trimble told me this story (It's pronounced Bee-jo, and yes, she did take a lot of kidding about

"the trouble with Trimbles . . .") about a friend of hers who was called "Nurse Enterprise" at the hospital where she worked. Of all the tribble stories, this is the best.

Bjo had organized STAR TREK's fan liaison, and was even responsible for handling the fan mail for a while; she set up STAR TREK Enterprises and even masterminded the "Save STAR TREK" campaign which inundated NBC with letters.* She was the second-most-intense STAR TREK fan I have ever met.

The first-most was a lady named Tim Courtney, a statuesque woman of magnificent proportions and deep internal beauty. For many years, Tim had been a fashion model in San Francisco—and a very good one too. After a while, though, she became dissatisfied with her life as a model and trained to be a nurse. Not just an ordinary nurse—but a special duties nurse, which means working with terminal and severely handicapped patients.

Bjo met Tim Courtney at—of course, it had to be—a "Save STAR TREK" rally in the Bay area. Bjo had planned it only as a small rally, but like all STAR TREK activities, it got out of hand—more and more people found out about it and wanted to attend; until finally, Bjo received a phone call from Tim, who asked if she and one of her small patients might attend.

Bjo describes Tim this way: "She had more vitality and energy and enthusiasm for life than any three or four other people could contain in one body. We immediately liked her.

"Our friendship with Tim continued even after we moved down to Los Angeles. I was getting little odds and ends of things from Gene Roddenberry—film clips and such that I could sell to help defray the costs of organizing the letter

---

*Bjo Trimble is also the lady responsible for *"The Star Trek Concordance."* A concordance is an index, and the STAR TREK concordance is an index to all of STAR TREK's episodes. It was an invaluable aid to the writing of this book, but it is also fun to read for itself—it's chock full of articles and illustrations about every imaginable detail of the show. (Can you identify Mako Root? Lirpa? The Symbalene Blood Burn?) You can get a copy of this 84-page, professionally printed index from Bjo for only $5.00. Write to: Bjo Trimble/ *Star Trek Concordance*, Box 74866, Los Angeles, Calif. 90004. Be sure to mention where you heard about it (it helps the bookkeeping.)

campaign—and I'd send some of them up to Tim, mostly film clips or stuff out of publicity, posters and pictures and such.

"Tim had a very big soft heart for the kids, and she would take the stuff into the children's ward, especially the permanently handicapped children who weren't going to get out of bed. Or even out of an iron lung. In fact, there were three children in sort of a half-circle position in iron lungs, and they put a really big poster of Mr. Spock, with the *Enterprise* behind him, on the ceiling so these kids could lie there and see him. Of course, there are little mirrors on iron lungs too—and they had little tiny pictures on those. I had managed to obtain some photographs that we could cut up, and they pasted little borders of all the STAR TREK people around the edges of the mirrors. And then we got a couple of big color posters, one was of Kirk and Spock, those went up on the ceiling too.

"Tim was insatiable. She kept asking for stuff—and all of it went out to the kids. All of it. She got 'Flight Deck' certificates for the kids, and every time a kid was especially good, she gave them a STAR TREK certificate—and if you think about it, there's not an awful lot you can promise a kid who is nailed down in bed permanently. The children are very aware they're not going anywhere, they're very aware there aren't any big treats in store—except maybe, ice cream for dinner, or something like this—and so, aside from promising them a new book or something, there's not a lot you can give a kid who's going to be on his back for the rest of his life.

"So these things perked up the children's ward a good deal. Now, this one case that came in—she was not on it herself as part of her job as a special duties nurse; she was on another case, waiting for a terribly rich, old person to die; but she would spend as much time as she could over in the children's ward—they brought in this girl. (Tim never told me her real name); she was thirteen years old and in practice for the Olympic trials in skiing, and she had been struck with one of the more virulent forms of meningitis. So they had her in an iron lung.

"Now, the girl's mother went to pieces. She would come in and stand around talking to her daughter for a few minutes, and all of a sudden, she would break down and start crying, 'My baby! My poor child!' The nurses would have to drag her out of the room.

"Now, remember, the girl was conscious—nothing had happened to her intellect. Her body was paralyzed, not her mind.

"Finally, one day, the mother had been reading, evidently waiting for the girl to wake up, a *Reader's Digest* article which was bannered on the front of the magazine, 'Will Your Child Live Through Meningitis?' When the little girl had awakened, the mother laid the magazine on a table nearby, and forgot it when she left—leaving the article where the little girl could see it. She turned her head and could read the cover very clearly. You can imagine the effect that had.

"Between her mother's hysteria and her complete paralysis —she had been a very physically active child, but only the iron lung was keeping her alive now—she began to decline. She was practically willing herself to die.

"She was as cooperative as ever—but she was visibly *sinking*. She had lost all will to live. She didn't care any more and nothing was working.

"Tim wrote me about her, because she was such a beautiful child it really distressed her. The loss of any kind of life was a very distressing thing to Tim anyway—but she was very tied up in this little girl, and she said, 'If she just had something, *something* to believe in . . .'

"The odd thing about it was, the doctors were fairly sure by this point that she *could* recover from the meningitis—but she wasn't doing her breathing exercises. She had to do these exercises to build up her lung strength, a little bit more every day—but she was convinced she was going to die, so she wasn't doing them. Between her mother and the *Reader's Digest* article and the complete paralysis, she had lost all reason to care.

"Now, I don't know whatever made me do it, it was one of these silly impulses, but we'd already sent Tim posters and this was the only tangible thing we had on hand—I sent her a tribble for this little girl.

"Tim took it in to her and said, 'Mr. Spock himself sent you a tribble. And this tribble is to help you get well. Because if you die, the tribble will die, he'll be so sad.'

"Well, this really got to the little girl—she loved that tribble. They put it on her pillow next to her head. And this was the turning point. She took up the exercises again; she began to cooperate, she began to listen and work and pretty soon she began to rally.

"Presently, she was out of the iron lung—she was keeping the tribble with her all the time—and she was progressing beautifully.

"Now, you know, when I'd gone over to the studio, I'd tried for something a lot more tangible, like a shirt or something, but I don't think it would have done nearly as well, because what could they have done except hang it on the wall? Instead, the tribble was a contact thing, the tribble was always there, she wore it around her neck. It was probably the best thing we could have sent her, she could see it and touch it whenever she wanted.

"She carried it around with her for all the weeks left in the hospital, rebuilding her strength, going through all the therapy exercises, but when she left, she went to Tim Courtney and said. 'I'd like to leave the tribble here at the hospital to help some other little girl.' And she did this *very* reluctantly, she had to do a lot of soul-searching because she really loved that tribble and she really wanted to take it with her, but she also realized that it could probably work for someone else.

"When she left, she was completely whole again, and as a matter of fact, there was nothing at all—except the dangers in extreme changes of temperatures—to keep her from going back and taking up for her Olympic trials again. (I don't know her real name, but this year I'm going to watch those trials very carefully for a fifteen- or sixteen-year-old girl . . .)

"The stranger part of this is that less than two weeks later, another child, a swimmer in this case, a thirteen-year-old girl, was brought into the hospital with the same thing, meningitis. And the first thing Tim did was bring the tribble in and introduce him and explain that Mr. Spock had sent this tribble in especially for this little girl—and started the whole cycle all over again.

"As far as I know, the tribble is still at the hospital and still helping children, and probably can continue to as long as children know about STAR TREK."*

*Interestingly enough, Bjo Trimble does not know the name of the hospital where Tim Courtney worked; she never told her. All she knows is that it's one of the local ones in Oakland. If I knew where it was, they wouldn't have to worry about ever running out of tribbles . . .

So, who needs a Hugo?

That little girl's faith is a much better award.

If it hadn't been a tribble though, maybe something else could have inspired her faith—but it *was* a tribble, and I'm honored that it was something of mine that could create such hope in another human being.

Every once in a while, I begin to feel that my existence is justified.

Acknowledgments

Books don't just happen.

They have to be researched.

I thought this book would be easy. I'd just sit down and write it. I'd dig out my file copies of my outlines and scripts, annotate them a little bit, and have a book. Right?

Wrong.

I had to do more research for this project than for almost anything I've written before.

I had to send a spy sneaking into the Cal State at Northridge Theatre Arts Department to *steal* my senior project from their files—there was only one copy in existence, and they had it. Without it, I wouldn't have had any of Gene Coon's notes or comments. So, thank you, spy—you shall remain forever nameless so they don't catch you.

I had to go over to U.C.L.A. and dig through their files. Gene Roddenberry donated all of the STAR TREK papers to their television library. I spent a fascinating two weeks one afternoon going through them. Thank you, Ruth Schwartz and U.C.L.A.

I had to secure releases from Paramount Pictures and Bantam Books. Thank you, Paramount and Bantam. And thank you, Tony Sauber, in particular.

I needed information from the STAR TREK fans. I made a phone call to a lady named Cheryl Etchison, secretary of the 1973 STAR TREK convention. One phone call, and within two days, fans from all over the country were sending me articles and fanzines about STAR TREK and tribbles. Unfortunately, space prevents their inclusion in this volume. But thank you anyway, Cheryl Etchison, Ruth Berman, Carol Lee, Mildred Broxon and all you others.

I had to talk to various STAR TREK people too. Thank you, Harlan Ellison and Gene Coon and Dorothy Fontana—for your reminiscences as well as your friendship.

And thank you, Bjo Trimble, for everything you've given me—especially the use of your film clips for the photo section. I didn't know how to end this book until you told me that story. So, thank you for that.

And thank you, Tim Courtney, for making the tribbles mean just a little bit *more* . . . I only wish you could have lived long enough for me to have gotten the story firsthand. But thank you, anyway.

And finally—thanks, Gene Roddenberry, for making it happen in the first place. It was fun, wasn't it?

COMMENTS ON THIS BOOK AND COPIES
OF REVIEWS MAY BE SENT TO:

DAVID GERROLD
Box 526
Hollywood, Calif. 90028

About the Author

DAVID GERROLD was born in Los Angeles in 1944. He majored in Cinema at the University of Southern California and minored in Art and Journalism. He graduated with a B.A. in Theatre Arts from California State at Northridge in 1967. Even before he graduated though, he was a working writer.

Gerrold had been submitting outlines and story premises to various television series, beginning in 1966. In early '67, the TV series, *Star Trek,* took an interest in one of his outlines and asked to see more. In the summer of 1967, he made his first professional sale; the story and script became *Star Trek*'s highly acclaimed episode, "The Trouble With Tribbles." It was nominated for the International Hugo Award for the best dramatic presentation in science fiction in 1967 and placed a close second in the balloting. Other sales to *Star Trek* included some rewrite work and an original story which became "The Cloud Minders" episode.

In 1969, David Gerrold turned his attention to the prose form, and in a short time had sold stories to *Galaxy* magazine and a serial to *If,* another science fiction magazine. He has been anthologized several times, most notably in Harlan Ellison's *Again, Dangerous Visions.*

David Gerrold has edited three anthologies of his own: *Protostars, Generation,* and *Generation Two.* He has written one collection of short stories, *With a Finger in My I* and several novels including *The Flying Sorcerers* (in collaboration with Larry Niven), *Space Skimmer, Yesterday's Children, When Harlie Was One, The Man Who Folded Himself,* and *Battle for the Planet of the Apes.* David Gerrold has also written two non-fiction books, both about *Star Trek, The Trouble With Tribbles* and *The World of Star Trek.*

The book on how to write for TV!

THE MAKING OF STAR TREK

Stephen E. Whitfield • Gene Roddenberry

The complete story on how the *U.S.S. Enterprise* was designed, her weaponry, equipment and power sources, the original concept behind the show, backgrounds of the characters, biographies of the stars, and photos, diagrams and illustrations—the whole authentic history.

". . . for would-be TV writers, directors and producers, this will be an education in itself, a polished but nonvarnished look at how TV really works."
—*Publishers Weekly*

THE WORLD OF
STAR TREK

DAVID GERROLD

Here are the worlds of *STAR TREK*:

GENE RODDENBERRY'S brilliant conception—the first viable science fiction world designed for a TV series

THE SHOW ITSELF and the people who created it—the writers, the stars, the technicians

THE FANS—the world the show created—and how they kept *Star Trek* alive in the face of network opposition

With sixty-four pages of pictures from the episodes themselves and with original photos by Stan Burns

To order by mail, send $1.50 per book plus 25¢ per order for handling to Ballantine Cash Sales, P.O. Box 505, Westminster, Maryland 21157. Please allow three weeks for delivery.

SCIENCE FICTION
from

BALLANTINE BOOKS

WALK TO THE END OF THE WORLD,
S. M. Charnas $1.25
ICERIGGER, Alan Dean Foster $1.25
UNDER PRESSURE, Frank Herbert $1.25
THE LEGEND OF MIAREE, Zach Hughes $1.25

THE BEST OF STANLEY G. WEINBAUM
With an INTRODUCTION by Isaac Asimov and an
Afterword by Robert Bloch $1.65

launching a new series of Sci Fi Greats

SCIENCE FICTION EMPHASIS 1
David Gerrold, Ed. $1.25
THE GINGER STAR
Leigh Brackett $1.25
A HOLE IN SPACE
Larry Niven $1.25
STAR TREK LOG ONE
Alan Dean Foster $ .95
PATRON OF THE ARTS
William Rotsler $1.25
THE BEST SCIENCE FICTION OF THE YEAR #3
Terry Carr, Ed. $1.50

available at your local bookstore